AF541334

Counterinsurgency in Afghanistan

Counterinsurgency in AFGHANISTAN

Col. T.N. Marwah (Retd.)

Gaurav Book Centre Pvt Ltd

Delhi

Publisher
GAURAV BOOK CENTRE PVT LTD
4832/24,Prahlad Lane,S-207 Ansari
Road, Daryaganj, Delhi-110002
Ph.: 43570976, 23278261
Email: gauravbookcentre@gmail.com

Edition: 2018

ISBN: 978-93-83316-36-6

Laser Typesetting
JEE-VEE Graphics, Delhi

Price: 1295/-

Printed
Neeta Press, Delhi

Preface

The insurgency in Afghanistan, the key challenges and successes of the U.S.-led counterinsurgency campaign, and the capabilities necessary to wage effective counterinsurgency operations. Since 9/11, two consecutive U.S. administrations have labored mightily to help Afghanistan create a state inhospitable to terrorist organizations with transnational aspirations and capabilities.

As long as the insurgency and warlordism exists, local communities will remain on the fringes of international and government beneficence. The principle of Subsidiarity forms the underlying approach to a counterinsurgency strategy for Afghanistan. In essence, Subsidiarity embraces decentralization of governance to the lowest level. Because this form of federalism has a long-standing tradition in Afghanistan (as well as the West), the populace readily accepts the concept. This concept permits the central government to focus on national issues.

The nature of the insurgency in Afghanistan, the key challenges and successes of the U.S.-led counterinsurgency campaign, and the capabilities necessary to wage effective counterinsurgency operations. By examining the key lessons from all insurgencies since World War II, it finds that most policymakers repeatedly underestimate the importance of indigenous actors to counterinsurgency efforts. The U.S. should focus its resources on helping improve the capacity of the indigenous government and indigenous security forces to wage counterinsurgency. It has not always done this well. The U.S. military-along with U.S. civilian agencies and other coalition partners-is more likely to be successful in counterinsurgency warfare the more capable and legitimate the indigenous security forces (especially the police), the better the governance capacity of the local state, and the less external support that insurgents receive.

In the areas of Afghanistan beset by insurgency, development spending has done little to increase popular support for the government, casting doubt on the counterinsurgency and development theories that have inspired this spending. Practitioners, however, have lacked access to viable alternative theories or principles on the use of development in COIN. This guide offers a comprehensive alternative approach, derived from the leader-centric model of counterinsurgency and based upon a wide variety of counterinsurgency campaigns in Afghanistan and previous conflicts. According to this approach, the primary purpose of development aid in counterinsurgency should be to improve local security and governance, because development is less important than security and governance and is effective only where security and governance are present.

This book offers an accessible introduction to counterinsurgency operations, a key aspect of modern warfare.

—*Editor*

Contents

1

Introduction

The Taliban insurgency began shortly after the group's fall from power following the 2001 war in Afghanistan. The Taliban forces are fighting against the Afghan government, which is led by President Hamid Karzai.

It is also fighting against the US-led International Security Assistance Force (ISAF). The insurgency has also spread to some degree over the Durand Line border to neighbouring Pakistan, in particular the Waziristan region and Khyber Pakhtunkhwa. The Taliban conduct low-intensity warfare against the Afghan National Security Forces and their NATO trainers. Regional countries, particularly Pakistan and Iran, are often accused for funding and supporting the insurgent groups.

The spiritual leader of the Taliban is Mulla Omar who heads the Quetta Shura. The Haqqani Network, Hezbi Islami, and smaller al Qaeda groups have also joined the insurgency. They often use terrorist attacks in which their victims are usually Afghan civilians. According to reports by the United Nations and others, the insurgents were responsible for 75-80% of civilian casualties between 2009 to 2011.

After the May 2011 death of Osama bin Laden in Pakistan, many prominent Afghan figures began being assassinated by the insurgents, including Mohammed Daud Daud, Ahmad Wali Karzai, Jan Mohammad Khan, Ghulam Haider Hamidi, Burhanuddin Rabbani and others. In response to this, major operations were started inside Afghanistan against the insurgents. These are intended to disrupt the network of the insugents and force them to the negotation table.

After the Invasion

After evading U.S. forces throughout the summer of 2002, the remnants of the Taliban gradually began to regain their confidence and launched the insurgency that Mullah Mohammed Omar had promised during the Taliban's last days in power. During September 2002, Taliban forces began a recruitment drive in Pashtun areas in both Afghanistan and Pakistan to launch a renewed "jihad" or struggle against the Afghan government and the U.S-led coalition. Pamphlets distributed in secret during the night also began to appear in many villages in the former Taliban heartland in southeastern Afghanistan. Small mobile training camps were established along the border with Pakistan by al-Qaeda and Taliban fugitives to train new recruits in guerrilla warfare and tactics, according to Afghan sources and a United Nations report. Most of the new recruits were drawn from the madrassas or religious schools of the tribal areas of Pakistan, from which the Taliban had originally arisen. Major bases, a few with as many as 200 men, were created in the mountainous tribal areas of Pakistan by the summer of 2003. The will of the Pakistani paramilitaries stationed at border crossings to prevent such infiltration was called into question, and Pakistani military operations proved of little use.

MAKE-UP OF THE TALIBAN

There are many players now in Afghanistan that are operating against the NATO coalition forces. In the general, the media use the term Taliban for all the insurgents in Afghanistan. However, in addition to Afghan insurgent groups with a separate history from the original pre-2001 Taliban – the Haqqani network and the Hezb-e-Islami Gulbuddin – there is also a Taliban group in Pakistan. The US military commanders call the Afghan Taliban Big T and they call the Pakistani Taliban Little T.The Afghan Taliban's main goal is to remove the foreign forces and their backed government from Afghanistan.

Their leadership councils are intact and they operate in almost all parts of the Afghanistan in one form or the other. The Taliban control most of the country side from Herat Northwestern Afghanistan to Qandahar (southern Afghanistan) to Kunar (Northeastern Afghanistan). Taliban fighters are also said to have started operations in the Northern city of Mazar-i-Sharif.

The Pakistani Taliban's main goals are very unclear. The Pakistani Taliban do cross border to Afghanistan to fight NATO forces but their main concern seem to be in Pakistani tribal areas. There is also the Hezbi-Islami militia which operates in Northeastern Afghanistan.

Financial support

While the pre-2001 Taliban suppressed opium production, the current insurgency "relies on opium revenues to purchase weapons, train its members, and buy support." In 2001, Afghanistan produced only 11% of the world's opium, today it produces 93% of the global crop, and the drug trade accounts for half of Afghanistan's GDP.

On July 28, 2009, Richard Holbrooke, the United States special envoy for Afghanistan and Pakistan, said that money transfers from Western Europe and the Gulf States exceeded the drug trade earnings and that a new task force had been formed to shut down this source of funds.

The United States Agency for International Development is investigating the possibility that kickbacks from its contracts are being funnelled to the Taliban.

A report by the London School of Economics (LSE) claimed to provide the most concrete evidence yet that the Pakistani intelligence agency ISI is providing funding, training and sanctuary to the Taliban on a scale much larger than previously thought. The report's author Matt Waldman spoke to nine Taliban field commanders in Afghanistan and concluded that Pakistan's relationship with the insurgents ran far deeper than previously realized. Some of those interviewed suggested that the organization even attended meetings of the Taliban's supreme council, the Quetta Shura. A spokesman for the Pakistani military dismissed the report, describing it as "malicious".

Poppy dilemma

In March 2010, after the ousting of the Taliban from the area of Marja in the Southern Afghan province Helmand in the Operation Moshtarak, the American and NATO commanders were confronted with the dilemma of on the one hand the need for *"winning the hearts and minds"* of the local population as well as on the other hand the necessity of the eradication of poppies and the destruction of the opium economy. Since opium is the main source of existence of 60 to 70 percent of the farmers in Marja, American Marines were ordered to initially ignore the crops to avoid trampling their livelihood.

SOCIAL CONTEXT: POVERTY AND CORRUPTION

In November 2010, a report with the results of an opinion poll of the Western aid group Oxfam indicated that 83 percent of the Afghan population does not consider the Taliban militants, but poverty, unemployment and government corruption as the main causes of war in their country.

After thirty years of war, the country remains one of the poorest and least developed countries in the world. It is also one of the most corrupt. Unemployment stands at 40 percent and more than half of the population lives below the poverty line. On top of that, violence then seemed to culminate since U.S.-backed Afghan forces ousted the Taliban in late 2001. Nearly half of those surveyed said corruption and bad government were the main reasons for the ongoing war. 12 percent said the Taliban insurgency was to blame. After the Taliban, the reason most people gave for the continued fighting was foreign interference, with 25 percent of respondents saying other countries were to blame.

2006 Escalation

Since the start of 2006 Afghanistan has been facing a wave of attacks by improvised explosives and suicide bombers, particularly after NATO took command of the fight against insurgents in spring 2006.

Afghan President Hamid Karzai publicly condemned the methods used by the western powers. In June 2006 he said:

And for two years I have systematically, consistently and on a daily basis warned the international community of what was developing in Afghanistan and of the need for a change of approach in this regard.

and

The international community [must] reassess the manner in which this war against terror is conducted. Insurgents were also criticized for their conduct. According to Human Rights Watch, bombing and other attacks on Afghan civilians by the Taliban (and to a lesser extent Hezb-e-Islami Gulbuddin), are reported to have "sharply escalated in 2006" with "at least 669 Afghan civilians were killed in at least 350 armed attacks, most of which appear to have been intentionally launched at civilians or civilian objects." 131 of insurgent attacks were suicide attacks which killed 212 civilians (732 wounded), 46 Afghan army and police members (101 wounded), and 12 foreign soldiers (63 wounded).

Timeline

Below are a few deaths (note:this is just a few NATO deaths)

- June 6: A roadside bombing leaves 2 American soldiers killed, the attack took place in the province of Nanghar. Also a separate suicide bombing in Khost leaves three US soldiers wounded.
- June 15: A bus carrying workers to an American base explodes killing 10 and wounding 15. The explosives were placed on the bus.
- July 1: 2 British soldiers arc killed when their base came under small arms fire including rocket propelled grenades.
- August 8: 4 Canadian NATO soldiers are killed in two separate attacks. And a suicide bomber targeting a NATO convey detonates killing 21 people.
- August 20: 3 American soldiers are killed and another 3 are wounded in a battle with Taliban militants after a roadside bomb hit an American patrol.
- September 8: A major suicide car bombing near the US embassy in Kabul kills 18 including 2 US soldiers.

- September 10: The governor of Afghanistan's southeastern Paktia province is killed alongside his bodyguard and nephew when a suicide bomber detonates himself beside the governor's car.
- October 14: A suicide attack in Kandahar city leaves 8 dead including one NATO soldier.
- October 15: 2 Canadian soldiers were killed when Taliban militants attacked NATO troops using small arms fire and rocket propelled grenades.
- December 6: A suicide bomber blew himself up outside a security contractor's office killing 7 including 2 Americans, the attack took place south of Afghanistan in Kandahar.
- December 19: Mullah Akhtar Muhammad Osmani, reportedly number 4 in the Taliban shura, is killed by an American airstrike in southern Afghanistan.

2007

The Taliban continue to favour suicide bombing as a tactic. In 2007 Afghanistan saw 140 more suicide bombings – more than in the past five years combined – that killed more than 300 people, many civilians. A UN report said the perpetrators were poorly educated, disaffected young men who were recruited by Taliban leaders in Pakistani madrassas.

Western analysts estimated that the Taliban can field about 10,000 fighters at any given time, according to an October 30 report in *The New York Times*. Of that number, "only 2,000 to 3,000 are highly motivated, full-time insurgents", the *Times* reported. The rest are part-timers, made up of alienated, young Afghan men angry at bombing raids or fighting in order to get money. In 2007, more foreign fighters were showing up in Afghanistan than ever before, according to Afghan and United States officials. An estimated 100 to 300 full-time combatants are foreigners, usually from Pakistan, Uzbekistan, Chechnya, various Arab countries and perhaps even Turkey and western China. They tend to be more fanatical and violent, and they often bring skills such as the ability to post more sophisticated videos on the Internet or bombmaking expertise. It has also been reported that the Taliban now control up to 54% of Afghanistan. In April 2007, Karzai admitted that he spoke to the Taliban to bring about peace in Afghanistan. He noted that the Afghan Taliban are "always welcome" in Afghanistan, although foreign militants are not. On April 15, 2007 the Afghan Government promised to end all hostage deals with the Taliban after two Afghan kidnapped victims were executed in an agreement to free an Italian journalist.

- February 27 – 2007 Bagram Air Base bombing

On May 12, Mullah Dadullah, a senior Taliban commander in charge of operations in the south of the country was killed in Helmand province, in what is seen as a great moral victory.

Timeline

- January 23: A suicide bomber blew himself up outside a US base in eastern Afghanistan killing 10 people who were waiting outside the base.
- February 2: Taliban forces raided a southern Afghan town destroying the government center and briefly holding some elders captive.
- February 19: The Taliban briefly seized a small town in western Afghanistan after police fled the town, the Taliban forces moved in for 30 minutes and seized three vehicles.
- February 20: A suicide bomber blew himself up during an opening hospital ceremony injuring 2 NATO soldiers and a hospital worker.
- February 27: 23 people are killed when a suicide bomber attacks an American military base, Bagram Airfield (BAF) in Bagram District, Parwan Province. The attack took place while US vice president Dick Cheney was in the compound, Cheney was unhurt in the attack and was the intended target of the attack as claimed by the Taliban. The dead included an American soldier, a Korean soldier, and an American contractor.
- March 4: A suicide bomber attacks an American convoy which leaves 16 civilians dead in the aftermath as the American convey begins to sporadically fire at civilian cars around them. In a separate incident, two British soldiers

were killed when a Taliban rocket was fired on them during clashes in Southern Helmand Province.

- March 17: A suicide bomber targeting a Canadian military convoy leaves one dead and three injured, including one NATO soldier. The attack took place in Kandahar.
- March 19: A car bomb blew up near a three-vehicle US embassy convoy injuring many in the convoy.
- March 27: Four police officers are killed in the southern Helmand province after a suicide bomber blew himself up outside a police station.
- March 28: A suicide bomber killed a top intelligence officer and three others in the capital Kabul.
- April 6: A suicide bomber struck a police checkpoint in Kabul leaving four dead and four others wounded.
- April 9: Six Canadian soldiers were killed in southern Afghanistan when they struck a roadside bomb. A separate roadside bombing, also in south Afghanistan, left another NATO soldier dead and one wounded. In another incident, a statement from the Taliban's spokesperson claimed that they had beheaded a translator for a kidnapped Italian journalist.
- April 15: A suicide bomber struck a US-private security firm, killing four Afghans working for the company.
- April 16: A suicide bomber ran onto a police training field and detonating his explosive device, killed 10 police officers and wounded dozens of others. The attack took place in the relatively quiet city of Kunduz. The Taliban claimed responsibility for the attack.
- April 20: Separate explosions in Southern Afghanistan leave two NATO soldiers dead.
- April 22: A suicide bomber blew himself up an eastern city of Afghanistan, killing six. A roadside bomb also hit an Afghan intelligence service vehicle, killing all four who were inside.
- April 30: Hundreds of Afghans took to the streets in western Afghanistan, accusing US soldiers of killing scores of

civilians in fighting which the coalition said killed 136 Taliban in a three-week operation.

- May 13: Mullah Dadullah, the Taliban's top military commander in Afghanistan, is killed in fighting in the south.
- May 23: The Taliban's newly-named top field commander, Mullah Bakht Mohammed, brother and replacement of deceased field commander Mullah Dadullah, makes his first public statement, saying the Taliban will "pursue holy war until the occupying countries leave."
- July 19: The South Korean hostage crisis involved the hostage taking of twenty-three South Korean Christian aid workers in the Ghazni Province which resulted in the death of two. The crisis ended on August 30 with the release of the remaining hostages as part of a deal with the South Korean diplomats of government.
- August 31: A suicide bomber detonated his explosive-laden vehicle after ramming three military vehicles at the military gate of the Kabul International Airport. Two Afghan soldiers were killed and ten people were injured.
- September 29: In an effort to reach a compromise with the Taliban leaders, the president, Hamid Karzai would make a quid quo pro by allowing militants to have a place in government if they stopped fighting. Taliban leaders replied by saying there would be no compromise unless intervening forces such as NATO and the U.S. left.
- November 2: Mawlawi Abdul Manan, an important Taliban figure, is killed by Afghan Security forces. His death is confirmed by the Taliban.

2008

The U.S. warned that in 2008 the Taliban has "coalesced into a resilient insurgency", and would "maintain or even increase the scope and pace of its terrorist attacks". Attacks by Taliban insurgents in eastern Afghanistan increased by 40% when compared to the same period in 2007.

Timeline

- February 24: Poor military intelligence leads to conflicted reports of a possible Taliban spring offensive.
- August 19:Taliban forces kill 9 French troops (with a 10th death in an accident) near Kabul.
- October 6: CNN reports that, via Saudi intermediaries, the Taliban is negotiating to end the conflict in Afghanistan, and that the Taliban has split from Al Qaeda.
- December 7: 200 Taliban armed with RPGs and automatic weapons attack two NATO supply depots outside of Peshawar destroying 100 vehicles packed with supplies intended to support the NATO effort in Afghanistan.
- December 8: 200 Taliban armed with RPGs and automatic weapons attack a NATO supply depot outside of Peshawar destroying 53 container trucks packed with supplies intended to support the NATO effort in Afghanistan.

2009

During 2009 the Taliban regained control over the countryside of several Afghan provinces. In August 2009, Taliban commanders in the province of Helmand started issuing *"visa"* from the "Islamic Emirate of Afghanistan" in order to allow travel to and from the provincial capital of Lashkar Gah.

Timeline

- June 30: US Army Private First Class soldier Bowe R. Bergdahl is captured by the Taliban in Southern Afghanistan.
- July 18: The Taliban release a video showing Bergdahl being interviewed by one of his captors.
- August 12: Taliban spokesmen threaten the public not to vote in the upcoming presidential elections.
- August 15: 2009 NATO Afghanistan headquarters bombing, A suicide car bomb explodes outside NATO headquarters in Kabul, killing at least seven and wounding almost 100. ISAF troops were reported among the wounded.

- August 25: A massive car bomb shakes Kandahar, killing at least 30 and wounding dozens as buildings collapse in the city's center. The attack comes after the first results of the presidential elections were announced. Four U.S. soldiers die in an IED explosion in southern Afghanistan bringing ISAF losses to 295, eclipsing 2008's coalition death toll of 294.
- September 4: U.S airstrike on two fuel tankers kill at least 70 people in Farah Province after it was hijacked by Taliban militants. Angry relatives of those killed claim civilians were collecting fuel from the tankers when the airstrike came.
- December 1, the U.S. President Barack Obama announced he would send an additional 30,000 troops to help battle the Taliban insurgency. The Taliban reacted to the President's speech by saying they will step up their fight in Afghanistan. A Taliban commander told the BBC that if more US troops came, more would die.
- Also in December 2009, after his disputed re-election, President Hamid Karzai announced to move ahead with a plan for a Loya Jirga to discuss the Taliban insurgency. The Taliban would be invited to take part in this Jirga.

2010

During 2010, the Taliban were ousted from parts of Helmand Province by the ISAF Operation Moshtarak that started in February 2010. In the meantime the Taliban insurgency spread to the northern provinces of the country.

The new policy of the Taliban was to shift militants from the south to the north, to show they exist *"everywhere"*, according to Faryab Province Governor Abdul Haq Shafaq.

With most Afghan and NATO troops stationed in the southern and eastern provinces, villagers in the once-peaceful north found themselves confronted with a rapid deterioration of security, as insurgents seized new territory in provinces such as Kunduz and Baghlan, and even infiltrated the mountains of Badakhshan Province in the northeast.

Timeline

- January 17: *"Kabul's day of terror"*, on which gunbattles near the presidential palace and other government buildings paralysed the Afghan capital for hours. As President Karzai was swearing in his new cabinet ministers inside the presidential palace, militants performed attacks on multiple locations in Kabul, including shopping malls, a cinema and the central bank. A team of gunmen launched a spectacular assault in "commando style" with two men detonating suicide bombs and the rest fighting to the death near the gates of the presidential palace, an operation by insurgents to terrorize the Afghan capital, further demoralizing the population and lending to the impression that virtually no part of the country could be safe. The Taliban said it had deployed 20 suicide bombers in explosive vests who were also armed with heavy and light weaponry A western security official estimated there is a security incident in Kabul, on average, every seven to 10 days.
- January 28: International Conference on Afghanistan in London
- February 26: Militants target hotels and guest houses in Kabul. Up to nine Indians, an Italian diplomat and a French film maker were among the dead in the worst assault on the Afghan capital for several months. A four-hour battle began with a car bombing and included suicide bombers and Taliban fighters throwing grenades. The attacks appeared to be aimed at Indian government officials and medical workers. Three Afghan police were killed, and six more officers were among the 38 people wounded in what was described as a well-planned and co-ordinated attack.
- June 2–4: The Karzai administration organized the Afghan Peace Jirga in Kabul that was announced after the 2009 presidential elections. The Taliban were not invited.
- July 20–29: International Conference on Afghanistan in Kabul
- August 6: killing of 10 members of a Christian charity's medical team in the mountains of Badakhshan.

- August 10: Amnesty International states that the International Criminal Court should open a formal investigation into crimes committed by the Taliban and other insurgent groups in Afghanistan.

2011

The insurgency continued strongly in 2011.

The Taliban continued attacking and ambushing NATO and Afghan troops as well as the targeted assassination of government officials.

On January 29, the deputy governor of Kandahar was killed in a suicide attack. Three months later, on April 15 the Kandahar chief police, General Khan Mohammed Mujahid was killed.

On May 28, Taliban assassinated one of their main opponents, Mohammed Daud Daud, in a bomb attack. Six others were also killed. He was the chief of the police for the northern of Afghanistan.

On July 12, the president's brother Ahmed Wali Karzai, the leader of the Kandahar province, was killed by his own bodyguard.

On July 18, President Karzai's advisor, Jan Mohammad Khan, was assassinated in Kabul by the Taliban in an attack that also killed an Afghan deputy.

The United Nations estimated that for the first half of 2011, the civilian deaths rose by 15% and reached 1462, which is the worst death toll since the beginning of the war and despite the surge of foreign troops.

As of July 22, 325 coalition fighters were killed, more than 55% of the deaths caused by IED's.

As of July 18, coalition forces started their plan of transition by handing power of several areas to the Afghan authority following their plan of future pull out of the country.

A Taliban militant who had infiltrated the Afghan police force killed seven other policemen in Lashkar Gah. The same day the police chief of Registaan district and three other policemen were killed in bomb attacks.

ISAF General Chief David Petraeus left his position with mixed results. During his time as the head of ISAF, 3775 insurgents were killed or captured in 2832 raids while 713 NATO soldiers were killed. Overall the level of violence in the country increased. He was replaced by General John Allen.

It is reported that in 2011, the United States was spending 2 billion dollars per week fighting in Afghanistan against the Taliban. In a 2011 forecast the war in Afghanistan was estimated at 108 billion dollars for the year, while the Iraqi War was estimated at 50 billion.

Between July 20 and July 22, NATO troops killed 50 Haqquani fighters in an attack on their camp.

A US military investigation discovered that a portion of the 2 billion dollars in funds given by the United States in contracts had fallen in the hands of the insurgency.

On July 27, the mayor of Kandahar, Ghulam Haidar Hameedi, was killed in a suicide attack.

On July 28, suicide bombers and snipers attacked the police headquarters of Tarin Kowt in a large-scale attack which killed more than 21 people including Afghan reporter Ahmed Omed Khpulwak. According to the Afghan interior minister, for the 2 year period between March 19, 2009 and March 19, 2011, 2770 Afghan policemen were killed and 4785 wounded while 1052 Afghan soldiers were killed and 2413 wounded.

On July 31, 10 Afghan policemen were killed in a suicide attack in Lashkar Gah where Afghan security forces had taken over from NATO a week before. The same day, 10 Afghan guards who were protecting a NATO supplies convoy were killed in the attack. One day before, 5 Afghans soldiers and 2 NATO soldiers were killed in a bomb attack on their patrol.

On August 6, 31 American Special Forces soldiers were killed in the crash of their helicopter probably shot down during a fight with the Taliban. Seven Afghan soldiers were also killed. This was the biggest death toll for NATO troops in the whole war. Most of the American soldiers killed were Navy SEALs.

On August 6, 4 NATO soldiers were killed, including two French Foreign Legion members, and 5 others were wounded.

INSURGENT ACTIVITY

From the beginning of the current Afghan insurgency in 2002, there was a gradual deterioration in the security environment—especially in the south and east of the country. R AND data show that the over-all number of insurgent-initiated attacks increased approximately 400 percent from 2002 to 2006, and the number of deaths from these attacks increased over 800 percent during the same period. The data incorporate insurgent-initiated attacks against Afghan civilians, international aid workers, and coalition forces. The U.S. military reported that the increase in violence was particularly acute between 2005 and 2006. During this period, the number of suicide attacks increased by more than 400 percent (from 27 to 139), remotely detonated bombings more than doubled (from 783 to 1,677), and armed attacks nearly tripled (from 1,558 to 4,542).33 In 2007, insurgent-initiated violence rose another 27 percent from 2006 levels. Helmand Province witnessed among the highest levels of violence, with a 60-percent rise between 2006 and 2007. The result was a lack of security for Afghans and foreigners, especially those living in the east and south. Road travel in many areas was dangerous, and crime was a major problem. Interfactional— or "greenon-green"—fighting continued among regional commanders, including those in the provinces of Herat, Nangarhar, Nuristan, Logar, Laghman, and Badghis. As one report by the National Directorate for Security concluded, Taliban cells in the south of Afghanistan developed good intelligence about individuals in villages and towns,

Individuals who flirt with the government truly get frightened as the Afghan security forces are currently incapable of providing police and protection for each village.... When villagers and rural communities seek protection from police either it arrives late or arrives in a wrong way.

Promoting disorder among the population is a key objective of most insurgents. Disrupting the economy and decreasing security helps produce discontent with the indigenous government and undermines its strength and legitimacy. Once insurgents establish a hold over the population, those who are hostile to the insurgents often become too fearful to oppose them. Some may be eliminated, providing an example to others. Some may escape abroad. Still others may be cowed into hiding their true feelings. By threatening the population, the insurgents give individuals a strong rationale to refuse or refrain from cooperating with the indigenous government and external actors.

As learning organizations, insurgent groups were successful at continually adapting their tactics, techniques, and procedures to confront counterinsurgency efforts. They conducted a wide variety of attacks against U.S., coalition, and Afghan security forces, as well as Afghan and international civilians. The insurgents relied heavily on asymmetric tactics, some of which were similar to those used by mujahideen forces against Soviet and Democratic Republic of Afghanistan army forces during the Soviet-Afghan war. Insurgent tactics included yielding the population centres to U.S. and Afghan forces, operating from rural areas, distributing propaganda to the local population and opposition forces, threatening and intimidating the local population, and conducting armed attacks. As Taliban military officials argued, this is classic guerrilla warfare: "Our military tactic is to control a district center, kill the government soldiers there, and withdraw to our mountainous strongholds, where it would be very difficult for the government to pursue us."

Examples of armed attacks by the insurgency included ambushes and raids using small arms and grenades; shelling using 107-mm and 122-mm rockets and 60-, 82-, and 120-mm mortars; and improvised explosive devices (IEDs). Most of their shelling and rocket fire was not accurate, though there is some evidence that insurgent forces considered harassment of enemy forces and populations as valuable. Insurgent groups, especially the Taliban, also succeeded in capturing government installations, villages, and district centres in the south, though usually for brief periods.

Taliban forces deployed in larger numbers over time, especially in such southern provinces as Helmand. In 2002, they operated in squad-size units. In 2005, they operated in company-sized units of up to 100 or more fighters. By 2008, they occasionally operated in battalion-sized units, though they deployed in smaller units as well. This suggests that the Taliban were able to move around with more freedom in the south without being targeted by Afghan or coalition forces as time wore on. They also shifted from hard targets, such as U.S. forces, to soft targets, such as Afghan police and international personnel perceived to be supporting the Afghan government or coalition forces. Examples include Afghans organizing or otherwise involved in election work, NGO workers, ANP, ANA, and Afghan citizens believed to be cooperating with coalition forces or the Afghan government. Major spikes in insurgent-initiated violence were usually a function of specific campaigns. Examples include the insurgent attempt to destabilize the October 2004 presidential elections and 2005 parliamentary elections in Afghanistan by targeting Afghan and international personnel involved in organizing, registering, and participating in the elections. Insurgents also conducted a major campaign tied to the U.S. handover of the counterinsurgency campaign to NATO in 2006. Attacks occurred throughout the country before and after the handover, though most were in the south and east around the provinces of Helmand, Paktia, Paktika, and Kandahar.

Some of the most brutal executions conducted by the insurgents were of "collaborators" with the Afghan government or coalition forces. These targets included the assassination of Islamic clerics critical of the Taliban, such as Mullah Abdullah Fayyaz, head of the Ulema Council of Kandahar. The primary targets included Afghan government officials, Afghan citizens, NGOs, educational institutions, and religious figures. Schools were increasingly targeted in such provinces as Helmand. As one Taliban night letter warned: "Teachers' salaries are financed by nonbelievers. Unless you stop getting wages from them, you will be counted among the American puppets." This rationale also included targeting election candidates and members of parliament, since "the elections are a part of the American program" and those who participate in the elections "are the enemies of Islam and the homeland."

External Support

One of the most significant reasons for the insurgents' success in perpetrating a greater amount of violence was the support they received from two types of external actors: states and the international jihadist movement. In most insurgencies, the insurgent's ability to achieve sanctuary in neighbouring countries presents a major challenge for indigenous governments. Opportunities for such sanctuary are often exploited by insurgents. It is more difficult for counterinsurgent forces to target insurgents who have retreated to these sanctuaries, which allow the insurgents to regroup, resupply, and recruit new members. Statistical evidence shows that mountainous terrain can provide a particularly useful sanctuary for insurgent groups because it is difficult for indigenous and external counterinsurgent forces to navigate and easier for insurgents to hide in. This presented a particular challenge in Afghanistan, since the border areas and sanctuary in Pakistan included some of the world's most rugged, mountainous terrain.

Support from External States

Insurgent groups were successful at leveraging assistance from external states—especially in Pakistan. There are indications that support from Pakistan included two major components: assistance from some officials in the Pakistan government and the freedom to operate on Pakistani soil.

Officials in the Pakistan government had ideological and geostrategic motivations. As Pakistan's former dictator General Zia-ul-Haq once remarked to the head of the ISI, General Akhter Abdul Rehman, "the water [in Afghanistan] must boil at the right temperature." Afghanistan has long been important to Pakistan policymakers because of its geographic location. Following the overthrow of the Taliban regime in 2001, officials in the Pakistan government were motivated to work with the Taliban for several reasons:

- to balance against India, especially in light of Delhi's close relationship with the Afghan government
- to hedge against a U.S. and NATO withdrawal, ensuring that if Western troops departed from Afghanistan, Pakistan would retain a proxy force in Afghanistan
- to preempt a movement among Pakistan's Pashtun population toward closer relations with Afghanistan should Afghanistan became more secure and prosperous.

The ISI provided assistance to the Taliban in the 1990s and early 2000s to ensure that it had an ally in Kabul. The motivation of those in the ISI assisting the Taliban in the mid-2000s was similar: to increase the likelihood over the long term that the government of Afghanistan (or at least those controlling the areas of Afghanistan near Pakistan) was controlled by allies. Balancing against India appeared to be a particularly strong impetus for Pakistan's support of the insurgents. Pakistan and India have long been involved in a balance-of-power struggle in South Asia. Both lay claim to the Kashmir region and fought at least three wars over Kashmir since 1947. Since September 11, 2001, India provided several hundred million dollars in financial assistance to Afghanistan, including funds to assist Afghan political candidates during the 2004 presidential elections and 2005 parliamentary elections. India also helped fund construction of the new Afghan parliament building and provided financial assistance to elected legislators. India's road construction near the Pakistan border was a significant point of contention between India and Pakistan. These projects were run by India's state-owned Border Roads Organisation, whose publicly acknowledged mission was to help "the [Indian] armed forces meet their strategic needs by committed, dedicated and cost-effective development and sustenance of the infrastructure." Finally, India established several consulates in such Afghan cities as Jalalabad, Kandahar, and Herat.

Pakistan accused India of using these consulates as a base for "terrorist activities" conducted inside Pakistan, such as fomenting unrest in the province of Baluchistan. The Indian-Afghan axis left Pakistan isolated among its South Asian neighbours. Before the September 11, 2001, terrorist attacks in the United States, Pakistan had a close relationship with the Taliban government in Afghanistan, which it had nurtured since the 1990s. Half a decade later, Pakistan was surrounded by hostile states. Consequently, for some Pakistani officials, assisting insurgents in Afghanistan was a way to balance against Indian influence in Afghanistan, maximize Pakistan's influence in the border regions, and prevent the Pashtuns on both sides of the border from developing a united front and pushing for integration into Afghanistan.

Some active and former Pakistan government officials from organizations such as the ISI and Frontier Corps provided logistical support to the Taliban and helped secure medical care for wounded insurgents in cities such as Quetta. They also helped train Taliban and other insurgents destined for Afghanistan and Kashmir in Quetta, Mansehra, Shamshattu, Parachinar, and other areas within Pakistan. To minimize its visibility, these individuals appeared to supply indirect assistance—including financial assistance—to Taliban training camps. NATO officials uncovered several instances in which ISI operatives provided intelligence to Taliban insurgents at the tactical, operational, and strategic levels. This included tipping off Taliban forces about the location and movement of Afghan and coalition forces, which undermined several U.S. and NATO anti-Taliban military operations.

In addition, General Hamid Gul and Colonel Sultan Amir Imam, pro-Taliban and pro–al Qaeda Pakistani leaders, gave widely reported speeches at government and military institutions in Pakistan calling for jihad against the United States and the Afghan government. In sum, individuals within the ISI and other Pakistan government agencies provided several types of assistance:

- ensuring that wounded Taliban and other insurgents received medical aid
- training insurgents at camps in Pakistan
- providing intelligence
- providing financial assistance
- assisting with logistics in crossing the border.

This assistance is consistent with the Pakistan government's past behaviour, especially the ISI. Throughout the 1990s, Pakistan's military and intelligence service provided arms, ammunition, supplies, financial aid, and training to the Taliban and Gulbuddin Hekmatyar. Pakistan also helped recruit fighters for the Taliban, sometimes working with domestic religious associations.

In addition, insurgent groups had substantial freedom to operate in Pakistan. The Taliban and other insurgent groups shipped arms, ammunition, and supplies into Afghanistan from Pakistan. Many suicide bombers came from Afghan refugee camps located in Pakistan. IED components were often smuggled across the Afghanistan-Pakistan border and assembled at safe houses in and around such provinces as Kandahar. The Taliban used roads such as Highway 4 in Kandahar Province to transport fighters and supplies between Afghanistan and Pakistan.

Pakistan's government failed several times to negotiate effective peace deals with militants in such tribal regions as North and South Waziristan. These deals called on tribesmen to expel foreign militants and end cross-border attacks into Afghanistan. In return, Pakistan's military promised to end major operations in the area and pull most of its soldiers back to military camps. The logic of these deals seems intuitive: In areas where tribes exert political, military, and economic power, the most effective long-term solution was to create incentives for tribal leaders to police their areas. After all, these tribal areas had been ruled indigenously for hundreds of years. And tribes often regard outside forces, including Pakistan's military, as unwelcome foreigners.

But there were several problems with this strategy. First, it rested on a false assumption, since it presumed that tribes actually controlled these areas. A closer look at the tribal areas indicated that insurgents and terrorists like the Taliban increasingly exerted control. In many cases, they usurped the power of tribes. Expecting tribes to police areas they did not even control was wishful thinking. Second, the tribal deals failed to curb cross-border activity and undermine the power of the Taliban and other militant groups there. NATO officials I inter-viewed argued that insurgents crossed the border in greater numbers.

As former Pakistan foreign minister Najmuddin Shaikh acknowledged in Pakistan's *Dawn* newspaper, "There is no doubt that the Waziristan agreement has led to increased Taliban influence." Third, there was no enforcement mechanism were the tribal deals to fail. Why should tribes cooperate, assuming they could, if there was no penalty for defection? Pakistan's military expressed a deep unwillingness to enter the tribal areas again.

Indeed, Afghan insurgents used Pakistan as a staging area for offensive operations. Taliban insurgents that operated in the southern Afghan provinces of Kandahar, Oruzgan, Helmand, and Zabol had significant support networks in such Pakistani provinces as Baluchistan and the Federally Administered Tribal Areas, including in Waziristan. Due to common ethnicity, they received political support from some of Pakistan's Pashtun tribes. The Taliban conduct much of their financing and recruiting operations on the Pakistani side of the border. There is also significant evidence that the Taliban leadership had a support base—commonly referred to as the Quetta Shura—in Quetta, Pakistan. As Zalmay Khalilzad, former U.S. Ambassador to Afghanistan, noted,

Mullah Omar and other Taliban leaders are in Pakistan. [Mullah Akhtar] Usmani, one of the Taliban leaders, spoke to Pakistan's Geo TV at a time when the Pakistani intelligence services claimed that they did not know where [the Taliban leaders] were. If a TV company could find him, how is it that the intelligence service of a country which has nuclear bombs and a lot of security and military forces cannot find them?"

In addition, Ali Jalali, former Afghan Interior Minister, argued, The Taliban have training camps, staging areas, recruiting centres (*madrassas*), and safe havens in Pakistan. The operations of a 70,000-strong Pakistani military force, deployed in the border region, mostly in the Waziristan tribal areas, have been effective against al Qaeda and non-Pakistani militants, but they have not done much toward containing the Taliban.

The Pakistani military conducted combat operations against foreign fighters—especially Central Asians and Arabs—in the Federally Administered Tribal Areas. But Pakistan was reluctant to conduct operations in Baluchistan against Taliban insurgents or their support network. As one Pakistani journalist argued, the Pakistan government "plunges into action when they know they can lay their hands on a foreign militant but they are still reluctant to proceed against the Taliban." Part of the reason may be that the Pakistan government was preoccupied with other security concerns in such provinces as Baluchistan, where it was fighting a counterinsurgency campaign against Baluch tribes.

In addition to Pakistan, Iran has historically been active in Afghanistan. Iranian policymakers have long been interested in securing strategic depth and influence in Afghanistan. Following the overthrow of the Taliban regime in 2001, the Iranian government funded reconstruction projects in Afghanistan (including road construction projects) and provided aid to some warlords. This behaviour was consistent with the activities of such regional powers as Pakistan, India, and Russia. Indeed, the Iranian strategy in Afghanistan after the overthrow of the Taliban is perhaps best characterized as a "hedging strategy."

The Iranian government preferred a close relationship with the Afghan government, which it enjoyed with key Afghan policymakers. Iran and Afghanistan cooperated in trying to crack down on drugs passing over their shared border. They also participated in joint trade, energy, investment, cultural, and scientific projects.

However, Iran also saw its involvement in Afghanistan as a hedge against a possible U.S. or Israeli strike against Iranian nuclear facilities. This meant that Iran was prepared to undermine U.S. efforts in Afghanistan in the event of further deterioration of U.S.-Iranian relations. There was some evidence that individuals from the Iranian government, including from the Iranian Revolutionary Guard Corps– Quds Force, provided some arms, money, and training to Taliban commanders and other insurgents. Examples included explosively formed penetrators, antitank mines, mortars, and small arms.

However, there were limits to Iran's willingness to support the Taliban and other insurgent groups. Iran historically had poor relations with the Taliban. As one Iranian diplomat noted in 1997, for example, Iran joined "Russia and the anti-Taliban alliance against Pakistan, Saudi Arabia and the Taliban" because it was concerned about the rise of Sunni extremist groups like the Taliban.

JIHADIST SUPPORT

Another source of support for the insurgency in Afghanistan was the international jihadist network, which enabled the Taliban and other groups to sustain their operations and helped them become more lethal in attacks against Afghans and coalition forces. This support came from a variety of different jihadist sources. One source was organizations such as the international al Qaeda network. Afghan insurgent groups also received assistance from the collection of *zakat* (the Islamic concept of tithing and alms) at mosques in Pakistan, Afghanistan, and the broader Muslim world.

Finally, much of the jihadist funding came from wealthy Muslims abroad, especially from such Gulf states as the United Arab Emirates, Saudi Arabia, and Qatar. For example, al Qaeda personnel regularly met with wealthy Arab businessmen during the Tabligh Jamaat annual meeting in Raiwind, Pakistan, which attracted one of the largest concentrations of Muslims after the hajj.

The Taliban and other insurgent groups established a major support base through their cooperation with Jamiat-e-Ulema Islam. This Pakistani political party had its roots in the Deobandi movement and had a following largely confined to the Pashtun border belt of the North West Frontier Province and Baluchistan (although it also has support in several of Pakistan's urban centres). The Deobandi movement developed in British-ruled India during the mid-1800s. It was an offshoot of the Sunni Hanafi legal school and took its name from the Indian Himalayan town of Deoband, the location of an influential religious school. The Deobandi movement aimed to reform and unify Muslims, preached strict adherence to the *Sunnah* (the way or deeds of the Prophet Muhammad), and emphasized the importance of *shari'a* law. Jamiat-e-Ulema Islam was split into two factions, led by Maulana Fazal ur-Rehman and Samiul Haq (a fervent supporter of Osama bin Laden). The party ran an extensive network of madrassas that trained most of the leadership and much of the early rank and file of the Taliban. Party links with the Taliban remained close, despite President Musharraf's talk of reforming the madrassas. Indeed, Afghan insurgents long targeted recruits at madrassas and Afghan refugee camps in Pakistan.

Al Qaeda played a critical role in the insurgency as a force multiplier, assisting insurgent groups such as the Taliban at the tactical, operational, and strategic levels. Groups such as the Taliban used support and training from jihadists to construct increasingly sophisticated IEDs, including IEDs with remote-control detonators. For example, there were a handful of al Qaeda–run training facilities and IED assembly facilities in such places as North and South Waziristan. They ranged from small facilities hidden in compounds to much larger "IED factories," which doubled as training centres and labs where recruits experimented with IED technology. These facilities were located in such remote places as the Bush mountains, Khamran mountains, and Shakai valley. Al Qaeda received operational and financial support from local clerics and Taliban commanders in Waziristan. They recruited young Pashtuns from the local madrassas and financed their activities through "religious racket"—forced religious contribution, often accompanied with death threats. Some of this IED expertise came from Iraqi groups, which provided information to Afghan groups on making and using various kinds of remote-controlled devices and timers. Indeed, there is evidence of cooperation between insurgents in Iraq and Afghanistan. Islamic militants in Iraq provided information through the Internet and face-to-face visits on tactics to Taliban, Hezb-i-Islami, and foreign fighters from eastern and southern Afghanistan and Pakistan's tribal areas. In addition, there is some evidence that a small number of Pakistani and Afghan militants received military training in Iraq; Iraqi fighters met with Afghan and Pakistani extremists in Pakistan; and militants in Afghanistan increasingly used homemade bombs, suicide attacks, and other tactics honed in Iraq.

The "TV bomb" is one example of an IED introduced to Afghan insurgents by Iraqi groups. This shaped-charge mechanism can be hidden under brush or debris on a roadside and set off by remote control from a distance of 300 yards or more. There is also some evidence that individuals such as Hamza Sangari, a Taliban commander from Khowst Province, received information from Iraqi groups that improved the Taliban's ability to make armour-penetrating weapons by disassembling rockets and rocket-propelled grenade rounds, removing the explosives and propellants, and repacking them with high-velocity "shaped" charges. Afghan groups occasionally adopted some of the more brutal tactics, such as beheadings, used by Iraqi groups. In December 2005, for example, insurgents posted a video to al Qaeda–linked Web sites showing the decapitation of an Afghan hostage—the first time a video of the beheading of an Afghan hostage was shown.

The Taliban also acquired new commercial communication gear and field equipment from Iraqi groups and received good tactical, camouflage, and marksmanship training from them as well. In addition, Afghan insurgents increasingly adopted suicide tactics, especially in major cities such as Kandahar and Kabul. The number of suicide attacks increased steadily: one in 2002, two in 2003, six in 2004, and twenty-seven in 2005. There were 139 suicide terrorist attacks in Afghanistan in 2006 and 140 in 2007.77 The use of suicide attacks was encouraged by al Qaeda leaders in Pakistan, such as Ayman al-Zawahiri, who argued for the "need to concentrate on the method of martyrdom operations as the most successful way of inflicting damage against the opponent and the least costly to the Mujahedin in terms of casualties." Suicide bombers included Afghans, Pakistanis, and some foreigners. Most suicide bombers through 2007 came from Afghan refugee camps in Pakistan.

They frequently attended Pakistani madrassas, where they were radicalized and immersed in extremist ideologies. Several factors can be attributed to the rise in suicide attacks. First, the Taliban successfully tapped into the expertise and training of the broader jihadist community, especially al Qaeda. Jihadists imparted knowledge on suicide tactics to Afghan groups through the Internet and in face-to-face visits. With al Qaeda's assistance, these militants helped supply a steady stream of suicide bombers. Second, al Qaeda and the Taliban concluded that suicide bombing was more effective than other tactics in killing Afghan and coalition forces. This was a direct result of the success of such groups as Hamas in the Palestinian territories, Hezbollah in Lebanon, the Tamil Tigers in Sri Lanka, and Iraqi groups.

Suicide attacks allowed insurgents to achieve maximum impact with minimal resources. Data show that when insurgents fight U.S. and coalition forces directly in Afghanistan, there is only a 5 percent probability of inflicting casualties. With suicide attacks, the chance of killing people and instilling fear increased several fold. Third, al Qaeda and the Taliban believed that suicide attacks increased the level of insecurity among the Afghan population. This caused some Afghans to question the government's ability to protect them and further destabilized the authority of local government institutions. Fourth, suicide attacks provided renewed visibility for the Taliban and al Qaeda, which previous guerrilla attacks did not generate. Because of their lethality and high-profile nature, every suicide attack was reported in the national and international media.

In sum, the international jihadist network provided significant support to Afghan insurgent groups. Al Qaeda effectively spread its extremist global ideology in Afghanistan and Pakistan. It played a critical role in providing encouragement and impetus for the utilization of suicide attacks and sophisticated IEDs. Al Qaeda also paid up to several thousand dollars to the families of suicide bombers who perished in operations in Afghanistan. In addition, some Taliban units included al Qaeda members or other Arab fighters, who brought with them tactics employed in such places as Iraq and Chechnya.

2

Counterinsurgency Strategy for Afghanistan

Of all the challenges that beset Afghanistan, the most dramatic is the lack of an integrated counterinsurgency strategy. Objectively, the coalition and the international community have provided admirable assistance to Afghanistan. Without exaggeration, Afghanistan's political, economic, and social situation has improved exponentially. Nevertheless, three interrelated challenges require resolution before Afghanistan can continue on its forward path—the insurgency, warlordism, and the neglect of the local communities.

As implied, an integrated strategy pursues tangible objectives which solve immediate problems, but it also contributes to the resolution of long-term menaces. Realistically, the Afghan insurgency is not a virulent threat to the government. The various insurgent groups have failed to extend their powerbase beyond their local powerbases and certainly cannot be construed as representing a unified front. Yet, Taliban groups, or those who claim to be Taliban for personal gain, do disrupt the necessary reforms essential to Afghanistan's progress. Similarly, endemic warlordism (local powerbrokers, drug lords, politicians, and other opportunists) resists government authority for the pursuit of personal gains. In the long term, warlordism represents a greater threat to the Afghanistan's liberal democracy. As in the past, the local communities (e.g., the thousands of hamlets, villages, towns, and city neighbourhoods) suffer the greatest neglect.

As long as the insurgency and warlordism exists, local communities will remain on the fringes of international and government beneficence.

The principle of Subsidiarity forms the underlying approach to a counterinsurgency strategy for Afghanistan. In essence, Subsidiarity embraces decentralization of governance to the lowest level. Because this form of federalism has a long-standing tradition in Afghanistan (as well as the West), the populace readily accepts the concept. This concept permits the central government to focus on national issues. However, it does not signify neglect. Rather, it permits federal, international, and coalition agencies to empower local communities in a decentralized manner without deleterious intrusion from above. In short, it shifts the counterinsurgency effort to the local communities.

Afghanistan's unique situation and how it forms the essential backdrop for the current challenges, underscoring pertinent historical considerations, the realities affecting the application of military power, and insurgency paradoxes. The explores a counterinsurgency operational paradigm as a systematic method for Clear-Hold-Build-Expand.

The operational paradigm is the most important element of the counterinsurgency strategy. Ironically, a good strategy cannot compensate for a failure at the operational level.

At best, partial success with clear and hold only makes the insurgency more manageable, but it cannot result in long-term success. The strategic considerations for the formulation of a counterinsurgency strategy. Many are supplemental initiatives (i.e., icing on the cake), which strengthen the strategy but are not necessarily essential to success.

The implications of a properly aligned counterinsurgency strategy are clear. Security operations are the sine qua non for separating insurgents from the populace, but they are not an end in itself. Instead, their success permits the other elements of power to operate without interference at the lowest level, to the benefit of the entire country over time. In addition, this approach recognizes the natural evolution from which modern, functional states have risen.

Pertinent Historical Considerations

In light of Afghanistan's history, sociopolitical background, and arrested development, a counterinsurgency strategy, which relies on a top-down execution, is likely to falter. A history of weak central governance, frequent political-military upheavals, and endemic tribalism has always been the dominant obstacle.

Promoting a strong central government to pursue strategic goals runs counter to the Afghan experience. Afghanistan is less a state than a collection of tribes and clans occupying the same geographic area. Historically, decentralized governance best describes the political tapestry of Afghanistan with local chieftains and councils (Shuras) providing the essential hierarchical needs to their tribal members.

This sociopolitical reality is partly due to geography and partly due to engrained decentralized governance. First, the majority of local communities are remote from Kabul due to the mountainous terrain and poor transportation networks. Second, with a history of foreign invasions combined with ubiquitous ethnic and religious strife creating socioeconomic and political upheavals, a strong federal government never truly evolved. The civil war of the 1990s destroyed any vestiges of a central government, and the Taliban regime was too short-lived to establish complete totalitarianism. The advent of liberal democratic governance as a result of Operation Enduring Freedom, without concomitant security to the local communities, created anarchy—Afghanistan in short became "The Wild West." Although Afghanistan will eventually evolve into a functioning state (contingent upon a continued commitment by the international community), it is also quite likely that the reach of the central government vis-à-vis the local communities will remain weak and tribal loyalty to the central government erratic for decades to come.

Afghanistan's tumultuous history most certainly undergirded tribalism as people depended on their family and local chieftains for self-preservation and various other needs. In this sense, the status of the central government became irrelevant to the average Afghan as long as the tribal ties remained unaffected. This arrangement also placed the monopoly on violence at the tribal level, resulting in the rise of local militias. In the absence of a strong central government, inter-tribal conflicts led to a predator-prey cycle. That is, the tribes enjoying predominance preyed on weaker tribes, causing the weak to bandwagon as a defensive mechanism or until the roles reversed. Paradoxically, this anarchical environment created mercurial balance of power arrangements of ever changing alliances. Hence, today's allies could easily become tomorrow's enemies and vice versa.

Military Power Realities

The most common nostrum for COIN is the predominate use of military action to defeat an insurgency. Despite the abysmal history of relying almost solely on the military solution, counterinsurgent governments habitually use it as the first option. This is not to say that there is no need for military power in counterinsurgency.* Successful counterinsurgencies learn to create the conditions for local security forces to protect their communities and only then do they

provide greater economic and political development. It therefore appears illogical in Afghanistan's case, to expand the Afghan National Army (ANA) and increase the number of U.S. military forces without a corresponding strategy which addresses the indispensible need for local security. The sheer number of local communities (i.e., hamlets, villages, towns, and cities) in Afghanistan makes it impossible for the ANA and American forces to establish a permanent presence in every community. And an attempt to do so would overextend these forces to the point of zero effectiveness.

Similarly, using military forces to seal off the border with Pakistan would require exorbitant numbers of troops. To provide perspective, the border length, not counting the mountainous terrain, is 1510 miles (2430 km). This length is 1.5 times longer the Eastern Front of World War II (994 miles). Hence, the sheer task of covering every possible infiltration point along the border is beyond any army. Small insurgent teams can effectively infiltrate into Afghanistan and remain inert in local communities (i.e., safe houses) until sufficient teams have accumulated in Afghanistan for operational effect. In such a situation, it becomes irrelevant how many infiltrators the military intercepts because over time, the insurgents can still infiltrate sufficient forces into the country to sustain the insurgency.

Afghanistan's history of decentralized governance has accustomed tribes and chieftains to self-sufficiency, and a concomitant suspicion of central government. Tribes have a long practice of accepting bribes from interventionist great powers in exchange for acquiescence or as a temporary ally against enemies. At best, bribing tribes is a short-term advantage. In the long-term such tactical arrangements militate against extending the authority of the central government and guarantee a resumption of the predatory-prey cycle.

The existence of warlord militias once the Taliban government was ousted were a source of great concern for the United States and was the reason for the disarming of non-government forces (e.g., warlord militias) under the DDR (Disarm, Demobilize, and Reintegrate), which evolved into DIAG (Disarmament of Illegally Armed Groups). Hence, rearming tribal militias willy-nilly would undo years of disarmament and stymie the authority of the central government.

An initiative relying on local Shuras to recruit, organize, equip, train and pay local militias may be effective against external Taliban threats. However, the initiative would have little or no effect on local warlords and drug lords, who likely overshadow the authority of the Shuras. One can assume these powerbrokers would infiltrate the Shura militias with their own men as a self-protection measure. Moreover, the Shura militia would not likely root out any Taliban indigenous to the local community (e.g., relatives and friends) as long as their activities were directed outside of the community.

Coalition authorities should recognize that individuals and tribes will use coalition military forces to attack their enemies. Hence, human intelligence on "Taliban" forces may be nothing more than personal revenge or the elimination of a tribal or criminal rival. Over time, unintentional military operations against non-insurgents are likely to create greater anti-government sentiment with the affected populace.

Insurgency Paradoxes

The Afghan insurgency is not attempting to compete with the central government for legitimacy. Instead, it has opted to stymie government economic and political development, adhering to a strategy of disruption and destruction. A paradox occurs, because the populace logically should blame the insurgents for causing mayhem. Instead, the populace blames the government for its failure to provide security, and by extension, economic and political development. The populace does not expect the insurgents to mend their ways; rather, it expects the government to expunge society of these societal parasites. And if the government is unwilling or unable to do so, the people demand a political change. Pressure from the people weakens the resolve and consensus of the government, planting the seeds of its own demise. Hence, a government in turmoil cannot help but advance the goals of the insurgency.

On the other hand, it would be wrong to conclude the Afghan insurgency is a zero-sum game. The various anti-government forces which call themselves Taliban cannot fill the political vacuum if the Afghan government falls. If the Taliban enjoy any popularity, it is confined to the single digits and even that is likely splintered among the various insurgent groups. The insurgency, as a political-military movement, has likewise foundered, leaving the insurgents no recourse but to rely on IEDs, suicide bombers, and limited paramilitary activities. If international forces withdrew, the Taliban would not become the uncontested challenger to the Afghan government. Rather, Afghanistan would slowly degenerate into tribal conflicts as the central government becomes increasingly irrelevant.

Whereas the Taliban are inept in the political and military sense, they have proven adept at creating the impression they represent a growing and virulent threat to Afghanistan. This is a partial consequence of journalistic romanticism of insurgents. The media embraces the simplistic notion that if the government cannot destroy the insurgency, the insurgents must be supermen. Second, collateral damage creates propaganda opportunities for the insurgents. Third, insurgents are not obliged to speak the truth, and since propaganda is often their greatest tool for defining reality, especially with no tangible successes, they rely on it profoundly. It would not be an exaggeration to state that if it weren't for the media's obsession with the insurgent mystic, the image of the Taliban would be properly relegated to the dustbin of historical incompetents.

One must bear in mind that the constraints on the government and coalition forces provide an advantage to insurgent propaganda. The media scrutinizes coalition and government statements and actions in search of a scandal. The coalition must investigate operations resulting in collateral damage or claims that targets were non-combatants. While the investigation is on-going, which can take days or weeks, the insurgents capitalize on the opportunity to issue false claims to the media, which accept the information without scrutiny. The results of the coalition investigation do not receive the same attention as the insurgent claims. At times, village officials claim or exaggerate collateral damage in order to receive blood money, that is, financial compensation for wrongful deaths. For the insurgents, it is a win-win situation. They have a platform for recruitment and financial aid from others susceptible to insurgent sympathies. Moreover, the coalition or government may place greater restrictions on the rules of engagement. From the insurgent perspective, any device which fetters coalition firepower simply shifts the correlation of forces in their favour.

THE COUNTERINSURGENCY OPERATIONAL PARADIGM

The counterinsurgency operational paradigm deserves special attention since it is essential to the success of the counterinsurgency strategy. The paradigm holds as its immutable, primary goal the permanent separation of the insurgents from the population. The paradigm is a systematic approach for gaining and retaining control of local communities, step by step until the entire population is secured. Implementation of the paradigm requires a mutually supporting effort tailored to the unique circumstances of each target area. The selection of target areas and the timing of operations becomes a matter of strategy. Naturally, the target area must be within the capabilities of the tasked unit. For example, a small district would likely be within the capabilities of a battalion; a brigade for a small province.

For Afghanistan, a proper integrated approach comprises four major components: military units, local security training cadre, counter narcotic teams, and construction and development facilitators. All components operate within close proximity both in time and space. Although some sequencing of events is necessary, most of the activities take place almost simultaneously.

The paradigm starts with the initial military sweep, with units occupying all population centres (e.g., hamlets, villages, towns, and cities) in the area of operation. The intent is to drive active guerrilla fighters from these communities and not to kill them per se. To minimize collateral damage, providing an escape route will likely induce guerrillas to flee rather than stand and fight out of desperation. However, the military may establish ambush sites outside of the community for the purpose of intercepting fleeing guerrillas. The military commander makes a proclamation to the community citizens to inform them of the operation, ask for their cooperation with the soldiers, and explain the subsequent planned initiatives. As the initial agent for information operations, the commander informs, reassures, and provides hope to the local population. He also takes the opportunity to rebut insurgent propaganda. He must realize that the local populace is susceptible to propaganda and rumours in the absence of competing information. The goal is to instill in the people hope for the future and self-confidence.

To assist the fledgling local security force, soldiers inspect every building, taking an informal census by residence and asking dwellers just two questions: who collects the taxes, and who recruits for insurgents. This information is collected and handed over to the training cadre.

The military commander's designated subordinate produces a sketch of the urban layout using a simple gridding system. In this manner, the military is able to create the foundations for urbanized order (e.g., street names, addresses, and residences). Satellite images of the urban area can be transformed into a sketch drawn-to-scale, which greatly enhances the accuracy of the urban sketch. This early groundwork yields great dividends as the government establishes greater control over the population.

As the military secures and canvases the community, the training cadre meets with the local authorities, either chieftain or Shura, to explain its purpose. The cadre seeks the approval of the local authorities to recruit, organize, equip, train, supply, and provide wages for a local security force. Those services are straightforward, but the real importance of the cadre lies in two essential qualities it provides to the security force: discipline and values. Without these two ingredients, a local security force can degenerate into a death squad, prey upon other communities, or become an oppressor to the community they are supposed to defend. Under the supervision of the cadre, the security force becomes a servant to the community.

U.S. Army Special Forces are the most proficient at training indigenous forces and should be employed in high threat areas whenever possible. American Special Forces have an illustrative and abiding history of training security forces throughout the world and are accustomed to working independently in austere environments. In medium and low threat areas, the military can use military police or contracted police as cadre. Similarly, Allied nations can provide sufficient numbers of cadres (including their own special forces) in their assigned regions without threatening competing requirements or sparking a political firestorm.

After the local security force is established and training begins, the military shifts its operations to the surrounding areas to hunt insurgents lingering in the area. Insurgents are at their weakest in the immediate aftermath of leaving their host community. The logic of this conclusion is clear. Insurgents expend extraordinary time and effort to bring the local population under their control. The community has provided insurgents with shelter, sustenance, money, intelligence, and other resources. Once they are thrust out in the hinterland, insurgents must find succour in base camps or safe houses elsewhere until the military forces depart the host community.

The military conducts small unit operations (squad, platoon, and company) in the surrounding areas for the purpose of discovering and destroying fugitive insurgents, base camps and caches. Gridding is a useful tactical tool for the methodical clearing of the surrounding areas. The principal purpose of these military operations is to keep insurgents away from the population centres during the formative period of establishing local security forces. Again, the ultimate goal is not to kill all the insurgents but to drive them to such despair that they abandon the insurgency and reconcile with the government.

Integral to the military operations is the use of psychological warfare. Prisoners and defectors are treated well with the intent of exploiting their knowledge of base camps, caches, and insurgent leaders. They are used to persuade their former colleagues to surrender through the use of the media, helicopters with their voice recordings, amnesty pamphlets, etc. The consistent message to convey is that the government does not intend to prosecute the rank and file, but only the hard-core leadership of the insurgency.

As the military starts small unit operations, the counter narcotics teams or a specially trained ANA counter narcotics unit begin poppy eradication and destruction of drug labs discovered by the military or already known. A military presence in the area acts as a deterrent against threats to the crop eradication teams. Should deterrence fail, the military eliminates the threats quickly. To accelerate eradication, the eradication teams hire local people to help burn the fields. The counter narcotic teams, in conjunction with the appropriate agencies, provide alternative crop seeds for the next growing season. The teams compensate farmers directly with crop losses, using the fair market value of a local, legitimate local crop (e.g., grain, produce, fruit, etc.) as the basis of payment. The teams issue warnings that failure to grow legitimate crops in the future will result in crop eradication without compensation and probable criminal charges. The team records persons involved in the drug trade for tracking or further investigation.

After a sufficient period of training for the local security forces, the training cadre identifies potential leaders for formal training (e.g., Regional Training Center), who assume leadership positions upon their return. At this point, the training cadres are released for operations in subsequent target areas and are replaced my mentor teams, which continue the process of inoculating the community from insurgent infiltration. Mentor teams can comprise conventional military personnel, international policemen, or trained civilian contractors. The greater abundance of such personnel are needed since Afghanistan will eventually need thousands of mentor teams if every population center is to receive the support needed for recovery.

Community inoculation is a series of measures to advance local government control of the local population. Control measures are tailored to the type of threats (i.e., insurgent, criminal, corruption, etc.) and the extent of threats (i.e., high, medium, or low). A formal census verifies and expands on the informal census. With the assistance of the local authorities, the mentors issue plastic identification cards with pictures and thumbprints to the residents. Using the urban sketch, the mentors pinpoint each inhabitant's residence, recording it on the ID card. To foster citizen cooperation, ID cards can serve as the basis for rations, labour, medical, and other assistance. To instill a sense of value, the authorities inform the people that the ID card is the only passport for aid and benefits.

A curfew is effective in controlling movement at night. Violators of the curfew are checked for ID card (to check residency) and brought in to the police station for questioning if suspicions are raised. Experience reveals that the vast majority of curfew violators are involved in insurgent or criminal activities. Swift questioning has a greater chance of arresting fellow conspirators before they are aware one of their own has been arrested. Thus, a curfew is a powerful tool for breaking covert insurgent and criminal cells.

The establishment of a neighbourhood watch permits the local authorities and security forces to detect insurgent attempts at infiltration as well as criminal activity. Using the gridding system of the urban area, the local authorities designate a neighbourhood watch czar at the top of an organizational pyramid. The czar splits the urban area in half and assigns two subordinates to monitor each area, who in turn replicate the process. The bifurcation process continues until a family monitor is responsible for three to five families. The monitor visits the families daily to check on their status and to learn of any changes (i.e., someone new living with them or reports of criminal activity). The family monitor reports changes through the organizational pyramid for situational awareness. If a family has someone new living with them, the family monitor escorts the new inhabitant to the local security authorities for ID cards and questioning.

To supplement the citizen reporting system, a cell phone hotline can permit people to report suspicious activities anonymously. For areas with internet connectivity, an internet website can also be used for reporting activities as well. A community reporting box can also be used for the anonymous passing of tips. Tapping into the community for information is a powerful tool because nothing escapes the scrutiny of the citizens. They just need a way to tip off the authorities without endangering themselves for retribution.

At some point, the local security forces morph into a community police force, complete with national uniforms and badges. Because they come from the community, the local police already have roots in the community and are trusted. Local police are invaluable for creating order in the community and maintaining control of the population. They should also be used for passing intelligence to mentor teams on suspected insurgent operatives and local criminals. However, mentor teams need to remain vigilant of police corruption or any deterioration in this trust. Although it appears easier to fire a suspect policeman, a formal investigation of the allegations is warranted because the accusations may be unsubstantiated (i.e., an attempt by local power brokers to get a troublesome policeman out of the way).

The mentor teams can accelerate the reintegration of society, which is usually rent asunder by insurgent occupation, through community activities. Clubs and sports are positive ways to create healthy interaction among the inhabitants and require little effort to organize and equip. Volleyball seems to be a sport the Afghans readily play and requires fewer people and space than soccer. In many respects, community centres, with a TV or radio room, a room for sewing circles, and a room for board games, etc, are effective centres for critical social interaction.

The mentor teams serve as the community middlemen for development and construction projects. Mentor teams submit their requests for projects to the appropriate Provincial Reconstruction Team (PRT) office. Projects are best identified by consultations with the local authorities. At times, various organizations have projects which the local communities do not need or want. If the mentors cannot dissuade an organization from building such a project, they should offer advice to the local authorities on alternative uses for the completed project. For instance, a school building may be laudable in broad terms, but without teachers, books, furniture, and supplies, it cannot be used. The mentors could recommend the local authorities turn it into a community center until it can be used as a school.

Construction projects offer great potential for improving the lot of local communities. Ideally, the construction agency builds something the community needs. This is an area which requires higher command scrutiny and influence because construction teams may want to do the projects themselves in order to meet self-imposed deadlines. A plethora of completed projects may brief well in terms of showing progress, but the process does little to advance the local societies.

Construction teams should provide the training, materials, equipment, supervisory expertise, and the salaries for local labour for projects. The payoffs are long-term but enduring. The local inhabitants begin to acquire skills, and the salaries boost the local economy. Nothing instills pride in ownership more than direct community interaction.

The presence of the Provincial Reconstruction Team assures continuity of effort after the military has moved on to other provinces. The PRT serves as the clearing house for construction and development agencies. It provides office space for such agencies (e.g., USAID, Department of State, UNAMA, medical etc.) to provide coordination and tracking of projects within the province. Additionally, the PRT is ideally suited to provide disaster relief assistance in many cases. A manoeuvre battalion is the ideal security force to serve as a quick reaction force and to provide security for construction and development projects as well as medical assistance events. This security requirement may seem unnecessary to American sectors because of the presence of brigade combat teams, but for the majority of allies in Afghanistan, a robust security element is sorely needed.

The potential of PRTs are limited only to the vision of the counterinsurgency commanders: a safe place for the holding of local police salaries and other funds; warehouses for disaster relief or humanitarian assistance surges; a refuge and amenities for mentor teams on a regular basis; a communications node for mentor team radios; clinics and medical civil assistance programs (MEDCAP); maintenance facilities and personnel when needed; and a first response to insurgent or criminal threats. Because of these diverse responsibilities, PRT commanders should be experienced manoeuvre commanders.

The operational paradigm establishes the mechanism for clearing an area of insurgent and criminal elements in addition to holding the area for economic and social development. Without this paradigm, any counterinsurgency strategy will only make limited progress and require extensive time at that. Nevertheless, the counterinsurgency commander must give due consideration to strategy in order to provide coherency to the moving parts.

COUNTERINSURGENCY STRATEGIC CONSIDERATIONS

The first consideration and initial effort must be given to securing strategic bases, such as Kabul, Kandahar, Gardez, and Ghazni.† They serve as the starting points for the oil spot strategy.

Because cities serve as the main theatrical stage for insurgent propaganda (hence their attraction for insurgent attacks), they must be denied insurgent access. In terms of the exigent threat elsewhere, the northern and western regions do not require urgent counterinsurgency action.

The timing and sequencing of areas to clear thereafter become a matter of strategy. Nesting the counterinsurgency strategy to the operational paradigm, the intent is to push insurgents and criminal organizations progressively farther from population centres: cities, towns, villages, and hamlets. This slow squeeze enervates the insurgents over time as their access to population centres becomes increasingly restricted.

As access to food, clean water, shelter, people, money, and other resources becomes limited, the ranks of the insurgency shrink accordingly. Additionally, without access to safe houses, the sophistication of improvised explosive devices and suicide bombs deteriorates as well. Although the goal is to push the insurgents to the border region, the secondary effects of the process is to create a sense of hopelessness in the insurgent ranks, increasing their rate of desertion.

The proposed increase of U.S. forces from 20,000 to 30,000 provides an opportunity to use the operational paradigm as a surge effort. However, if these reinforcements are reserved only for clearing operations, their added value to the counterinsurgency will remain limited.

The influx of troops will require extensive engineering assets for construction or expansion of Forward Operating Bases, which will likely adversely affect construction timetables for the ANA expansion as well as construction projects for local communities. To compensate, the United States may need to deploy more construction assets than earlier anticipated.

Similarly, the expansion of the ANA to 122,000 makes strategic sense if the rationale is to devote more units to the operational paradigm. If the expansion solely leads to military clearing operations, there is little added value. Similarly, a counterinsurgency strategy which attempts to place garrisons in local communities rapidly leads to an overextension of the military and exorbitant budgets due to overhead costs.

More importantly, the 122k-expansion must not set precedence for subsequent expansions. There comes a point where the size of the ANA assumes an offensive capability, creating a potential security dilemma in the region.

Increased threat perceptions among neighbouring countries can easily lead to regional instability. Assurances of current intent are no insurance against potential future aggression. Hence, as the conflict winds down and as a mollification of its neighbours,

Afghanistan should adopt a national security policy to convert selected units into the reserves, in the form of round-out brigades.

To bolster the operational paradigm, the ANA could station ANA units in high threat areas, thereby providing operational reserves in response to insurgent threats that are beyond the capabilities of the local police forces and PRT quick reaction forces.

More importantly, they can increase public confidence through periodic anti-insurgent and counter narcotic operations. ANA units can also increase public confidence and insurgent dismay by frequent visits to the local communities. Hence, the greatest expression of government authority is the presence of ANA soldiers in the local communities.

In the case of counter narcotics, the ANA counter narcotics battalion could provide an effective capability for poppy eradication, destruction of drug labs, and arrest of local drug lords.‡ The counter narcotics battalion commander must initiate operations in coordination with ANA corps, regional Afghan National Police, and the provincial governors, rather than waiting for a request beforehand.

Because insurgent and criminal activities represent a civil threat rather than a military threat, the Afghan National Police (ANP) should take precedence over the ANA in the counterinsurgency. What this means in effect is that the ANP should be the first responders to insurgent and criminal activity rather than the ANA.

This also implies that the local police forces should eventually fold into Afghan law enforcement institutions. Keeping the local police forces under the watchful eye of mentor teams will underscore the need for discipline and values, staving off the petty corruption that currently plagues the ANP. As the first line of defense for their communities, the local police force is in the best position to mitigate predatory practices on the population. In this regard, mentors can alert the central office at the PRT of warlord predatory incidents or government malfeasance for investigation.

To keep the insurgents off balance, deep raids into insurgent enclaves are necessary. These strategic thrusts keep insurgent enclaves in a weakened state and easier to clear later. Attempting to eliminate the insurgent sanctuaries in Pakistan are currently not worth the risk of escalation. In this sense, the cure is worse than the disease.

If the insurgents are confined to conducting operations from their sanctuaries in Pakistan, the conflict is confined to the border region without affecting the population centres. Again, without this access, the insurgency in Afghanistan withers. The use of coalition air power, armed UAVs, artillery, and infantry operations provides a distinct edge in the interception of insurgent infiltrations without the risk of collateral damage.

With the local communities inoculated from insurgent access, insurgent infiltrators successfully passing through the border region soon find themselves in dire straits as their supplies dwindle. Forced to attack local communities in order to gain access, insurgents are susceptible to air power and artillery. This situation significantly reduces the amount of collateral damage, thereby robbing the insurgents of their greatest propaganda device. Even if they do gain access, the quick reaction forces would quickly expel insurgents before they can fortify or exploit their gains. And once expelled, they need to make the long trek back to their Pakistani sanctuaries.

Coalition SOF and Afghan commando battalions provide a lethal threat to key insurgent leaders, to include al Qaeda and the Taliban in Pakistan. In this regard, killing and capturing the top al Qaeda and Taliban leadership are important goals, but just as important, keeping them pre-occupied with their own survival rather than planning and coordinating attacks serves national security purposes. The reconciliation program, which Afghanistan started several years ago, should continue with the promise of amnesty for insurgents, payment for weapons, payment for information, and reintegration into society. A reconciliation office in each PRT provides an immediate vehicle for insurgents to surrender.

Strategic Communications requires continual review and adaption. The medium used for Strategic Communications must have entertainment value first and foremost in order to gain and maintain an audience. Afghan entertainers (e.g., musicians, comedians, actors, etc.) must be employed for this cause. Although the Coalition can provide assistance and recommendations for Strategic Communications operations, only the Afghans provide the essential cultural and linguistic knowledge for the listening audience. Strategic Communications themes and messages are interwoven into the entertainment. Reconciled insurgents can contribute to the effort by informing insurgents of the reconciliation program and exposing insurgent propaganda techniques. To this end, the local community centres with TVs or radios assume paramount importance. Of course, news programs are an important part of this medium, and the government must issue statements through the news agencies to refute insurgent propaganda as well as informing the public of government development and construction programs.

Lastly, the Coalition must integrate combat cameras into every operation so as to videotape targets and the extent of collateral damage. Because insurgent propaganda issues immediate claims of civilian casualties after each Coalition attack, the coalition command can counter these claims immediately through the release of film footage. The command can then conduct investigations without the suspicion of a cover-up. Strategically, PRTs offer a politically palatable way for allies to increase their contributions to the Afghan conflict. Unlike the laissez faire approach with existing PRTs, a standardized contingent package is required. The package should approximate the size and capabilities of the PRT. Allies also need to provide training teams and/or mentor teams for the creation and maintenance of local police forces in their assigned areas.

Because of the existing stability in the north and west, the need for accompanying military operations preceding the insertion of training teams is predicated on the threat. The north serves as a rest and rehabilitation for Taliban elements in certain enclaves, such as Kunduz and Sar e Pol, so denying them to the Taliban is an important goal. Likewise, greater efforts against criminal organizations in the north and west warrant the use of the operational paradigm.

Major Afghan cities require greater attention because they are dense population centres and in need of urban renewal. PRTs dedicated to cities would provide that welcome relief. Another initiative with great potential is the adoption of sister cities, which the United States and Europe adopted in the aftermath of World War II.

Since many modern cities in the world have a plentitude of excess resources, Afghan cities could use the donations and other benefits which mayors can offer to their sister cities. This initiative might be a suitable mission for the Department of State to manage. The issue of free-riding among some ISAF partners requires a policy resolution. Basically, free-riding concerns the subtle practice of contributing governments shifting security burdens to other countries.

A long-standing practice in NATO, partner governments employ various stratagems to sub-optimize contributions: not following through with stated promises; claiming their forces are already overstretched; and shifting attention to other governments' free-riding.

Because of its status as a superpower, the United States has and will continue to shoulder the greater burden in most conflicts. That reality comes with the territory.

However, the countries, which have shouldered a greater burden in Afghanistan, (e.g., United Kingdom, Netherlands, Australia, and Canada), should rotate to the northern and western regions. Accordingly, the affected partners in the north and west would shift their PRTs to the southern region. In the long-term, the benefits of keeping active partners engaged in Afghanistan far outweigh the status quo arrangements. Again, this is a policy decision, but its impact on counterinsurgency strategy is profound. The time has come for UN Assistance Mission—Afghanistan (UNAMA) to manage the various construction and development activities in Afghanistan.

As this represents a momentous task, the UN Special Envoy to Afghanistan should lay the foundation of establishing a Reconstruction and Development Agency for the purpose of eliminating redundant projects, harmonizing efforts among the various organizations, and reducing fraud, waste and abuse (e.g., fraudulent NGOs, corrupt contractors, and power broker patronage). Working through the PRTs, the assistance effort can acquire greater coherency and effectiveness.

Ultimately, a counterinsurgency strategy seeks to balance available resources, the realities on the ground, and the expectations of the beleaguered populace. It follows then that a measurement of success entails the number of population centres inoculated from insurgent infiltration rather than the nebulous shibboleth of "hearts and minds."

Conclusions

No easy solutions exist in Afghanistan for defeating the insurgency while conducting state building. The operational paradigm and strategic considerations as outlined in this chapter seek to separate insurgents, criminal organizations, and corrupt power brokers from local communities in a systematic manner.

Heretofore, the counterinsurgency effort in Afghanistan has predominately focused on clearing insurgents from local communities but has been unable to prevent insurgents from infiltrating back.

Even though a blanket policy of rearming local militias may lead to a short-term solution of separating insurgents from the local communities, in the long term, warlord militias will undercut the authority of the central government and reverse the previous militia disarmament programs. Under the operational paradigm, the local community police, ANP, ANA and coalition forces provide the necessary security sphere for society to prosper. Without the security component, all other lofty programs—capacity building, development, and reforms—become irrelevant in terms of building citizen trust and loyalty to the government, in addition to instilling self-confidence and hope for the future.

Since 2006, Afghan insurgents have shown an amazing capacity of incompetence. Despite ample opportunities and the support of Islamic extremist sympathizers, the insurgency has been unable to gain any momentum. Thus far, the counterinsurgency effort has focused more on state building, in the mistaken belief they trump basic security needs. As long as this imbalance between security and development remains, the various insurgent and criminal groups will continue to survive. And in an insurgency, survival counts for much in the end.

Counterinsurgencies do not require large numbers of conventional troops, leading to the creation of a garrison state. Nor do they require multiple, large headquarters coordinating complex operations. Insurgencies do not have the operational tempo to warrant that need. In reality, insurgency/counterinsurgency requires finesse not firepower, with the victor being the one who best achieves control over the population.

3

Soviet Counterinsurgency in Afghanistan

The Soviet Union was at a disadvantage going into Afghanistan. Soviet leaders misunderstood the social and political dynamics of the country's situation, and entered the country expecting a relatively quick war against predominantly foreign backed fighters. Temporary military help, it was hoped, would install a more effective regime, put an end to foreign meddling and allow the Kabul government to proceed forward with support from the people. Instead, Soviet troops faced an increasingly popular insurgency that had widespread support throughout the country. Soviet leaders also lacked a doctrine and a military force suited for counterinsurgency. This was partly a result of focusing on conventional threats in the context of the Cold War.

As Robert Cassidy notes, large powers are forced to retain high level conventional capabilities to maintain parity with rivals. Due to the conditions of the Cold War, Soviet focus on conventional capabilities was especially strong. The situation in Afghanistan was considered primarily through the lens of the struggle against the United States and NATO – Soviet leaders were afraid of 'losing' Afghanistan to the influence of the West. Rumours that President Hafizullah Amin was making overtures to the CIA may not have been central to the decision to deploy Soviet troops, but represented underlying concerns of Soviet leaders. In a Politburo discussion, Andrei Gromyko demonstrated this Cold War mentality, arguing that "under no circumstances can we lose Afghanistan.... If we lose Afghanistan now, it will move away from the Soviet Union, that will be a blow to our politics". Soviet ideology at the time cultivated a perception that actions in Afghanistan were in support of workers and peasants, which promoted the underlying assumption that counterinsurgency was not all that needed, because Soviet policies aligned with the desires of the 'people'.

Therefore, due to distractions of the Cold war and ideological bias, Soviet leadership initially did not pay necessary attention to the requirements of conducting an effective counterinsurgency in Afghanistan. After the invasion in 1979, the Soviets quickly felt the effects of misreading the situation. The Kabul regime did not win widespread or enthusiastic support, and Soviet actions were sharply criticized in the international community. The Soviet army found its heavy equipment and conventional tactics of little use against irregular forces in challenging terrain. Continuing support from outside Afghanistan funded a largely Afghan insurgency that benefitted from open borders between Afghanistan and sanctuaries in Pakistan and Iran. Ultimately, the Kremlin was unable to address the causes of the insurgency adequately. Despite some successes, the Soviet side was unable to outlast and outdo the mujahedeen in the struggle for Afghanistan.

They were not forced to leave due to military necessity, however. Soviet forces regularly dominated the field, and the stalemate between the Soviets and the mujahedeen was a result of a combination of factors. The popular argument that Stinger missiles tipped the balance is also problematic. Gorbachev had already expressed the need to withdraw from Afghanistan in October of 1985; Stinger missiles took down the first Soviet helicopter in September of 1986. Many accounts imply that the Soviet side attempted to rely only on brute force to deal with the situation, mindlessly pursuing ineffective political and military policies, and counting on the overwhelming might of the Soviet Union to force the desired outcome. Soviet initiatives addressed the 'three pillars' of counterinsurgency, that have been outlined by David Killcullen: political, economic and military. Soviet political and military leaders developed a counterinsurgency strategy covering all these categories, including initiatives aimed at winning the support of the Afghan population through political means.

Brute force and mindlessness did not characterize the substantial attempts at encouraging strong governmental and social institutions and a less repressive regime in Kabul. The Kremlin put forth considerable effort to support unity within the PDPA, and to influence it to broaden its base of support through active broadcast of a positive and accommodating political message. Soviet initiatives were also designed to stimulate the Afghan economy as a way to support the government, win support with the population and sustain military gains. Although initially unprepared, Soviet military leaders worked to adapt the army to the situation in Afghanistan.

Some conventional and harsh tactics did persist. However, strategy, force structure and tactics were re evaluated and adjusted to the conditions in Afghanistan. Improved and specialized training, changes in military formations, organization of efforts and increased use of non linear tactics were all designed specifically for the Afghan theatre. These adjustments correspond with the advice of both classical and modern counterinsurgency theorists and practitioners. While Soviet leaders pursued many effective policies, there are several factors that limited their success.

First, many of the policies were poorly implemented. For example, despite significant Soviet pressure on the PDPA and insistence that the party be unified, internal divisions between Parcham and Khalq factions persisted and severely impeded all political efforts. Likewise, in the military context, new training and tactics were not sufficient to cultivate a pervasive ethos of initiative and independent action within the officer corps or instill comfort within motorized rifle troops for working in small units away from armoured vehicles. Second, resources were limited due to political concerns. As evidenced in the name, the Soviet 'Limited Contingent' did not have the numbers to effectively control all the borders and regions of Afghanistan. Third, lack of coordination between military and political efforts caused Soviet gains to be consistently reversed. As General Akhromeev noted in a Politburo session in 1986, "there hasn't been a military task that... hasn't been completed.... our military successes have just not been supported by political ones". Political initiatives were likewise often left unsupported by military action.

Despite lack of success in implementing policies, claims that the Soviets ignored the fundamental ideas of counterinsurgency are inaccurate. Many Soviet efforts both in political and military areas align with the recommendations of counterinsurgency theorists, who actively stress the importance of political work, information campaigns and non conventional military techniques. Soviet leaders addressed all of these aspects of counterinsurgency.

PROPAGANDA WITHIN AFGHANISTAN

Even before the invasion in 1979, the Soviets were very active in Afghanistan and aware of the importance of propaganda. A Soviet analysis of the situation in the spring of 1979 criticized Afghan PDPA members for being outdone by the 'counter revolutionaries', whose work was "much more active and on a larger scale than the work conducted by party members". After the deployment of Soviet troops, Soviet leaders made it even more of a priority to supply the Kabul government and the PDPA with all the tools necessary to spread their message and compete in information warfare both domestically and in the international arena.

As noted in 1980 in a resolution of the Secretariat of the Central Committee of the Communist Party of the Soviet Union (CPSU), "with the permission of the CPSU...Soviet ideological institutions began to provide operational help to the PDPA in propaganda... aimed at counteracting the anti afghan campaign in the UN and in the media abroad". In 1981, the Soviet government passed a resolution *On the Support for the People's Democratic Party of Afghanistan in Propaganda Work.* Development of the propaganda effort was a central aspect of the USSR's relationship with the Democratic Republic of Afghanistan (DRA). The Soviets worked hard to develop newspapers, journals and radio stations that supported the Kabul government.

Radio, in particular, was emphasized both by Afghan and Soviet government leaders due to the high rate of illiteracy in Afghanistan. As early as March 1979, president Taraki asked Leonid

Brezhnev for help in creating capabilities for a radio station in Afghanistan. A few days later, Yuri Andropov repeated the need to supply the Afghans with means for radio broadcasting. In January 1980 Soviet officials approved the building of a radio station in the region of Kabul, allocating ten million rubles for the job and agreeing to send equipment and specialists to facilitate the project. In December of 1980 Soviet leaders approved the distribution of megaphone and loudspeaker assemblies to all administrative zones in Afghanistan as a way to facilitate spreading information. The Soviet government also made efforts to broadcast radio programs from nearby Central Asian republics in Afghanistan. In 1981, Soviet leaders approved the broadcast of programs in Uzbek for the benefit of listeners in Afghanistan. Moscow also ordered the support of other forms of media. In one instance, the Soviet media agency Tass was tasked with sending materials and equipment for creating a dark room and photo studio for the Afghan news agency Bakhtar. Initiatives in television were discussed between the USSR and Afghanistan as well.

In a 1980 resolution of the Secretariat of the Central Committee there were conversations regarding the relay of broadcasts from a Tajik TV studio to Afghanistan. In the same year, the film "Conspiracy Against the Republic" was filmed with Soviet help in Dari and Pashto, clearly for government use as a propaganda tool. An agreement between the two countries for 1983 established cooperation on creating three TV studios in Afghanistan. Several Afghan newspapers were set up under Soviet guidance. Khambastegi was created in 1980, based on the Soviet newspaper "Socialism: Theory and Practice", and had a circulation of 3000 copies.

Soviet programs were also formulated for the purpose of training Afghan specialists in the skills necessary for media and propaganda operations. The Soviet Union sent many advisors and trainers in journalism to help strengthen Afghan capabilities. This had been an ongoing effort for many years but intensified after the April Revolution and the subsequent Soviet invasion. For example, from November 1980 to February 1981 ten Afghan media interns (five in radio and five in television) were sent to the USSR for training. The Soviet government also directed leading press agencies to send personnel to train their counterparts in Afghanistan. Editors from the newspapers Pravda, Izvestia, and Komsomolskaya Pravda were each ordered to send a representative to train and advise cadres in the Afghan newspapers Pravda Aprelskoi Revolutsii, Khivad and Znamya Molodyozhi.

Soviet political leaders also discussed the promotion of journalism amongst Afghan students, working out plans to send professors in Journalism from the USSR to Kabul University. The Ministry of higher education was directed to send professors to work directly with the PDPA on journalism, clearly indicating that the subject was understood as a tool for use in the political context.

Substantial amounts of media and propaganda materials were sent from the USSR to Afghanistan to explain and spread the message of the PDPA. In 1980, the publishing house 'Plakat' was instructed to send 50,000 rubles worth of flyers and other publications in Dari and Pashto. The newspaper Novosti was directed to publish a series of brochures in Dari and Pashto that explained the principles of domestic and foreign policy of the DRA, with the specific instructions that they be oriented towards the 'average' Afghan. In October of 1980 a Soviet news agency created the textbook "Course in the Basics of Politics" in Pashto and Dari. The textbook "Guidebook of a Party Worker" and "Political Parties of the World" were also created around the same time.

Soviet leaders persistently advised their Afghan counterparts in propaganda, reminding them to be sure to broaden their base of political support through engaging key segments of the Afghan population. The Soviet intention was that the PDPA explain their platform in terms understandable and compelling to the average Afghan. This dovetails with David Galula's point that the counterinsurgent should avoid abstract policies that do not interest the population, and that it is important for the counterinsurgent to ascertain what the people really want, and then promote corresponding policies.

Soviet leadership pushed this same recommendation with the Afghan government. One example is Soviet advice that PDPA members articulate clearly to Afghan peasants that they receive land due to the reforms of the PDPA, and that this land will remain with them only if the government remains strong. For the purpose of continuing to explain the Kabul government's policies, the publication Novosti published 10,000 of each of the following brochures in Dari and Pashto: "Domestic Politics of the DRA", "Stories about the Reforms" and "Speeches of Babrak of Karmal". One Soviet document refers to the number of copies of varying pamphlets, books and other publications sent from the USSR to Afghanistan at 290,00 in 1979, and at 720,000 in 1980.

These Soviet PDPA programs came in the context of an active propaganda campaign on the part of the mujahedeen. As General Gromov recounts in his memoirs, there was "active anti Soviet propaganda, which was conducted amidst the whole population in Afghanistan. In every village and small city they set people against us". It was of vital importance to convince the Afghan people that the Kabul government meant well and would bring them good things. This objective was not fully achieved, but certainly strived for as evidenced by the many programs enumerated above.

PROPAGANDA DIRECTED AT THE INTERNATIONAL COMMUNITY AND SOVIET POPULATION

International propaganda surrounding the conflict in Afghanistan cannot be separated from the realities of the larger Cold War. The war in Afghanistan was yet another reason for the United States and other countries to discredit the Soviet Union, and, in turn, a reason for the Soviet Union to strike back. This was an expected aspect of international relations at the time. This propaganda struggle was also a battle for legitimacy and global sympathy for which both the mujahedeen and the Soviet backed PDPA were vying.

The Soviets were seeking to gain tolerance for their actions in Afghanistan in the international community; they were also interested in sustaining support for the effort within the USSR. The mujahedeen were seeking to erode the will of the Soviet leaders and people, to gain sympathy and funds internationally, and to win support within the Afghan populace. Success or failure in the propaganda struggle would have major consequences for both sides. The politics of Pakistan and Iran and the larger powers working with them had a very real effect on the Soviet counterinsurgency effort. Mujahedeen forces made use of these governments' finances, equipment and sanctuaries.

The Soviet population also played an important role in the Soviet counterinsurgency. Although living in a society of restricted press and having limited effect on government processes, the Soviet population was the source for the conscript 40th Army deployed in Afghanistan, and the sentiments of the people did ultimately influence Soviet policymakers. Winning the 'hearts and minds' of these audiences, therefore, would be a significant advantage in the struggle for Afghanistan. In discussing evolved insurgencies in the context of fourth generation warfare, Colonel Hammes highlights the importance of international information campaigns even in localized conflicts, noting that a wide variety of international institutions and networks can spread a political message quickly throughout the world, and with great consequences. Soviet strategy took into account various international institutions when considering the information campaign for Afghanistan, placing great importance on achieving success in this area. Soviet leaders repeatedly discussed the Afghanistan situation in the context of the global arena and their standing vis à vis competing powers.

This is illustrated in a letter from Leonid Brezhnev to Fidel Castro in march of 1980: "You are right, Fidel, that in the current complicated circumstances, there is an opportunity for Cuba to move towards implementing a more active attempt... to support international security. This is even more important, because the imperialistic powers try to place all causes of international tension in Afghanistan, using it to distract attention away from their own dangerous activities". In a conversation with a western reporter in 1981, the Soviet representative expressed the government stance and prevailing understanding of the situation at the time, "literally everyday in the US there is spread new fabrications about the foreign policy of the USSR, and this is done not only by the press, but even more by official representatives of the administration". During the war in Afghanistan Soviet analysts would often mention that the United States and China saw the situation simply as an opportunity to hurt the USSR and promote the spread of anti Soviet sentiments around the globe. The Soviets viewed such countries to be uninterested in stabilizing Afghanistan, and focused primarily on inflicting damage on the Soviet Union. Afghan leaders felt themselves to be victims of propaganda aimed at weakening their government as well.

In a conversation with A. N. Kosygin on 20 March 1979, President Taraki complained that "Pakistani propaganda twisted our programs regarding social freedoms for women... and turned to politics of sabotage...against us". This battle for propaganda, of course, was conducted with greater global political objectives in mind, but it was also an important aspect in insurgency and counterinsurgency. The information battle is vital in counterinsurgency: the insurgent wins if he can convince the counterinsurgent's population or policymakers that the pursued "strategic goals are either unachievable or too costly for the perceived benefit". The counterinsurgent must therefore attempt to thwart such an information campaign. In the context of the Soviet Afghan war, the Soviet Union had to counteract attempts conducted by a broad and powerful coalition of countries. Accordingly, Soviet leaders undertook substantial measures in propaganda directed toward international audiences.

These strategies included exploiting the differences between the allies in NATO and hindering the development of ties between the United States and China in an effort to weaken solidarity on the question of Afghanistan. Also, there were initiatives to gain support for the Soviet Union amongst the leaders of Socialist countries and other large socio political organizations. The Central Committee of the CPSU sent letters of explanation of the Afghanistan situation to communist affiliated organizations all over the world; in one document forty six such organizations are listed as recipients of such a letter. The Soviets also sought to court Middle Eastern countries in hopes of preventing Islamic movements from assuming an anti Soviet posture. In 1980 the Soviet government encouraged the Kabul regime to publicize their political platform because it "would be timely from the perspective of... having an effect on the positions of countries that are participants in the... session of ministers... of Islamic governments". The support for anti American elements in Iranian foreign policy was also encouraged, as it would potentially weaken support for the US backed opposition movement in Afghanistan. It was also noted that it would be helpful to discredit pro mujahedeen leaders in the Afghan émigré community, as well as highlight the destructive effects of US and Chinese backed fighters in Afghanistan. The effort to uncover and discredit foreign support for the Afghan insurgency had been part of policy since the beginning of the conflict.

Even before the invasion, top Soviet leaders agreed that an element of their Afghan strategy would be "preparing materials, revealing meddling in Afghanistan's affairs on the part of Pakistan, Iran, the U.S., and China, and publicizing these materials through a third party". Soviet ambassadors received explicit instructions about how to present the issue of Afghanistan. These instructions urged them to point out that Soviet and Afghan cooperation against insurgent groups was consistent with article 51 of the UN's charter, which supports the right of individual or collective self defense in the case of an attack. The Soviet representative at the United Nations was explicitly ordered to thwart all attempts at including the issue of Afghanistan in the daily agenda. A list of explanations and arguments was provided in case the matter was accepted for formal discussion. In such a circumstance, it was to be emphasized that Soviet troops were in Afghanistan only for the purpose of helping the government and people of Afghanistan against outside aggression in accordance with the Soviet Afghan treaty of 1978, and that these troops would leave as soon as the threat subsided.

In 1980, the Central Committee of the CPSU gave special instructions for lobbying the Soviet perspective on Afghanistan at a conference of the Inter Parliamentary Union in response to anti Soviet bias in the organization. Afghan representatives were advised to send a letter of protest to the Union's chair, declaring such discussions to be meddling in internal Afghan affairs. Overall, the Soviet leadership supported the propaganda campaign on all fronts. In a document of the Central Committee of the CPSU a plan was outlined to "continue the broad publication of counter propaganda materials of Soviet and foreign authors, that expose the falsifications of the western media".

Media coverage of the Afghan conflict was tightly controlled by Soviet leaders, who were interested in cultivating a positive image of the war in the USSR and abroad. Soviet government officials approved various restrictions and guidance for the portrayal of events in Afghanistan. This guidance was clearly aimed at shaping the opinions of the Soviet population. The retaining the Soviet people's support for the war was important for leaders whose policies entailed continuing financial expenditures and human sacrifice. Central committee documents specify that Soviet troops were to be portrayed primarily in their daily activities and training alongside their Afghan counterparts; describing Soviet troops providing medical help to Afghans was specifically mentioned. Stories, pictures and other mention of PDPA party members and government officials meeting with Soviet troops were also encouraged. Describing the danger of surprise attacks on Soviet and Afghan units that were conducting routine activities was encouraged in order to show the destructive nature of the opposition movement. Description of the heroism and sacrifice of Soviet soldiers was also to be emphasized, as were award ceremonies, though discussion of actual combat was discouraged. Soviet press sources were also directed to accentuate the constructive nature of the presence of the Soviet troops: depictions of Soviet troops building and protecting economic infrastructure were encouraged. The Soviet government also encouraged stories and reports about Soviet aircraft and other vehicles disbursing goods and services to local populations.

These restrictions were clearly meant to preserve positive impressions of the situation in Afghanistan amongst the Soviet people. In a 1981 meeting of the Politburo, Yuri Andropov was careful to adopt measures downplaying Soviet combat losses, advising against too many memorials and mentioning that notifications to the families of fallen soldiers "ought to be brief and as standard as possible". Soviet leaders allowed only limited discussion of the sacrifice of Soviet soldiers in the media. The press was authorized to report only one account of a soldier wounded or killed per month.

Soviet leaders pursued numerous initiatives in the area of information warfare, aimed at various audiences that influenced the outcome of the Afghan conflict. While these measures did not necessarily result in the overall success desired by the Kremlin, it is clear that the Soviets were diligent in their efforts in propaganda as a part of counterinsurgency strategy. These efforts indicate that the Soviets were not relying on force alone, but were cognizant of the need to win support by means of persuasion.

COUNTERINSURGENCY IN THE SOVIET AFGHAN WAR

Current conflicts in Iraq and Afghanistan have directed considerable focus to the questions of insurgencies and counterinsurgencies. Understanding the historical examples of insurgency conflicts and the regions in which they have occurred is of vital importance for those who wish to understand present day events.

The Soviet Afghan war is one such historical example. Attempts at drawing direct parallels between the Soviet and U.S. experiences in Afghanistan are problematic, as there are many substantial differences between the two cases. Nevertheless, understanding the Soviet case is useful for identifying basic themes that are common in the experience of large powers conducting counterinsurgency campaigns. The Soviet Afghan war also represents an important step in the evolution of insurgency warfare in the context of globalization and accelerating technological progress. Many current phenomena such as transnational extremist networks and information warfare were in a unique stage of development during the Soviet Afghan war. Announced understanding of this conflict, therefore, is helpful for comprehending current insurgencies and counterinsurgencies.

In February of 2009 we found myself at the corner table of a popular Cambridge pub, translating for a group of Russian and

American generals. In the midst of facilitating conversation during their cocktail hour, the conversation turned to the Soviet Afghan War. One of the senior Russian Generals at the table, a veteran of the conflict, said to me, 'let me tell you the thing about Afghanistan, the Afghans – mostly they loved us – we were able to do whatever we wanted every day, we owned the place, but at night, everything would change... the night was all theirs'. Regardless of the bias or oversimplification of this statement, it does represent a valuable metaphor for the Soviet Afghan conflict of the 1980s.

The Soviet efforts in Afghanistan generally followed the paradigm of 'three steps forward and three steps back'. On the one hand Soviet forces were able to dominate in the field, but on the other hand they could never achieve the level of organizational coordination necessary to sustain their gains. Tactical accomplishments were routinely reversed whenever and wherever Soviet forces were absent.

The reversals and ultimate failures of Soviet policies in Afghanistan are well documented. The Soviet Afghan war is often described as a victory for the mujahedeen over the larger, but ineffective, Soviet army. There is much attention given to the ingenuity and resilience of the Afghan mujahedeen and the Soviets' inability to defeat them. Many analyses of this conflict have dwelled on the mistakes made by Soviet leaders and the inability of Soviet forces to defeat the Afghan insurgency.

The strategy and conduct of the Soviet counterinsurgency in Afghanistan from 1979 1989 certainly lend themselves to negative critiques. Over the course of the conflict, the Soviet armed forces killed or maimed some 2.5 million civilians, were the cause of millions more displaced persons and refugees and lost a reported 14,453 killed, 53,753 wounded, and millions of dollars worth of equipment. In 1989 when General Gromov evacuated the country with the last troops in a highly orchestrated show of propaganda, the situation was far from optimal from the Soviet point of view. Most key urban centres were under the control of Soviet supported government troops, while the rest of the country was subject to the influence of an insurgency that was supported by the majority of the population.

The Kremlin had taken on a challenging mission by invading a Central Asian country known for its resistance to outside influence and centralized rule. Moreover, Soviet troop levels were limited by political considerations, and trained and equipped to do battle with NATO forces in the European theatre and not with irregular fighters in a mountain environment. Partly due to the ideological origins of the Red Army and to simple negligence, the Soviet military initially did not have an adequate counterinsurgency strategy. An enduring insurgency was not anticipated; it was presumed that Soviet forces would win a 'quick war' in similar fashion to the actions in Hungary and Czechoslovakia.

While the Soviet 'Limited Contingent' was clearly not ready for the mission in Afghanistan, it is an oversimplification to fault the Soviet security forces for the overall failures of Kremlin policies in Afghanistan. It is undeniable that flaws in Soviet counterinsurgency strategy and deficiencies in Soviet military capabilities seriously hindered operations against the mujahedeen. However, from the earliest moments of the invasion of Afghanistan, Soviet military leaders began to transform the 40th Army into a more effective force for counterinsurgency missions in challenging terrain, and political leaders worked to strengthen the Kabul government through political programs. Partially due to the complex nature of counterinsurgency operations, the lack of success of Soviet policies in Afghanistan is sometimes attributed to utter incompetence on the part of both military and political leaders. Counterinsurgency requires a delicate balance of both political and military efforts. While the military aspect of counterinsurgency operations is crucial, complementary political progress is necessary for success. Highly developed cooperation between military, intelligence and political actors is essential for lasting gains. This coordination was lacking in the Soviet effort, and disconnects between military and political actions led to efforts that did not result in the synergy necessary for counteracting persistent insurgency movements.

Nevertheless, many aspects of the Soviet political and military campaign held promise. My research and analysis show that, although the Soviets were at times quite severe in their actions, they did not rely solely on military might and conventional power to achieve their goals; they attempted to develop effective military and political counterinsurgency initiatives. This chapter will identify and analyse those aspects of the Soviet counterinsurgency that were effective, and put them in the context of counterinsurgency theory, noting where Soviet policies were consistent with accepted counterinsurgency approaches. These aspects of the Soviet effort are often overlooked.

SOVIET-AFGHAN WAR

Centrally located amidst large countries with competing interests, Afghanistan has often been the location of proxy struggles between rival governments and ideologies. Afghanistan has seen the armies of Alexander the Great, Genghis Khan and the British Empire. The interests of Tsarist Russia and the British Empire chaffed at one another in Afghanistan in the 19th Century – an episode that is popularly known as the 'Great Game'. After World War II, the United States and the Soviet Union both projected influence into Afghanistan, undertaking a variety of projects and aid programs. During this time American money was supporting various efforts in the country, such as the Helmand Valley Project, and there were attempts on the part of the United States to bring Afghanistan under Western influence. Concurrent to these efforts, the Soviet Union was cultivating a relationship with Kabul based on trade and military aid.

In the period after World War II Afghanistan turned to the Soviet Union for support for a variety of political and economic reasons. This support came largely in the form of military aid. In this context, economic and cultural ties between Moscow and Kabul strengthened. Afghan leaders began to rely more and more on Soviet military supplies and support. Growing numbers of Afghans travelled to the USSR for education and training many for military instruction. For example, in 1979, before the Soviet Union invaded Afghanistan, there were 460 Afghans studying in Soviet military institutions. In this way, officers and other urban elites were increasingly exposed to Soviet life and ideologies, and added new vitality to progressive socialist urban movements in

Afghanistan. Many of these movements were centered on Kabul University and consisted of Marxist pro Moscow students. In 1965 these groups and others formed the People's Democratic Party of Afghanistan (PDPA), which was a communist organization with strong ties to the USSR.

In April of 1978, the PDPA wrested control of the government from Mohammad Daoud Khan in a coup and emplaced Nur Muhammed Taraki as the leader of Afghanistan. The new regime went ahead with a program of economic and social reform inspired by socialist Marxist ideas. Many of the new initiatives, which related to issues such as agriculture, landowning, and literacy, were foreign to the majority of the Afghan population that lived in a society governed by tribal and Islamic traditions. The PDPA government alienated many segments of the population through ""administrative inadequacy, as well as...regimentation which did not compensate for the absence of legitimacy". The PDPA was also severely hindered by an internal division between the Parcham and Khalq factions. Opposition movements that worked against the PDPA run government had developed in parallel – in counterbalance to those of the communists of the PDPA.

Men who would later fight the Soviet Army in the 1980s, such as Ahmad Shah Massoud and Gulbuddin Hekmatyar, had mounted a failed attempt at a coup in July 1975, before Soviet troops even deployed to the region. The armed struggle between the mujahedeen and the Soviet supported PDPA government was a conflict that had been developing for some time and was not entirely a spontaneous response to the appearance of Soviet forces in Afghanistan, "The conflict between the communist government and the mujahedeen resistance was as much a manifestation of political polarization in the country as a struggle for the liberation of Afghanistan from Soviet occupation. The dominant groups that led the Afghan resistance represented an old ideological conflict which took shape during the constitutional period (1964 73)".

In the face of growing opposition the PDPA leadership sought to tighten links to the USSR, and asked for increased military aid, as well as the arrival of Soviet troops. Soviet leaders initially refused these requests, but after significant unrest in the city of

Herat and the murder of Taraki and seizure of power by Hafizullah Amin in September of 1979, Soviet leadership decided to take military action in Afghanistan. Select special units were already in the country near Kabul, and in December 1979 Soviet units stormed the presidential palace, killed Amin and installed Babrak Karmal as president of Afghanistan. Soviet troops streamed into the country, working quickly to secure provincial capitals and to quell opposition from the Afghan army and other resistance units. By January 1980, Soviet troop levels in Afghanistan were over 50,000.[55] Initially the Soviet aim was to keep a low profile, secure main infrastructure and urban centres, and give the Afghan army the freedom to focus on crushing the resistance. It turned out, however, that the presence of Soviet troops inspired increased support for the mujahedeen and that the Afghan army proved incapable of effectively engaging and destroying mujahedeen forces. It soon became clear that Soviet units would have to undertake most of the combat missions. Soviet troop levels subsequently increased to 110,000 120,000 by 1982, which was the level at which they remained for the duration of the conflict.

The fighters that opposed Soviet troops were diverse. Among the factions of the Afghan mujahedeen there was a varying emphasis on Islam, nationalism and other ideologies. The Russian General Staff reports that in the Afghan resistance in 1982 there were seven Islamist parties, allied in the 'Group of Seven', and three Traditionalist parties, allied in the 'Group of Three'. The presence of Soviet troops served to overcome many internal divisions in these groups, and inspired support for them with many segments of the Afghan population. In addition to financial support from the U.S., Europe, China and the Middle East, many Muslims came to join in the fight against the Soviets.

Leaders such as Abdullah Azzam and Osama bin Laden established organizations and training sites in Pakistan to facilitate the Muslim world's participation in the fight against the Soviets. These foreign fighters did not make a very large impact tactically, but their presence spoke to the broader themes and implications of the Soviet Afghan War. In 1979 Azzam issued a fatwa, *Defense of the Muslim Lands*, which formalized Islamic support and encouragement for the jihad against the Soviets in Afghanistan. Azzam traveled the world even to Europe and the US inspiring audiences with elaborate descriptions of the Afghan jihad in order to win their monetary and political support. The narrative that ensued from this aspect of the Afghan resistance was important for the broader propaganda campaign and represented a growing tendency in insurgencies to direct information campaigns towards global audiences. This manner of information campaign had been a factor for the United States in the Vietnam conflict as well. Despite the large powers that supported the mujahedeen, however, most fighting was conducted by Afghan combat units organized in the context of tribe or village.

Early in the conflict Soviet troops mounted large conventional offensives that encountered very limited success. Soviet troops, equipment and tactics were ill suited for the terrain and enemy in Afghanistan. As Soviet forces became familiar with the conditions in Afghanistan, many adjustments were made. It became clear that there would be no quick victory in Afghanistan and that battling the mujahedeen would take years. The Soviets attempted to implement a counterinsurgency strategy that involved political and military components, but lack of resources and coordination caused these efforts to yield limited results. Some successes were sustained, however, due to increased use of specialized units and utilization of KGB trained Khad units.

Increased bombing of the Afghan countryside as an effort to destroy mujahedeen sources of support resulted in many civilian casualties and millions of refugees both inside the country and in neighbouring Pakistan and Iran. Mujahedeen forces, however, were able to survive due to extensive outside support from a coalition of anti Soviet countries. This support was predominantly funnelled through Pakistan. Soviet attempts to close the border with Pakistan were extensive, but ultimately did not succeed due to long distances, exceedingly difficult terrain, and lack of sufficient numbers of troops. Babrak Karmal, who had dissatisfied leaders in Moscow by his unresponsiveness to recommendations and inability to remedy divisions within the PDPA, was removed from power in 1986.

He was replaced by Mohammad Najibullah, the former head of the Khad. Najibullah pursued a program of national reconciliation, aimed at widening support for the government and finding a way to end conflict within the country. This effort was unsuccessful, as foreign backed mujahedeen sought a decisive victory in Afghanistan, and foreign powers saw continued fighting in Afghanistan as furthering their objective of weakening the Soviet Union. The Soviet government, led by Mikhail Gorbachev, increasingly saw the troop commitment to Afghanistan as an impediment to both foreign and domestic political objectives. In the context of unsuccessful political initiatives in Afghanistan and lack of a decisive military victory, Soviet leadership decided to withdraw its troops. Withdrawal was completed in February of 1989.

SOVIET-AFGHAN WAR AND COUNTERINSURGENCY

The Soviet counterinsurgency and the Afghan insurgency of the 1980s occupy an interesting place in the development of insurgencies and counterinsurgencies. This conflict can be viewed as a pivotal step between the traditional insurgencies of the earlier twentieth century and the more modern insurgencies, which are sometimes categorized as fourth generation war. Both the mujahedeen insurgency and the Soviet counterinsurgency included elements of the older paradigm mixed with elements of emerging new forms.

The Afghan insurgency was a movement of the people like many traditional insurgencies, but did have transnational elements, being significantly affected and supported by outside funding and the influx of Muslim fighters from around the world. While most operations were conducted by Afghan tribesmen who were fighting the Soviet invader, the insurgency was affected by a globally oriented Islamic ideology that transcended the particular fight for Afghanistan. While most of the fighting was carried out by small mujahedeen units and military superiority was not the determining factor in the struggle between insurgent and counterinsurgent, some insurgent organizations fielded sizable military formations and functioned in ways similar to conventional military units.

Although the press and the freedom of speech was significantly limited in Soviet Russia, persistence on the part of the insurgents did affect the will of Soviet policy makers and the populace through various means. Even though the internet was not a factor and insurgent forces were not able to broadcast victories or messages to the world instantaneously, propaganda campaigns were conducted throughout the world with the purpose of attracting funds, volunteers, and broadcasting the insurgent ideology against the Soviets. Soviet counterinsurgency – as a reaction to the insurgency that contested the government supported by the Kremlin – was also a synthesis of varying approaches. On the one hand, Soviet forces adopted many enemy centric principles into their strategy: they sought to engage and kill as many insurgents as possible and went to great lengths to bring the fight to their enemies. Often unable to apprehend elusive insurgent forces, Soviet forces routinely decimated crops, livestock, and villages in an effort to weaken insurgent supply sources and sanctuaries. On the other hand, Soviet strategy did include non coercive principles aimed at persuading the population to support their cause. Significant funds were invested in Afghan infrastructure and education in an effort to build institutions and human capital. Soviet politicians worked to influence the Kabul government to support reforms aimed at improving conditions in Afghan society. Soviet leaders supported substantial propaganda initiatives for promoting and publicizing the message and interests of the Kabul government. It is interesting to note that earlier Soviet counterinsurgency experience in Central Asia against the Basmachi movement was characterized by a similar synthesis of 'soft' and 'hard' approaches.

The nature of the Afghan insurgency as an indigenous and international movement with mixed ideologies and motivations was extremely hard to counteract. The hybrid form of the mujahedeen movement highlighted the need for a comprehensive, adaptive and tailored approach to counterinsurgency. The challenge that the Afghan resistance posed to the Soviet Union vividly underscored the requirement that the counterinsurgent use political, economic and military measures in good proportion in order to achieve success. Soviet strategy coincided with many of the accepted theories outlined in this chapter, and to what extent Soviet leaders used the necessary tools of counterinsurgency in the Afghan conflict.

Many aspects of the Soviet strategy corresponded to the general advice outlined by experts in counterinsurgency. However, lack of coordination between the various players in the Soviet effort, disjointed execution, and differing visions of the conflict, the mission and the strategy led to ineffectiveness despite the promise of many Soviet initiatives.

4

Counterinsurgency, Circumstances Structure in Afghanistan

INTRODUCTION

In the context of the Afghan security transition of 2014, when the bulk of foreign military forces are due to withdraw, policy debates have focused on the role and capabilities of the Afghan National Security Forces (ANSF). Much effort has been devoted to building up and bureaucratizing the means of violence in Afghanistan with a view to establishing a legitimate monopoly over the means of coercion. Yet this has been paralleled by a series of government and North Atlantic Treaty Organization (NATO) experiments in arming local defense forces, including local militias under the ALP, to fight the insurgency and provide security at the local level.

Frequently, notions of Afghan ownership, local solutions, and cost-effectiveness are invoked to justify such programs. This strategy is not without controversy, however. It has prompted concerns about the efficacy and impact of such interventions on the Afghan state's capacity to rein in armed groups, impose a monopoly over the means of violence, improve security, balance civil-military relations, enforce the rule of law, create political stability, and end the internal conflict. These debates on the role of irregular forces tend to be driven by agency interests and based on limited or disputed evidence.

This report attempts to provide an empirically based and independent analysis of the ALP program. It aims to show how the program and its previous iterations evolved and its impacts at the local and national levels. The research addresses the roles and impacts of the ALP program on security and political dynamics in the context of ongoing counterinsurgency and stabilization operations and the transition of security responsibilities from Western forces to Afghan security forces.

Background

International intervention in Afghanistan has been driven and shaped by different (and competing) logics, justifications, and modalities. Although it is often claimed that all good things come together, in practice, major contradictions and trade-offs are involved in pursuing multiple objectives simultaneously. The most fundamental contradiction is attempting to build peace while fighting a war. This contradiction manifests itself in the sphere of policing in the form of tension between a U.S. focus on paramilitary policing to pursue the war and a European focus on civil policing to consolidate the peace.

In addition to a complex range of often contradictory interests, the international response has shifted over time. Intervention began as a relatively minimalist endeavor involving a limited presence of U.S. ground forces fighting al-Qaeda and the Taliban through local proxies.

This changed over time to a more expansive, top-down form of statebuilding—encompassing all the transformative ambitions and recognized deficiencies of what is generally called liberal peacebuilding—radical institution building, good governance, reconstruction, security sector reform, rule of law, and so forth. This was followed by a third phase, returning in some respects to a modified version of the first phase, in response to the intensification of the insurgency and the evident failures of statebuilding. The terminology, if not always the practices, changed to incorporate what are known as more bottomup, Afghanled, culturally appropriate, quick-impact stabilization measures. This approach was influenced by wider trends in military doctrine, shifts in personnel—particularly the arrival of General Stanley McChrystal as the commander of the International Security Assistance Force (ISAF)—and imperatives from the field. This was paralleled by a massive surge in international troops and financial resources aimed at turning the situation around.

Thomas Barfield (2012) nicely captures the shift in how the international community defined and responded to the 'Afghan problem': In 2002, the absence of a strong centralized state was viewed as the driver of insecurity and terrorism, yet by 2011, a corrupt, illegitimate central state was considered the core of the problem.

A fourth and most recent phase has been transition, the drawdown of foreign troops by 2014 and the handover of ownership to the Afghan government, including responsibility for fighting the Taliban and providing security for the population. This latest phase has involved a further and hasty redefinition of the problem and the criteria for success—leading to a search for pragmatic solutions—and the ALP can perhaps be understood as one manifestation of this shift toward expediency. This phase has also been marked by the surfacing of longstanding tensions between the Afghan government and international actors, particularly the United States. President Hamid Karzai has openly distanced himself from the U.S. war agenda and emphasized Afghan sovereignty and independence.

Shifting Safety and Policing Surroundings

International intervention at the end of 2001 marked the mutation of thirty years of conflict into a new phase rather than the beginning of a transition from war to peace. The preceding war years had seen the growing decentralization of the means of violence, associated with the emergence of a new class of military entrepreneurs and a political economy shaped by military patrimonialism. The collapse of the Najibullah regime was followed by a demodernization of the army, in which, over time, fragments of the regular army in the north gradually assumed the character of militias, similar to other military forces in the rest of the country. The Taliban regime to some extent centralized the means of violence, including through an effective disarmament campaign, a process that was reversed by internationally promoted regime change, leading to the further fragmentation of the political-military landscape.

International military intervention, the exclusive elite pact forged in Bonn in 2001,10 the failures of statebuilding, and the absence of meaningful reconciliation efforts galvanized the insurgency, which over time intensified and spread geographically. Although patchy attempts at disarmament were attempted in the north and less so in the south, as the insurgency intensi-fied, the U.S. military embarked on arming Pashtun rivals of the Taliban in the south. If war is, as Ariel Ahram suggests, "an effective auditor of institutional performance", the growing insurgency exposed deficiencies in the capacity and legitimacy of the Afghan state.

Western efforts to regulate what was in effect a security market have been contradictory and often ill considered. On the one hand, interventions were directed toward bureaucratizing coercion by building up a monopoly on the means of violence through security sector reform, which was defined as the five related pillars of the Afghan National Army (ANA) and ANP; judicial reform; disarmament, demobilization, and reintegration (DDR); and counternarcotics. On the other hand, foreign forces continued to support and fund local power brokers, creating militias and deploying private security companies, who operated either above or below the law. Unsurprisingly, given the continued high levels of insecurity and the absence of real socioeconomic opportunities to encourage the reintegration of fighters, DDR programs were a failure. Warlord democratization by absorbing jihadi factions into key ministries succeeded in relation to some of the senior figures within the northern alliance. However, many provincial strongmen resisted the extension of centralized state power into the periphery, while mid-to low-level fighters had few options beyond military-patrimonial networks or engagement in the drug economy. The underlying structural conditions that explain the continued persistence of illegal militias, far from being transformed, have intensified over time. Programs that attempted to centralize the means of coercion and establish effective policing were a threat to the interests of many, both within and outside the state.

Efforts to invest in policing reflect and have contributed to this security environment. Initially, investment in policing was limited and muddled, though in 2006, the Afghanistan Compact stated that by the end of 2010 there would be a fully constituted, professional, functional, and ethnically balanced ANP and Afghan Border Police (ABP) with a combined force of up to 62,000 that had the ability to meet the security needs of the country and be increasingly fiscally sustainable. The ANP's growth targets expanded, paralleling the increase in size of the ANSF more generally, and the ANP numbered some 148,500 personnel in February 2013.

Between 2001 and 2011, the international community spent more than $15 billion on Afghanistan's police. The focus for the United States, however, was primarily on the paramilitary dimensions of policing rather than on building an institution to enforce the rule of law. As the United States became more involved in funding and organizing policing, the strategic goal was increasingly to fight off organized challenges to state power. This emphasis on training and using the police in offensive counterinsurgency roles reflected the institutional preferences of the U.S. Department of Defense, which has had primary responsibility for police assistance in Afghanistan since 2005. Between 2005 and February 2013, the United States, the largest donor in this sector, spent some $14 billion to train and equip the ANP. Efforts directed at restructuring and training the police achieved mixed success, and even by 2011, the uniformed police "was still more like a fragmented coterie of militias than either a paramilitary police or a civilian police force".

This combination of protracted conflict and invasive international intervention has led to a militarized and volatile security landscape inseparable from the wider regional conflict system, given that both Afghanistan and Pakistan use asymmetrical warfare to pursue statebuilding goals.

The decentralization of violence and remobilization has arguably accelerated in the runup to the transition deadline. When

General David Petraeus took over for McChrystal in 2010, the rules of engagement shifted from counterinsurgency back to counterterrorism. This shift was reflected in an increased reliance on night raids, aerial bombardment, and drones. Some argue that Afghanistan has increasingly become a dirty war whose brutality has increased insecurity, which in turn has been used to justify the arming of communities by U.S. Special Operations Forces (SOFs), the Afghan state, or regional strongmen. A negative spiral is in evidence as concerns about a chaotic post-2014 scenario contribute to a spontaneous rearmament by communities and militias.

APPEARANCE OF THE ALP

Historically, state formation has involved the creation of a military specializing in the monopoly of large-scale violence. Policing, which tends to occur in the shadow of this process, involves the management of small-scale violence. The increased provision of state policing has often gone hand in hand with the gradual disarmament of the population and the expropriation of policing capacities from the communities.

This is associated with what Michael Mann characterizes as a shift from states that rule through despotic or raw coercive power to those that govern through infrastructural power associated with policing and technologies of governance, such as census making and mapping, that make society more legible and therefore more manageable (1984). However, the creation of a military and police force is costly in financial and political terms. Historically, states and imperial powers have frequently acted as brokers rather than monopolists, seeking to extend their control through franchising the means of coercion. This pattern was typical of feudal Europe and the norm for pre-twentieth-century states in much of Asia. Imperial powers such as the British developed a policy of indirect rule, which involved creating irregular armies to police and administer the empire, particularly in frontier zones. Such armies and constabularies were less costly in manpower, resources, and political risks. One example is the Sandeman system, developed on the northwest frontier in the nineteenth century and recreated in the form of the watch and ward system in the early twentieth century and echoed in U.S. counterinsurgency strategies in the Philippines and Vietnam. Policing by tradition is therefore not new. The Sandeman system of frontier management introduced and institutionalized the *jirga* system, irrevocably changing Baluch society in the name of its preservation. Contemporary counterinsurgency (COIN) and development policy literature on Afghanistan similarly reinvent and reify local traditions, including older forms of community policing, such as *arbaki*.

Historically, a symbiotic relationship between bandits, warlords, and states has been common. The assumption that building a Weberian monopoly over the means of violence is a necessary condition for state formation is not always born out by historical experience. As Ariel Ahram notes, violence devolution can be seen as a mode of military development rather than as a defective mode of state formation. In Burma, for example, the state has deployed militias effectively to regain control over and pacify its unruly border-lands. Similarly, the Sri Lankan state created Tamil militias to fight the Liberation Tigers of Tamil Eelam (LTTE) and police the Tamil population in the north and east.

This body of literature suggests that militias are not necessarily a manifestation of state breakdown or agents of *statecide*, to borrow Antonio Giustozzi's term (2009b). They may contribute to disintegrative or integrative dynamics, depending on context. Critics of the ALP point to the Najibullah period as a warning about the danger of militias, given that government-created militias ultimately contributed to the downfall of the regime once Moscow ended the external subsidies that held the system together. However, the relative importance of militias was much greater during Najibullah's time, leading to a symbiotic relationship between government and irregular forces. Furthermore, Western donors are unlikely to suddenly curtail subsidies to the Afghan state as the Soviets were forced to do, which made the militias defect and sealed the downfall of the Najibullah regime.

States and empires have frequently deployed surrogate forces to extend their control and counter violent resistance to their rule. How these forces are deployed and the forms they take vary from place to place. The term *militia* is frequently used as a catchall that lumps together dissimilar phenomena. For this study, the distinction between home guards and militias is important. The former are recruited from a particular locale and are responsible for policing that locale. Their role is primarily defensive and policing. This most closely resembles the arbaki model, which was meant to maintain law and order and defend the borders and boundaries of the tribe or community. In the context of counterinsurgency operations, home guards are meant to secure control over the population and minimize insurgent abilities to establish a support network among civilians. On the other hand, militias are larger and more powerful than home guard units and combine policing with an offensive military role and frequently operate over a wider geographical area. The boundaries between the two structures may frequently be blurred, particularly given that organizations have a tendency to mutate over time.

Antecedents

International actors have funded and supported efforts to disarm factions and centralize the means of coercion. DDR was launched in April 2003 in the form of the UN-created and Japanese-funded Afghan New Beginnings Program (ANBP), which targeted what was known as the Afghan Military Forces. This program was followed by the Disarmament of Illegal Armed Groups (DIAG) program. Both, however, were largely failures in terms of achieving stated aims. The opportunities for rank-and-file combatants were limited; only a few went into the newly constituted ANA, and many joined local militias or semiprivate police forces.

In parallel with these programs, other international actors were supporting rearmament and contributing to the further decentralization of violence. This support occurred from the time of the invasion, when the CIA channeled funds to Northern Alliance warlords to pursue the war on terror. This model—promoted by Secretary of Defense Donald Rumsfeld—of deploying special forces and arming local proxies, initially appeared to be successful in achieving regime change. It was followed in subsequent years by a succession of experiments in local policing or community militias, including the Afghan National Auxiliary Police (ANAP), Afghan Public Protection Program (APPP or AP3), Community Defense

Initiative (CDI), Local Defense Initiative (LDI), arbaki, Critical Infrastructure Program (CIP), counterterrorism pursuit teams, the Kandahar Strike Force, and the Khost Protection Force. Some of these programs were locally initiated—sometimes spontaneously by provincial governors, regional strongmen, and local communities as the growth of the insurgency increased the demand for paramilitary policing, particularly in the north—and others were pushed from the center or the provinces by foreign forces. The management of the various militia groups was located in different parts of the Afghan government (although they often had closer relationships with foreign forces than with the government), including the Independent Directorate for the Protection of Public Properties and Highways by Tribal Support, Ministry of Interior (MOI), President's Office, and National Directorate of Security (NDS). The rationale for their formation was linked to a range of tactical and strategic objectives, including fighting the Taliban, winning election campaigns, strengthening local power bases, pursuing local vendettas, strengthening the central government, or promoting Taliban reintegration.

The experiments reflected wider developments in COIN doctrine, which as a body of knowledge and set of practices appeared to mesh with the statebuilding and stabilization agenda. The dissemination of this practical knowledge was associated with a number of what David Miller and Tom Mills (2010) call warrior intellectuals and associated policy institutes and academic institutions, which at the end of the Cold War were influential in helping carve out a new role for Western militaries in relation to expeditionary forces, statebuilding operations, and counterinsurgency campaigns. COIN doctrines involved reframing warfighting, from being conceived as purely a military task to primarily a battle for governance. Counter-insurgency is understood to be "an umbrella term that describes the full range of measures that governments take to defeat insurgencies. These can be political, administrative, military, economic, psychological or informational, and are almost always used in combination". Soft power is deployed alongside hard power to win local hearts and minds and to engage in more announced ways with the local terrain. This requires deep knowledge of civilian populations.

COIN represented a shift from the Weinberger-Powell doctrine of using overwhelming force to achieve a decisive victory, but U.S. COIN doctrine does not hide the fact that, as Kilcullen concedes, "There is always a lot of killing, one way or another" (cited in Gregory 2008, 19). Nor ultimately does it provide a convincing answer to what happens when the priorities of the military occupation are not aligned with those of the host political system. For example, the arming of Sunni militias in Iraq or the military's involvement with traditional justice institutions in Afghanistan are in tension with the putative establishment of a monopoly of force or the state's universal legal jurisdiction. Afghanistan, like Iraq, became a testing ground for this supposedly new but actually very old doctrine. It was picked up and embraced enthusiastically by military planners, special forces, and politicians desperately seeking solutions to what they saw as the lack of progress in Afghanistan and seeking to justify and legitimize what had become an increasingly difficult enterprise to package and sell to Western electorates.

Yet there was a growing perception among Western policymakers that the state was part of the problem, especially the formal policing structure. Furthermore, as the insurgency expanded and changed tactics to target major population centres, the regular police were increasingly deployed to either protect urban centres or to fight in operations alongside or in support of the ANA and foreign forces. Consequently, the police were taking heavy casualties, an estimated twice as many as the ANA. Attrition rates for the ANP have remained at an annual rate of 25 percent overall with rates up to 70 to 80 percent in some units. One of the rationales for militia programs such as the AP3 and Afghan Public Protection Force (APPF) was to free the regular police force from protecting government installations and officials and return them to civilian policing and rule of law duties. COIN experts also drew on—or reinvented—Afghan traditions of community policing to justify the promotion of such programs. Since 2006, the United States has supported several efforts to establish militias. The first was the ANAP, when in February 2006 the Afghan Ministry of Interior and Ministry of Finance approached the Americans with the idea of creating a new force involving an additional two hundred to four hundred police per district. Under this plan, provincial governors could recruit 11,271 men from 124 high-risk districts in twenty-one provinces. The program aimed to train villagers for ten days and equip them with guns. By July 2007, some 8,300 ANAP members received training. They were then sent to secure checkpoints and conducted operations with coalition forces in Helmand, Zabul, Kandahar, Farah, Uruzgan, and Ghazni, reaching a strength of nine thousand men. It was ostensibly managed by the MOI in close collaboration with the U.S. Combined Security Transition Command-Afghanistan (CSTC-A). However, the force was widely criticized for reversing the effects of DIAG. Many of its participants were thought to be Taliban agents, and nearly all were members of forces loyal to provincial power brokers. The force was disbanded in May 2008.

In 2009, MOI and U.S. special operation forces piloted the AP3 in Wardak. It was funded and implemented by SOFs until mid-2010, when U.S. regular forces took over. The plan initially provided for between one hundred and two hundred guardians to be recruited in four insecure districts, but no more than a total of twelve hundred in the entire province. The AP3 was in theory part of an integrated, sequenced program to improve security that included four elements: deployment of U.S. troops that were part of the surge, training of locally based ANP officers under the Focused District Development program and their interim replacement by the ANCOP constabulary, the recruitment of an AP3 cadre, and provision of development assistance from the Commander's Emergency Response Program (CERP). Districts that cooperated were eligible for an additional $500,000 in CERP funds as an incentive to participate.

Haneef Atmar, the minister of interior at the time, saw the AP3 as a pragmatic solution to the problem of local insecurity. However, he also explicitly linked it to the wider project of centralization and institutionalization and therefore emphasized the need for central control and regulation of surrogate forces. Local *shura* were to select local recruits, who were to be vetted by government institutions, trained by SOFs, paid directly by the MOI, and required to report to the district police chief, bypassing their commanders.

Atmar's preference was for small groups linked to local shuras and not for either commanders pursuing personal agendas or large militias that could pose a military risk to the government. Paying local recruits directly through the bank and not through their commanders was one way of engendering loyalty to the state rather than to militia commanders. Further, Atmar envisaged the gradual replacement of private security companies (PSCs) with the APPF. The AP3 and APPF were envisaged as two sides of the same coin. The AP3 were to serve guard duties as a defensive force at the provincial and district level to free regular police from those tasks. The model envisaged a government-controlled stopgap measure tied to the growth of the ANSF, whereby militia units would be demobilized or integrated into regular forces as the ANP and ANA developed. This was a pragmatic way of building state power by extending control over armed groups and the means of violence. Atmar saw AP3 as a means of registering existing weapons belonging to local villagers willing to join the force and in so doing promoting the goals of DDR and DIAG. However, the gap between the theory and the practice was wide, largely because the theory was based on an outmoded set of assumptions about the capacity of tribal leaders to command the loyalties of local villagers. In practice, it was the militia commanders who held the real power in post-2001 Afghanistan.

INTER-AGENCY ASSESSMENT OF THE SITUATION EMERGENCE

In 2009, General Stanley McChrystal, commander of the ISAF and U.S. Forces Afghanistan, conducted a thorough inter-agency assessment of the situation. It concluded that the insurgents had increased their control of territory in most parts of rural Afghanistan, in particular the Pashtun areas in the south, west, and east. As the AP3 was getting under way in March 2009 in Jalrez district in Wardak province, U.S. and Afghan officials began discussing options to establish rural militias under the CDI, later branded the LDI. U.S. planning was led by Combined Forces Special Operations Component Command—Afghanistan (CFSOCC-A) under the leadership of Brigadier General Edward Reeder. The program's goal was to "identify local communities that seek outside help against insurgents" and to "assist the local population to provide their own security with defensive 'neighbourhood watch' type programs." Reeder's staff claimed to have analyzed the history of militias in Afghanistan. It was, they claimed, a "model built consciously on Afghanistan's previous stable periods".

The CFSOCC-A plan involved deploying U.S. and Afghan special operations teams to live and operate in villages that had decided to resist insurgents. They would focus on three tasks: improving informal governance through village shuras, establishing or co-opting village defense forces, and improving development. The militia had to number fewer than three hundred, be defensive, fall under the oversight of village jirgas, and be closely monitored by the Afghan government and NATO. The deployment of U.S. and Afghan SOFs to villages facilitated oversight. At this stage of the program, no formal role was envisaged for the MOI or any other Afghan central state institution, which meant that the SOFs would work with local shuras they either found or established for that purpose. It was thus presented as a truly local initiative, far removed from the corrupting influence of Kabul.

Four criteria were set down to determine where CDI-LDI units would be established:

1. The locals had already resisted insurgents.
2. The area was strategically important for the Taliban and other insurgent groups.
3. The area was strategically important for the Afghan government and NATO.
4. An assessment team found that it was feasible, based on local support, terrain, and population density.

In July and August 2009, CFSOCC-A briefed McChrystal and won his approval for the concept. In August, CFSOCC-A briefed the ministers of interior and defense, Haneef Atmar and Rahim Wardak. Both ministers reportedly supported the formation of local militias. It was also in August that CFSOCC-A deployed a special operations team to Nili in Daykundi province to train forces with the help of the ANP. By December, the United States had teams training a total of one hundred militia members in four other districts.

However, the CDI-LDI initiative proved controversial with Afghan officials and the U.S. political leadership in Kabul. The LDI was never a full-scale program but more a series of experiments tried in Arghandab (Kandahar), Nili (Daykundi), Achin (Nangahar), Gereshk (Helmand) and parts of Paktia. The program, which Haneef Atmar later called illegal, involved turf battles between the Independent Directorate of Local Government (IDLG), the MOI, and the Independent Directorate for the Protection of Public Properties and Highways by Tribal Support led by Wolesi jirga member Aref Noorzai, a relative of Hamid Karzai.

Nevertheless, in mid-November, U.S. ambassador to Afghanistan Karl Eikenberry reported that CFSOCC-A was conducting survey work and tribal engagement and outreach to local shuras on CDI-LDI. Although ISAF had sought ministerial approval for the scheme, by the end of October, Karzai had not given the Afghan government's formal approval. The ambassador insisted on a firm approval by the president and the cabinet before implementation, even though by August, CFSOCC-A had already deployed special operations teams to four provinces. The U.S. political leadership in Kabul feared that local militias set up by SOFs outside the framework of Afghan institutions would come at the expense of formal institutions and distract from efforts to build the Afghan army and police by potentially undercutting popular and international support for funding formal security forces, especially in the absence of plans to eventually reintegrate them into the ANSF or disarm and disband them. They could also reverse the rather modest progress made under DDR and DIAG programs in disarming mujahideen militias.

In April 2010, Brigadier General Scott Miller took control of CFSOCC-A and, though the Afghan government had not yet granted a formal approval, began a significant expansion of the program with the support of McChrystal. He coined the term 'Village Stability Operations' to capture the governance and development aspects of the program. When Petraeus took command of the ISAF that July, he pushed for and succeeded in extracting a formal agreement from Karzai. Keen on expanding the ISAF's local militia initiatives to fight the insurgency, Petraeus must have realized that an expansion of the program could not have gone ahead without the approval of the Afghan government. He needed legal cover and political legitimacy for the operation. Following intense wrangling between Karzai and Petraeus, the program was officially authorized in August 2010 under the MOI, calling the militia members Afghan Local Police. As a result, most of the existing militias were eventually incorporated into the ALP. For example, the MOI directive of June 2011 affirms that the aim of the ALP program was to incorporate all previous village and district defense programs. The U.S. Department of Defense stated that the ALP program incorporated previous village-level defensive programs, such as the CDI-LDI. In many places, the ALP label became a seal of approval to legitimize existing local militias that SOFs often set up outside any agreed framework. It was an attempt to "legitimize what was really a militia program by calling it 'police' and making it part of the MOI." By December 2010, the ALP had three thousand men in fifteen districts. By December 2011, it had ten thousand in fifty-seven districts.

The idea of the APPF, as noted earlier, developed in parallel with the ALP. It was discussed in July 2010—about the same time that negotiations over the ALP heated up—but was actually created in early 2011 to replace the hundreds of private security companies that had protected institutions and infrastructure throughout the country. President Karzai issued a decree in August 2010, ordering the disbanding of all PSCs by December 2010. However, following pressure from the ISAF and development contractors and non-governmental organizations (NGOs) that depended on PSCs for their security, a one-year extension to March 2013 was negotiated. These firms had operated without government over-sight, and the majority of them were owned by Afghan power brokers allied with Karzai. The APPF is supervised by the MOI and operates under the presidential decree that disbanded private security providers. The APPF's fourteen thousand Afghan personnel are a static guard force that protects public buildings, development projects, and vital infrastructure.

The ALP, as described by the Department of Defense, is a village-focused local defense initiative that complements the ISAF's counterinsurgency efforts by targeting rural areas affected by the insurgency to enable conditions for improved security, governance, and development. The ALP is a complementary component to the VSO program. It focuses on rural areas that have limited ANSF and ISAF presence, where Afghan communities were already resisting the Taliban and providing for their own security. However, before the ALP was formally launched, the U.S. military's priority of containing the insurgency at the local level empowered militia commanders who received direct U.S. military patronage, such as former PSC commander Azizullah in Urgun, whose forces were eventually transitioned into the ALP. The Afghan government perceived such armed units as a threat to its authority and aimed to bring U.S.-supported local militias under central government control. The ALP and the APPF were thus seen as instruments to further the goal of centralizing the means of coercion.

The ALP, in its final manifestation, was a compromise solution. On the one hand, it allowed the U.S. military to legalize and legitimize its existing network of ad hoc local militias and expand it in support of its counterinsurgency strategy. On the other hand, the Afghan government, at least in principle, managed to put an end to such ad hoc initiatives as the CDI-LDI and extended its control over the means of coercion by reining in U.S. military patronage. Two important questions to ask in relation to the CDI-LDI and ALP are why the U.S. military chose to adopt the CDI-LDI model following the AP3 and why the Afghan government, in particular President Karzai—who initially raised objections—agreed to U.S. plans to expand its local militia program and make the ALP a national force, albeit with a local mandate.

The answer to these questions can be partly found in the SOFs' experience with AP3 in Wardak in 2009. U.S. military officers in Wardak argued that setting up "local defense forces is done better when SOFs live and work with them and are under their direct control."

However, this model "lacked broader legitimacy and links to Afghan government institutions." The ALP as a presidentially approved and MOI-run program had "strategic level buy-in and legitimacy, but at tactical level," as military officers noted, "it is a mess, and MOI is unable to service it properly." As a result, the LDI program was launched to overcome the limited success of the AP3. The general conclusion among the SOF community in Wardak was that the bureaucratic nature and the centralized control by the MOI had complicated AP3 implementation.

The LDI was launched to remove the central government's control and free the hands of SOFs to experiment with more locally driven initiatives to raise village-based militias. With the rollout of the LDI, the view that local militias independently operated by SOFs were more successful gained traction within U.S. military circles and paved the way for Petraeus to propose its expansion nationally. However, when he presented the idea to Karzai, he faced opposition. As Karzai's national security advisor admitted in early 2012, there were intense negotiations and numerous disagreements between Karzai and Petraeus on this issue. To some extent, this was also a fight over control of patronage and the people it empowered.

The Afghan government had objected to what it perceived as unilateral efforts by U.S. SOFs to create local militias outside the control of the central government. Furthermore, the government's objections may have been linked to Karzai's preference for and prioritization of rebuilding the ANSF. In fact, in 2005, Karzai proposed increasing the size of the national police to improve security in the border areas with Pakistan, indicating a preference to train and equip more ANA and ANP to meet the security needs of the population and to fight the insurgents. When his request was turned down by U.S. and NATO officials, he then proposed creating what he called community or local police, modeled on the arbaki concept. His plan was to arm local villagers in those areas so they could provide their own security and protect their homes. They would receive funds and military equipment in exchange for agreeing to operate under the control of the MOI.

It appears that Petraeus was not in favour of international forces or of the ANSF conducting COIN operations in insecure areas. According to Afghan officials involved in the negotiations,

Petraeus's proposal was influenced by his experience with the Sons of Iraq program in Iraq. It involved setting up small anti-Taliban local armed groups paid by the U.S. military to work directly under SOFs command without links to central government institutions. Karzai argued that such a plan would lead to *militiasazi* (proliferation of militias), the destruction of the state, and a new form of warlordism. To prevent this outcome, Karzai argued for Afghan government control and proposed an alternative in the form of the ALP, which allowed the creation of thousands of local police under the command of the MOI. This option enabled the Afghan government, at least in principle, to exercise some control over SOF-supported militias while legitimizing the U.S. expansion of its existing militia program.

The future of the ALP by early 2013 was unclear. Some argued for its absorption into the regular police, others for its disbandment, and others still for its extension. The Afghan government did not articulate a clear policy on whether to keep, expand, or disband it. The U.S. military indicated that it had plans to expand the more costeffective ALP and to shrink the more expensive army and police units. The ALP's strength in January 2013 stood at 19,600 in more than one hundred districts, covering roughly 17 percent of the Afghan population, some five million people being protected by ALP units according to the Special Operations Command. These numbers were projected to increase to twenty-two thousand in July 2013 and thirty thousand by July 2015. In February 2013, plans were revealed for the Special Operations Command to extend a financial lifeline from the Pentagon to the ALP for at least five more years, providing $1.2 billion to train, arm, and pay forty-five thousand fighters. Although the expansion plans won the approval of U.S. commanders, and Afghan officials from the MOI also gave their support, Karzai and his cabinet did not officially approve the request, and the president remained critical of the program.

Rationalities and Incentives

In practice, the way that the ALP program emerged and was implemented was the result of a complex bargaining process involving international actors, national political elites, and provincial level elites. For international actors, the ALP was attractive because of cost efficiencies and risk transfers. It helped overcome manpower shortages while reducing costs and political risks. Like colonial systems of policing, the metropolitan centres of power seek to reduce the costs of policing the periphery by devolving these responsibilities to the periphery itself. As William Rosenau notes, local police are in effect low-cost trigger pullers (2008).

Militias were revived or created because of a perceived tactical deficit—the inability of regular forces to respond effectively and efficiently to insurgent activities in remote insecure areas where government and ISAF forces had no or limited presence. As well as being more cost-effective, according to their special forces mentors, they do not desert, have low attrition rates, and tend to win their battles, though their casualty rates are three times higher than those of regular forces. Their lack of institutionalization ensures a more rapid response, they know the local terrain, and they can generate effective intelligence—all critical factors in counterin-surgency operations.

European donors were more skeptical about what they perceived as the paramilitarization of the police force. Whereas the American military was mostly concerned with increasing the capabilities of the police force to suppress the insurgency, Europeans were mostly worried about the weakness of the rule of law. Afghan reformers, on the other hand, were intent on strengthening the institutions of the Afghan state (Giustozzi and Isaqzadeh 2011, 17).

Therefore, from the beginning, their role, status, and institutional home were ambiguous. Should they be a military or paramilitary force or a policing force? What should be their duties? Should they enforce the law or bring security? What was their legal status? Should they be subject to criminal or military law? Should they be housed in the Ministry of Interior or the Ministry of Defense? The Americans and Europeans had different answers to these questions, with the former wanting them to be more of a paramilitary force and the latter a civilian policing force. As one European official noted, "If they're police, they shouldn't be on the frontlines or manning checkpoints."

For national elites, the calculations were quite different. It is important to distinguish between centralizers like Karzai, who have sought to build up their power base through brokerage and patronage, and centralizers like Atmar and former finance minister Ashraf Ghani, who are essentially donor-dependent reformers and have sought to build the institutions of the central state and to disempower the men of violence in the periphery—in the process making enemies who contributed to their downfall. There are also political elites who are physically located at the center but are there primarily to strengthen their power bases in the provinces. Each of these types of actors had different reasons to support or oppose the ALP.

Karzai was initially very outspoken against all militia formations but ultimately backed the ALP. He appears to have seen it as an opportunity to regularize and assert control over the various militia experiments. In addition, earlier forms of militia creation were linked with attempts at building a stronger electoral base, including, for example, Aref Noorzai's election militias and the IDLG's Afghanistan Social Outreach Program (ASOP) shuras, both of which were vehicles for strengthening patronage relationships in relation to the 2009 presidential elections. The issue subsequently became mixed up with a number of other questions that set the president on a collision course with the United States, including the issues of regulation of PSCs, Afghan control over the Bagram prison, night raids by SOFs, and civilian deaths caused by NATO air strikes. These can also be seen as bargaining chips, used by Karzai to increase his regime's control of the means of coercion and patronage and to bolster his domestic legitimacy, countering his image as a Western puppet.

Reformers such as former interior minister Atmar had a different take on the ALP and its previous iteration, the AP3. He conceptualized the AP3 as a border force based on the arbaki model to prevent incursions by the Taliban across the Afghan-Pakistan border. As mentioned, he saw it as having a specific and limited role in relation to a broader state institutionalization and state legitimation strategy, which in practice would have amounted to indirect rule, using tribes as brokers in security arrangements in the border areas.

Massoum Stanekzai, the president's adviser on reconciliation and integration, saw the LDI, which evolved into the ALP, as an opportunity to reintegrate fighters and pave the way for a political settlement with insurgents. This perspective to some extent was in conflict with the goal of the U.S. SOFs, who saw them as an instrument in defeating the Taliban militarily, rather than as an inducement to reintegrate existing or former Taliban.

Initially, therefore, some SOF officers wanted to delink militias from reintegration, but government officials overseeing the Afghanistan Peace and Reintegration Program (APRP) saw it as a funding disbursement mechanism in the absence of viable employment or liveli-hood opportunities in the provinces. As the case studies show, SOFs in practice gave in to the temptation to reintegrate insurgents into the ALP, arguing that "the north was too difficult, we had no choice but to accept them?"

Provincial elites, including members of parliament (MPs), provincial governors, and regional strongmen, saw the ALP as another resource flow that could be captured to consolidate their power bases.

Further down the political chain, local commanders and ALPers, who were trying to access resources and employment, drew on the ALP for this purpose. This attitude can be understood as part of a complex coreperiphery bargaining relationship. For example, local commanders elected to parliament felt the need to maintain their power base in their districts and tried to use the ALP to reinforce their power but ended up clashing with former interior minister Bismillah Mohammadi, who refused to recruit some groups into the ALP.

Those who felt disempowered and excluded from the formal provincial security archi-tecture saw the ALP as a way to protect themselves and as a bargaining chip with provincial elites. In the provinces, roads and infrastructure are strategic resources, or sources of rent, and the ALP can act as force multipliers for local elites who want to extend their control over these assets. The program can also enable local power brokers to access their constituencies, which would otherwise be too insecure for them to visit.

ALP in the Regions

The selection of the three case studies was based on the following criteria. Wardak constituted the first joint U.S.-Afghan government effort to set up local militias under the MOI and provided the intellectual soil for similar initiatives elsewhere. Both Baghlan and Kunduz were strategically important in relation to the insurgency after 2008 and became sites of militia formation, leading to very different outcomes. The three cases therefore allow comparison between geographical spaces, over different time periods, and with varying outcomes.

Wardak

With an estimated population of more than half a million, and lying a mere thirty-five kilometers from Kabul, Wardak province is divided into nine districts and borders Kabul and Logar in the east, Parwan and Bamyan in the north and west, and Ghazni in the south. It is home to an ethnically mixed population of Pashtuns, who constitute a majority in the province, and Hazaras and Tajiks. Areas along the Kabul-Kandahar highway are more densely populated.

Despite its strategic value to Kabul, Wardak is graded as a third category province, which means that it does not attract the same level of financial and political support as grade one provinces like Kandahar and Balkh. In relative terms, it is resource poor, given that it has no border with a neighbouring country to generate custom revenues, little industry, and few large-scale commercial enterprises, though an unexplored mining sector holds modest economic potential in the future. The majority of the population lives in rural areas (97.7 percent), and about half of those live in remote mountainous areas. Wardak's economy is based mainly on revenues from subsistence and commercial agriculture (46 percent of households) and labour migration and remittances (16 percent); moreover, 21 percent of household income is derived from livestock, 24 percent from trade, and 45 percent from nonfarm labour. The predominately Hazara district of Behsud-e-Markazi is responsible for the bulk of the agricultural production, including wheat, vegetables, and animal products. The Kabul-Kandahar highway through the provincial capital Maidanshahr and Sayedabad is a major transport route for commercial goods and ISAF supplies as well as a source of instability and rent-seeking by both government officials and insurgents.

Wardak is politically and strategically important because of its proximity to Kabul and its status as gateway to the south. This explains why the province has remained so insecure and why, since 2009, it has become a testing ground for local governance and local defense initiatives as part of U.S. military efforts to bring stability to Wardak in order to secure Kabul.

The politico-military environment in Wardak has been shaped by a succession of armed groups dating back to the years of conflict before 2001, including Hizb-e-Islami, Harakat-e-Inqilab-e-Islami, Itihad-e-Islami, Hizb-e-Wahdat-e-Islami, and the Taliban. Competition for power among the different armed groups frequently led to open conflict.

For example, factional rivalries in the 1980s and 1990s between Hizb and Harakat resulted in more than three thousand deaths in and around Maidanshahr alone. Political and military fragmentation continued as a result of power struggles among mujahideen factions after the fall of the Taliban in November 2001. This fragmentation was reflected in the structure of the provincial administration in late 2001 and early 2002. Commander Abdul Ahmad of Sayyaf's Itihad-e-Islami faction took the provincial police chief 's post. The governor's authority was disputed by commander Ghulam Rohani Nangyalai of Hizb-e-Islami (Khalis). The Shura-e-Nizar-dominated government in Kabul appointed a local Tajik as head of the intelligence bureau. Military control fell to General Muzafaruddin, a former Hizb-e-Islami commander close to Shura-e-Nizar. He took over the army's 42nd division, which numbered 4,300 personnel. In this capacity, Muzafaruddin received support from the Northern Alliance security structures in Kabul during the power struggle against commander Nangyalai. Mohammad Musa Hotak and his brother Ghulam Mohammad Hotak maintained significant quantities of weapons and armed men under their command and were believed to be more powerful than the provincial governor.

According to Ghulam Mohammad, he commanded more than three thousand armed men before they were demobilized in 2004.55 Months later, the two brothers were arrested by U.S. forces and detained in Bagram. Ghulam Mohammad spent two and half years in U.S. detention and following his release was appointed commander of the U.S.-supported AP3.

Apart from Pashtun power brokers, a prominent Hazara politician from Hizb-e-Wahdat, Vice President Karim Khalili, is from Wardak and has a strong political base in the Hazara areas of the province. Relations between Pashtun nomads and settled Hazaras have frequently erupted in conflict, particularly in Behsud-e-Markazi, Hesa-e-Awal Behsud, and Daimirdad districts. Armed clashes between the two groups have intensified since they were first reported in April 2008. In response, thousands of Hazara took to the streets of Kabul demanding government action. Karzai issued a decree banning Kuchis (Pashtun nomads) from entering the Hazara areas of Wardak and the central highlands. Despite attempts by Kabul to settle the issue, renewed clashes in 2010 coincided with parliamentary elections, which increased external meddling and contributed to violent riots in Kabul with protesters firing at the police.

When the Taliban retreated toward Kandahar in late 2001, Wardak was handed over to local mujahideen groups, including Ghulam Mohammad and Haji Musa Hotak. Maidan-shahr remained under the control of commanders loyal to Kabul, but most other districts were controlled by Hizb-e-Islami and Harakat fighters. Signs of insecurity appeared in the lead-up to the 2004 presidential and 2005 parliamentary elections, mostly in the districts of Sayedabad and Nerkh, where Hizb-e-Islami initially enjoyed military superiority. However, its dominance gradually declined as the Taliban intensified their military campaign, and by the end of 2008, most parts of Wardak were under Taliban control. This rising power was linked to a broader expansion of the insurgency from the south to central and northern Afghanistan. However, the district of Nerkh remained divided. Jalrez district, which is home to a number of prominent local power brokers, emerged as the most contested region, with both Hizb-e-Islami and the Taliban carrying out attacks against NATO and government forces. When American forces set up a base there in 2009, they nicknamed it "the valley of death". Likewise, Maidanshahr also remained insecure. After his appointment as governor of Wardak in July 2008, Halim Fidai traveled to Maidanshahr to assume his duties. The security situation there had deteriorated to the extent that insurgents were able to fire fifteen rockets into the governor's compound on the day of his inauguration. The insurgents had become so confident that they frequently carried out attacks against government offices located a few hundred meters from the governor's compound. Fearful of Taliban retaliation, civil servants rarely stayed overnight in Maidanshahr, preferring to escape to the safety of Kabul. The governor of Nerkh district (eight kilometers from Maidanshahr) relocated his office to a shop in the local bazaar because the district center had fallen under Taliban and Hizb-e-Islami control. Although security improved, insurgents were still able to stage a devastating bomb attack in the Maidanshahr bazaar in December 2012.

Reliable aggregate figures on the level of aid to the province are difficult to obtain. The Swedish Committee for Afghanistan has been working in Wardak for decades providing assistance in education, health, and rural development. U.S. Agency for International Development (USAID) aid funding to the province between 2002 and 2012 was around $112.8 million and included assistance to agriculture, education, health, and stabilization initiatives. The Turkish government established a provincial reconstruction team (PRT) in Wardak in 2006 to promote health, education, agriculture, women's rights, and police training, among others. The Turkish PRT, consisting of a limited number of military and police officers, presented itself as a nonbelligerent and development-centered organization and therefore avoided an active role in the security sector except in police training. In 2009, for example, the Turks provided police training to more than one hundred ANP throughout Wardak. The Turkish PRT did not take part in any military operations against insurgents, and in general avoided contact with U.S. forces. Governor Fidai was unhappy with the Turkish PRT because of its limited reach and poor quality of projects. For example, of the fifty-six projects approved by the Turkish government for 2009, only five were launched. One reason was the deteriorating security situation. Another was the passive approach of the Turkish PRT. The PRT had a seventy-man security teams to support the civilian development team. In 2009, Governor Fidai asked the United States to take over the PRT from Turkey, possibly motivated by the lure of far more resources coming into Wadak than what the Turkish government could provide. The arrival of U.S. forces in early 2009 as part of President Obama's minisurge signified the importance of Wardak to the ISAF's counterinsurgency campaign and opened the flow of additional U.S. resources to the province.

LABORATORY FOR COALITION FORCES

In response to rising insecurity and the ineffective implementation of the ANAP program from 2006 through 2008, Afghan and U.S. officials began planning in October 2008 to establish a 1,200-strong force of the AP3 in four districts in Wardak province: Jalrez, Nerkh, Maid-anshahr, and Sayedabad. Each district was to have between one hundred and two hundred armed men. In March 2009, the implementation of AP3 began in Jalrez district. The AP3 guardians, as the U.S. military called them, received twenty-one days of training, AK-47 rifles, and a small quantity of ammunition. They also received a vehicle for every twenty-five men and one radio for every ten men. Individual pay was $170 per month and sometimes not paid for months. By 2010, the AP3 had 1,100 recruits. The initiative, at least on paper, was part of a broader security effort that included deployment of additional international troops, training of the ANP, recruitment of AP3 cadres, and development assistance of up to $500,000 per district from CERP funds as an incentive to participate in the program. The AP3's mandate was a product of competing interests and rationales. Among other things, it sought to improve security by denying insurgents safe havens in rural villages that had been cleared in ISAF and ANSF military operations, prevent insurgent attacks on government and NATO forces, protect infrastructure, and build the peoples' trust in their government. Once security had been established and the government's authority expanded into remote areas, the program intended to improve not only development outcomes but also government legitimacy.

The AP3 faced many of the same problems as the ANAP, especially in terms of recruitment, logistics support, and appropriation by local commanders. The central government and provincial authorities sought to use the unelected ASOP shuras to recruit AP3 members. However, European donors objected to the use of ASOP, as did provincial council members and local elders. This objection, combined with the insecurity, meant that ASOP shuras played a limited role in the process. The AP3 was funded by the U.S. military because European donors objected to payments to a paramilitary force. The European objections were also related to a broader U.S. plan to encourage villagers to form local militias against the insurgency, a step that seemed to undermine earlier disarmament efforts. As a result, the AP3 was seen from the beginning as an American program designed to defeat insurgents rather than to improve policing or the rule of law. Initial recruitment in Jalrez began positively where the Tajik population was encouraged by the local NDS chief to take up arms and Hazaras were eager to access weapons and resources to use in their ongoing clashes with Pashtun nomads in both Behsud districts. On the other hand, recruitment among Pashtuns was slow and met with resistance in southern Pashtun-dominated districts, where locals feared Taliban retribution. In addition, skepticism was widespread in Wardak and based largely on people's bitter experiences with local militias during the 1980s and early 1990s.

Early Beginnings

As insecurity increased in 2008 and posed a threat to Kabul, provincial authorities demanded more regular police to protect government offices, senior officials, and public infrastructure. The AP3 emerged partly as a solution to overcome the manpower gap given the shortage of regular police. Accounts differ as to the origins of the demand for AP3. Governor Fidai claimed it came from elders, yet in a today meeting in Kabul in October 2008, tribal elders and representatives of district shuras and provincial council members rejected a government declaration that intended to show popular support for the initiative. Instead, local elders asked for the deployment of more ANA and ANP units in Wardak. The U.S.

military and Afghan government pushed ahead with the AP3 implementation regardless. The lack of local support and Pashtun fear of Taliban retribution help explain why recruitment was a problem and largely limited to the Tajik and Hazara populations.

After almost a year of limited progress, the U.S. military and Afghan officials, including Fidai, reached out to Ghulam Mohammad Hotak, former Taliban commander and Bagram inmate, to rescue the program by taking up arms against his former colleagues. A rival of Wardak Police Chief General Muzafaruddin, Hotak reportedly brought five hundred of his supporters to the force, but after a few months of poor government support through the MOI, he quit the program. Hotak bitterly regretted his decision to join the AP3 and accused the government and U.S. forces of harming his reputation among the people of Wardak. He added that funding for the program was always late, and he had to buy basic supplies for the force. As a result, he accumulated considerable personal debt. Many other local commanders also became heavily indebted because of late payments and inadequate logistical support, forcing them to dig into their own pockets to support their men, resources for which they allegedly were never properly compensated.

In interviews, former commanders and their men complained about the lack of weapons, ammunition, and winter supplies, as well as the late salary payments. Although part of a plan that required additional U.S. and Afghan forces to clear areas before the AP3 was deployed to those areas and hold them, most AP3 units said they were used for clearing purposes and were described by local commanders as 'shields of meat,' stood up to receive Taliban bullets. As a result of poor support from the MOI, the AP3 remained dependent on U.S. SOFs and was in turn relied on for joint operations, including outside the province. Despite Fidai's repeated attempts to get the U.S. military and the MOI to intervene to address the emerging problems with the AP3, he was largely ignored. The main points of concern were the lack of trust and support both from the Afghan government and local communities, unclear operational procedures, poor coordination among stakeholders, lack of sustainable resources, poor logistics, weak command and control structure, and lack of strong backup or Quick Reaction support from the ANSF.

The impact of the AP3 is difficult to assess. Mathieu Lefèvre, who wrote the first comprehensive report on the AP3, came up with mixed conclusions: The U.S. military considered it a success but remained skeptical of expanding it to other provinces because it was slow to take off, resource intensive, and bureaucratically cumbersome.

They had hoped for a more nimble approach that would bring about rapid improvement in security and win hearts and minds, which did not unfold in practice. Although security along the roads had improved, especially in Jalrez where AP3 was most heavily deployed, and people could visit the districts, government officials did not consider district centres safe enough to spend the night. Although even the critics of the AP3 admitted it had helped bring about relative security, Afghanistan NGO Safety Office data showed that violence levels had in fact increased in 2010, when the AP3 had reached its full strength. Proximity to Kabul also meant that central state elites had greater influence in destabilizing the situation as support flowed to competing armed groups for military and political dominance, as the case of Hizb-e-Islami illustrates.

Shift from aP3 to aLP and Beyond

By summer 2010, the AP3 had transitioned into the newly approved ALP. However, the problems inherited from the AP3—including limited popular support, insufficient resources, poor recruitment and logistics, and weak command and control—were considered so serious that the ISAF finally took steps in the winter of 2011 to address them. In the summer of that year, the MOI had established new guidelines for the implementation of the ALP. This led the U.S. military to announce an ambitious plan to fix the ALP and "redo it all over again," according to newly established operational guidelines. The first step in reforming the ALP in Wardak involved the demobilization of 260 members of the AP3 from Maidanshahr and Sayedabad, who had earlier been transitioned into the ALP.

They were demobilized because they did not meet the new ALP recruitment guidelines, which stipulated among other things that the ALP recruits should be recruited from local villages through shuras and vetted by local elders and government institutions and report to the district police chief. Most of the targeted recruits were from Bamyan, Laghman, and Jalalabad, though some belonged to other parts of Wardak where the ALP had not yet been established. In violation of procedure, most of them served guard duties in Maidanshahr and provided personal protection to provincial officials, who were not happy to have their personal guards dismissed as part of the reform process.

The application of the new ALP guidelines paved the way to establish ALP units in other districts. However, the U.S. military's attempts in the spring and summer of 2012 to expand the ALP to Wardak's insecure southern districts of Chak, Daimirdad and Jaghatu petered out when the program encountered similar problems as before. The U.S. military's figures indicated only a handful of new recruits in Chak. The difficulty of expanding ALP to southern districts in Wardak had been evident in February 2012 when Governor Fidai and the U.S. military tried, unsuccessfully, to persuade the elders of Sayedabad to "give their sons" to the ALP. In response, the local elders requested more army and police in place of the ALP and indicated their readiness to send their sons instead to the ANP.

A prominent member of the provincial council, echoing the sentiments of his people, pointed out that "the people wanted more ANA and ANP, but the Americans forced AP3 and ALP on them?" Realizing that public opinion was coalescing against the ALP, by the summer of 2012, Fidai had given up trying to fix it in Wardak. With pressure mounting ahead of the Taliban's spring offensive, he wrote to Karzai on March 12, pointing out that the ALP had not worked in Wardak and recommended that the 1,600 strong ALP force be disbanded and replaced with one thousand regular police (at the time, Wardak had slightly more than eight hundred ANP personnel). The governor argued that the ALP was not suitable for Wardak because tribal structures had been decimated by years of conflict, the tribes remained internally divided, and factional rivalries and conflicts among local power brokers ran deep. Most important, because the Taliban insurgency remained strong in most parts of Wardak and the government could not guarantee sufficient security, people generally feared for their lives and avoided a controversial program like the ALP.

In private, senior U.S. military officers and the political leadership in Kabul had more or less come to the same conclusions as Fidai. However, the government did not immediately react to Fidai's recommendation, possibly to avoid souring already tense relations with the U.S. military locally. Subsequently, Fidai suggested an alternative strategy to defeat the Taliban insurgency in Wardak. This occurred in early Spring 2012 amid closely guarded discussions with local elders and SOFs allegedly involving the idea of supporting local Hizb-e-Islami factions in Nerkh district, and possibly other areas, against the Taliban in a war that had been going on between the two factions for the past two years. In 2010 and 2011, skirmishes broke out between the two sides, which observers believed had been supported by the provincial government and the U.S. military. By late 2012, the suggested alternative to the ALP had failed to materialize, possibly because of U.S. objections and the unwillingness of key Northern Alliance power holders in Kabul to empower their historic rival in the process of fighting the Taliban. More important, the strategy of building up the ANA and ANP, as advocated by Karzai, would likely have been undermined by relying on groups like Hizb-e-Islami to defeat the insurgency.

The difficulty of reforming and expanding the ALP to the southern districts in Wardak finally convinced local officials and SOFs to try a different approach. This was the clearest indication of the failure of the strategy to use a government-backed militia to bring about security in a contested environment.

Meanwhile, Fidai had become increasingly scathing in his criticism of U.S. military strategy in Wardak, especially over the question of transitioning security responsibilities to Afghan forces, which he claimed was irresponsible because the Afghan forces were not ready, and for its overreliance on the ALP. As early as February 2012, a month after the U.S. military started transitioning security responsibilities to Afghan forces in Wardak, Fidai aired his views publicly, describing Wardak as a "laboratory for coalition forces" and criticizing U.S. plans to transition security responsibilities to poorly trained and poorly equipped Afghan forces in Wardak.

The failure of the ALP in Wardak in the summer of 2012 and the purported plans to arm local anti-Taliban factions perhaps indicated a shift away from McChrystal's population-centric counterinsurgency, which claimed to protect the population against insurgents, and toward a new strategy of exclusively fighting America's enemies through targeted killings by SOFs and the CIA's counterterrorism pursuit teams, as well as working with local proxy forces like Hizb-e-Islami as part of an attempt to mobilize the population for offensive operations against insurgents. This shift, in turn, may be understood as part of the strategy for extracting Western forces from Afghanistan by leaving behind a rural paramilitary force to hold the ground and fight the insurgency, rather than prioritizing the more demanding task of building regular forces to do so instead.

However, these plans were partly thrown into disarray when, in late February 2013, allegations of abduction, torture, and extrajudicial killings by SOFs and Afghan units associated with them in Wardak emerged, prompting Karzai to order all SOFs out of Wardak within two weeks. Provincial authorities claimed that around seven hundred families had been displaced as a result of insecurity created by the abusive actions of SOFs and their Afghan proxies. The incidents in Nerkh and Maidanshahr districts indicate that the problem of militias in Wardak extends well beyond the ALP program. One implication of restrictions placed on SOFs as a result of these incidents is that without their presence in villages, support to and further development of the ALP has become difficult. Moreover, it can be expected that the risks to local villagers who participated in the ALP will increase as foreign forces are pulled out.

One interpretation of events is that Hizb-e-Islami-affiliated politicians close to Karzai, in an alliance of convenience with local power brokers, manipulated popular sentiments to persuade Karzai to evict SOFs from Wardak, especially Nerkh district, where Hizb-e-Islami and the Taliban had been involved in a prolonged power struggle. The aim of such an intervention would have been to protect Hizb-e-Islami from U.S. military action to safeguard its military capabilities against the Taliban. Meanwhile, allowing Hizb-e-Islami some breathing space while the government sought to reach a peace settlement with the Taliban could also be a key reason political pressure on SOFs increased during this period. By March 10, when Karzai's deadline for pullout came into effect, SOFs had not withdrawn from Wardak. In response, the government mobilized the Ulema Council, the country's highest clerical body, to issue a statement calling on the U.S. government to respect Afghan sovereignty and implement Karzai's decree without further delay. However, a day later, media reports indicated that it looked likely that a compromise solution was on the table, with the government allowing SOFs to stay in Wardak in exchange for a U.S. agreement to hand over control of the Bagram detention facility.

Finally, on March 20, reports indicated that the U.S. military had agreed to start the withdrawal of its SOFs, first from Nerkh district and later from other parts of the province. In their place, the government deployed Afghan special forces to work alongside regular Afghan army units to ensure security in Nerkh.

Impact of aP3 and aLP

The impacts of the AP3 and the ALP were mixed. Security along roads from the provincial capital of Maidanshahr to district centres like Jalrez and Nerkh, previously considered too risky, had seen visible improvement from 2009 onward. Villagers and government officials started traveling more frequently to these two districts. The Nerkh district administration returned to its compound in the district center after months of operating from a rented shop in Maidanshahr. When, in 2008, security had deteriorated in Nerkh and travel to the district center was not possible, the Nerkh district was relocated to the Maidanshahr bazaar. In 2009, amid tight security, the governor along with members of his administration took a symbolic walk from the provincial capital to the Jalrez district center. The return of the district administration to Nerkh and the symbolic walk showcased some of the improvements in security along the roads.

In Sayedabad district, security incidents dropped noticeably in 2012, although the majority of the insurgent attacks in Wardak continued to occur in Sayedabad, through which the highway passes. More generally, insurgent attacks nationwide declined by more than 25 percent in 2012. However, declining attacks do not necessarily translate into improved security for the population, given that most attacks occurred on ISAF troops and strategic highways. It could also mean that foreign forces leaving rural villages meant fewer targets. Afghan forces shoul-dering most of the responsibility for fighting insurgents certainly meant that their casualties soared in 2012 and 2013. In December 2012, the Afghan ministry of defense reported very high casualty figures of army and police personnel: about three hundred ANA and ANP per month, an average of 110 soldiers and 200 policemen. This is on top of an annual attrition rate of 25 percent for the ANP and close to 30 percent for the ANA. In February 2013, it was revealed that the U.S. military had suffered no casualties in a month, yet the war continued unabated, and Afghan civilians and security forces were its primary victims.

Measuring the success of the ALP from a narrow security perspective may be possible, but the governance and development outcomes are much harder to assess. The empowering of abusive commanders and rival factions and human rights abuses committed by some ALP units have intensified concerns about the long-term impact of militias and undermined the program's main intent—to increase the population's trust in the government, expand government authority in insecure areas—where the Taliban offer a repressive but more predictable order—and to improve governance and development outcomes. Reports of extortion by AP3 members have also been documented along the Maidanshahr-Jalrez road, where Hazara members of the AP3 repeatedly harassed Pashtun travelers. Although in public most government officials put on a brave face, in private discussions, provincial council members often reminded visiting dignitaries from Kabul and the governor of Wardak about the dozens of cases of murder and extortion involving AP3 and ALP members and the obstacles faced by the families of victims and the provincial military prosecutor in prosecuting the perpetrators.

They argued that unless the government applied the rule of law and arrested these individuals, the local population would be unlikely to change its negative views about government-backed militias in Wardak. Despite improved security along the roads, most AP3 units in the vicinity of Maidanshahr and Nerkh remained particularly vulnerable to insurgent attacks. The AP3, like the ALP later on, acted as a magnet for insurgent attacks. Casualty figures attest to this: One AP3 commander in Nerkh lost more than half of his 150 men to insurgent attacks in less than a year.

The strategically vital Kabul-Kandahar highway remained insecure for most of the period. Although in 2012 insurgent attacks in Sayedabad decreased overall by 35 percent, 90 percent of all attacks in Wardak were concentrated in Sayedabad, along the Kabul-Kandahar highway. By design, the AP3 and ALP were not trained or equipped to seriously weaken the insurgency, and in that sense, the overall impact on security was limited.

It would take many more conventional Afghan and U.S. forces as well as SOFs and night raids targeting key commanders to achieve a shift in the security environment during the period studied. Even that was no guarantee of success. On its own, the ALP has limited strategic value; it is too small and in proportion to the ANSF has suffered greater casualties: five hundred as of early 2013, twice as many as the ANA and ANP. It remains highly dependent on SOFs and ANSF support to remain effective. The warning by the U.S. military that if SOFs working with the ALP are pulled from insecure villages where the ALP is deployed, they could fall into the hands of insurgents—with serious consequence for villagers who have participated in the program—is a tacit admission of its vulnerability.

It also suggests that after a decade of fighting and an increase of thousands of U.S. troops as well as the expansion of the ALP to 136 districts and billions of dollars spent on training Afghan security forces, the security situation in much of the country remains extremely tenuous. The ISAF nevertheless claimed in late 2012 that 80 percent of the Afghan population lived in secure areas. Such claims were challenged by reported abuses in late 2012 and early 2013 by SOFs in Nerkh and Maidanshahr districts. Alleged victims included young children, women, elders, government workers, doctors, nurses, and school and university students. Neither the Afghan government nor the ISAF identified which armed group or groups had perpetrated the abuses. Perhaps the lack of attribution of responsibility in this case was intentional, because off the books and unaccountable militias provide plausible deniability to those who rely on them. In other words, by outsourcing violence and repression, states can reduce international and domestic legal and political liability. Therefore, reports in early 2013 about the long-standing roles of the CIA and SOFs in arming and using Afghan paramilitary units for counterterrorism missions intensified concerns about the post-2014 presence of U.S. intelligence and military assets in Afghanistan.

Baghlan

Baghlan province lies 250 kilometers from Kabul along the north-south axis connecting both sides of the Hindu Kush. Its fertile valleys and strategic roads link Kabul to northern Afghanistan. The province has fifteen districts; the provincial capital is in Puli Khumri. It borders Kunduz and Takhar in the north, Parwan and Panjshir in the south, and Bamyan and Samangan in the west. It has an ethnically mixed population of about 741,690, a substantial number of whom are Pashtun settlers from southern and eastern Afghanistan who arrived there toward the end of the nineteenth century. Its main source of wealth is agriculture, boosted by the water sources of the Baghlan-Kunduz river system and the proximity to markets in Balkh and Kabul. Baghlan's energy plants and modest industrial enterprises—notably the Ghori cement factory, the sugar mill, hydropower plants, and coal mines—make it an important industrial zone. With the fall of the Taliban, Jamiat-linked mujahideen commanders from Andarab district returned to power in Baghlan. Although the former rulers of Baghlan, the Ismaili clan of Sayed Mansoor Naderi, briefly captured power in the confusion surrounding the fall of Taliban, his forces were quickly driven out of Puli Khumri by a coalition of Jamiat and

Hizb-e-Islami commanders. The Andarabi commanders at the head of this coalition occupied most of the powerful positions in the local administration, especially in the security sector. As head of the Highway Police in 2003, General Khalil Andarabi awarded two-thirds of all senior positions in the Highway Police to his supporters from Andarab, 90 percent of whom were Tajik, and only one Pashtun. During Mir Alam's, and later Kabir Andarabi's, tenure as provincial police chief—in 2005 and 2009, respectively—the police were primarily drawn from Jamiat supporters. According to Alam Jan, the total ANP force in Baghlan numbered some eighteen hundred policemen. In 2009, the provincial ANP headquarters, the Komandani, was staffed by forty-six senior officers, six of whom were junior Pashtun officers. To overcome dominance by one faction, the central government appointed General Abdul Rahman Rahimi, a professional Pashtun officer, as police chief in Baghlan in early 2010.

He replaced Kabir Andarabi, and though his appointment signaled the change of leadership at the top, the rank and file of provincial police force remained loyal to Mustafa and Kabir Andarabi. The domination of the post-2001 provincial security architecture by Northern Alliance factions reversed the fortunes of local power brokers who had benefited from Taliban rule between 1997 and 2001. Most of these Pashtun commanders were cut off from government patronage and protection. Northern Alliance commanders with links to power brokers in Kabul folded their militias into the local security structure and avoided the UN-sponsored DDR program, but many Pashtuns were targeted, accused of having Taliban or al-Qaeda sympathies. The Andarabi-dominated police force disarmed Pashtuns they suspected of previous ties to the Taliban or otherwise perceived as a threat to their power. Although a few Pashtun commanders such as Amir Gul joined Jamiat commanders in power, others were hunted down by the security forces in the name of al-Qaeda and Taliban, thus driving them into the arms of the Taliban insurgency.

With the rise to power of Jamiat factions, rival groups in the central government have tried to weaken their power by appointing governors and police chiefs with links to Hizb-e-Islami factions from the local Pashtun community or trusted political allies from Kabul. In the last decade, Baghlan has had more governors (by one count more than ten in nine years) than any other province in the country. The rapid turnover indicates the difficulty faced by the central government in maintaining political stability in the province. Vice President Fahim maintained links to Mustafa and Rasoul Andarabi, and Karzai relied on the support of former Hizb-e-Islami commanders such as Amir Gul, Mullah Alam, and Alam Jan to check the power of Tajik strongmen. Centrally appointed governors often found it difficult to work with the provincial police chief and local strongmen from Jamiat factions.

On more than one occasion, local demonstrations organized by Jamiat strongmen forced Kabul-appointed governors from office, notably the pro-Pashtun former military commander of Hizb-e-Islami in Balkh and the current governor of Paktia, Juma Khan Hamdard. During his brief governorship of Baghlan in 2005, Hamdard tried to rally disaffected Hizb-e-Islami supporters against Tajik strongmen from Andarab. He also played a key role in regional politics. For more than a decade, Juma Khan has stood in opposition to the governor of Balkh, Atta Mohammad Noor, who emerged as the north's undisputed strongman with an active influence in Baghlan and Kunduz.

Atta has been accused of fanning insecurity and arming local militias to disrupt elections in Pashtun areas and undermine the incumbent's electoral chances and boost his rival Abdullah, a political ally of Atta. However, the Andarabi clan is not a monolith. Political fragmentation among Andarabi factions has resulted in the creation of several armed factions, some loyal to Mustafa and Rasoul Andarabi, who rely on them to undermine their rivals during elections and to exert control over licit and illicit economic activities. Other factions are loyal to General Kabir Andarabi. They have resorted to highway robbery, setting up roadblocks and taxing traffic and other criminal activities while fearing no retribution. The insurgency is therefore not the only source of instability in the province.

5

The Age of Insurgency

Insurgencies are not new to Afghanistan. This chapter briefly examines Afghanistan's recent history of insurgency and argues that governance, the capacity of indigenous security forces, and external support have been critical factors in the outcome of these insurgencies. This finding has significant implications for understanding the resurgence of the Taliban that began in 2002.

In 1973, the royal dynasty that had ruled Afghanistan for more than two centuries fell. Mohammed Daoud deposed his brother-in-law, King Zahir Shah, and declared Afghanistan a republic. Daoud became president, abolished the monarchy, and forced Zahir Shah into exile in Rome. Marxist army officers helped consolidate Daoud's position, although this process was hampered by splits between the two main communist factions in Afghanistan: Khalq [the masses] and Parcham [the flag]. In 1978, Khalq army officers engineered a bloody coup, which led to the death of Daoud and his replacement by Nur Mohammad Taraki. Violence between the rival factions—including the murder of Taraki—coincided with wider rural revolts by Islamist opponents of the communist regime. Moscow grew increasingly concerned about the deteriorating security situation and feared that Tara-ki's successor, Hafizullah Amin, would turn to the West for assistance. Thus began Afghanistan's age of insurgency.

A LEGACY OF WAR

Over the next three decades, Afghanistan experienced at least four major insurgencies: the mujahideen wars against the Soviet

Union (1979–1994), the rise of the Taliban (1994–2001), the U.S.-backed overthrow of the Taliban regime (2001–2002), and the return of the Taliban. The objective of each of these insurgencies was to overthrow the existing regime and replace it with one more palatable to insurgent forces and their state sponsors. Many of the insurgent leaders—including Gulbuddin Hekmatyar, Abdul Rashid Dostum, Jalaluddin Haqqani, and Mullah Mohammed Omar—played key roles in most or all of the insurgencies.

The Mujahideen Period

In December 1979, the Soviet Union invaded Afghanistan, overthrew the Afghan government, and installed Babrak Karmal as leader. But a disparate collection of mujahideen insurgent groups resisted the Soviet occupation.

The Soviets were successful in controlling the major cities and provincial towns in the country, but they never managed to take control of the countryside. Indeed, the situation in rural areas worsened for the Soviets and the Afghan government as mujahideen forces steadily gained popular support. Support for the mujahideen from Pakistan was a critical variable. Pakistan's Inter-Services Intelligence Directorate (ISI) provided money, weapons, training, and other assistance to Afghan insurgent groups, funneling aid to the mujahideen from a variety of other countries such as the United States and Saudi Arabia. Pakistan also provided sanctuary to mujahideen groups, where they were generally safe from Soviet forces.

Soviet losses mounted steadily, despite the Soviets' repeated efforts to defeat the mujahideen through the widespread deployment of mines, carpet-bombing of rebel areas, and the use of scorched-earth tactics. In November 1986, Mohammad Najibullah was elected president of Afghanistan. He attempted to introduce a "national reconciliation" program, but with little success. When the Soviets withdrew in February 1989, the country was devastated. An estimated 1 million Afghans had been killed, more than 5 million had fled abroad, and 2–3 million were internally displaced. Nearly 15,000 Soviet soldiers had been killed, and as many as 500,000 had become sick or were wounded.

The Soviet withdrawal raised hopes both within Afghanistan and abroad for an imminent end to the conflict. However, fighting continued as the former anti-Soviet mujahideen coalition splintered along ethnic and political lines into competing factions. As a result of this in-fighting among the mujahideen forces, the pro-Moscow regime of President Najibullah was able to cling to power for three years after the Soviet withdrawal. In April 1992, Kabul finally fell to elements of the mujahideen, who then established a new government for the renamed the Islamic Republic of Afghanistan. Mujahideen leaders agreed to introduce a rotating presidency, starting with Burhanuddin Rabbani. However, disputes broke out over the division of government posts, and the fighting flared again. Pashtun leaders were particularly concerned about the makeup of the government and resented having to hand power over to other ethnic groups after more than 250 years of uninterrupted Pashtun rule.

THE RISE OF THE TALIBAN

By 1994, Afghanistan had disintegrated into a patchwork of competing groups and shifting alliances. The predominantly ethnic Tajik government of President Rabbani held Kabul and the northeast of the country, while the northern provinces remained under the control of Abdul Rashid Dostum and other warlords. Ismail Khan controlled the western provinces around Herat, and the area to the south and east of Kabul were in the hands of warlords such as Gulbuddin Hekmatyar. The eastern border with Pakistan was held by a council of mujahideen, and the south was split between scores of ex-mujahideen and bandits, who used their control of the roads to extort money from the cross-border trade with Pakistan.

In late 1994, a new movement emerged in the south, seizing control first of Kandahar and then of the surrounding provinces. Its leaders took the name of their group, Taliban, from the plural of talib, an Arabic word denoting an Islamic student. Many members were drawn from madrassas (Islamic theology schools) that had been established in Afghan refugee camps in northeastern Pakistan during the 1980s. The Taliban leadership, headed by Mullah Omar, presented itself as a cleansing force that would rid the country of the factionalism, corruption, and violence that had predominated since the Soviet withdrawal. Due to frustration and war-weariness among the population in the south, the Taliban was initially well received. Its forces advanced rapidly through southern and eastern Afghanistan, capturing nine out of thirty provinces by February 1995. The movement received strong backing from Pakistan's ISI, which assisted in the recruitment of members and provided weapons, training, and technical assistance. In 1996, the Taliban captured Kabul and, despite temporary setbacks, conquered the northern cities of Mazar, Kunduz, and Taloqan in 1998.

By 2001, the Taliban controlled virtually all of Afghanistan. The only exception was a small sliver of land northeast of Kabul in the Pan-shjir Valley to which Ahmed Shah Massoud and his Northern Alliance forces had retreated. The Taliban instituted a repressive version of *shari'a* law, banning music, banned women from working or going to school, and prohibited freedom of the press. Afghanistan also became a breeding ground for jihadists and terrorists intent on attacking the United States and other nations. Osama bin Laden and his al Qaeda network used their money and influence to support the Taliban regime and, in return, received permission to train operatives and plan operations on Afghan soil.

Operation Enduring Freedom

After the September 11, 2001, terrorist attacks in Washington, New York, and Pennsylvania, the United States military launched Operation Enduring Freedom, helping Northern Alliance forces led by Abdul Rashid Dostum, Atta Mohammad Nur, Mohammad Qasim Fahim, and other local commanders mount a successful insurgency against the Taliban. Over the next several months, U.S. and Afghan forces conducted a series of offensive operations, such as Operation Anaconda in the Shah-i-kot valley of eastern Afghanistan, against Taliban and al Qaeda forces. The result was that most Taliban, al Qaeda, and other foreign jihadists resettled across the border in Pakistan. Although fighting continued for several years, the United States and other international actors began to assist Afghanistan with reconstruction by December 2001. As the Taliban's power base collapsed, international and local attention turned to nation-building. The UN helped organize a meeting of Afghan political leaders in Bonn, Germany, in late November 2001. On December 5, 2001, Afghan leaders signed the Bonn Agreement. It established a timetable for a transition to legitimate power structures, which culminated in the establishment of a fully representative and freely elected government. The UN Security Council endorsed the outcome the following day in Resolution 1383.[9] Under the Bonn Agreement, the parties agreed to establish an interim authority comprising three main bodies: a 30-member interim administration headed by Hamid Karzai, a Pashtun, which took power on December 22; a supreme court; and a Special Independent Commission for the Convening of the Emergency Loya Jirga.

In January 2002 in Tokyo, international donors pledged over $4.5 billion for reconstruction efforts. The parties present at Bonn had also asked the United Nations to "monitor and assist in the implementation of all aspects" of the agreement. To that end, Security Council Resolution 1401, passed on March 28, 2002, established the UN Assistance Mission in Afghanistan (UNAMA). In addition, the United Kingdom agreed to be the lead nation for counternarcotics, Italy for justice, the United States for the army, Germany for police, and Japan for the disarmament, demobilization, and reintegration of former combatants. The Emergency Loya Jirga, which was attended by approximately 2,000 people, took place between June 12 and 19, 2002, following extensive preparations and countrywide consultations. At the conclusion, Hamid Karzai was chosen as president of the transitional administration and head of state. His nominees for key posts in the administration were also approved by the Emergency Loya Jirga. The defense and foreign affairs portfolios were given to the mainly Tajik Northern Alliance, while the Ministry of Interior went to a Pashtun regional governor.

THE RETURN OF THE TALIBAN

In the spring and summer of 2002, Taliban and other forces began to conduct offensive operations to overthrow the Afghan government and coerce the withdrawal of U.S. and coalition forces. In April, for example, Taliban and jihadist forces conducted a series of offensive attacks in Kandahar, Khowst, Nangarhar, Kabul, and other Afghan provinces. This marked the beginning of the latest insurgency. After 2002, insurgent groups waged an increasingly violent campaign in Afghanistan despite political progress. In January 2004, for example, Afghans adopted a new constitution. In October 2004, they elected Hamid Karzai as president, despite efforts by the Taliban and other insurgent groups to target those involved in the election. In September 2005, Afghans elected a new parliament, which included a number of ex-Taliban ministers. At least several individuals formerly associated with the Taliban won Wolesi Jirga (lower house of the National Assembly) seats in the September 2005 elections, including Abdul Salam Rocketi. President Karzai appointed the former Taliban deputy religious affairs minister, Mawlawi Arsallah Rahmani, to the Meshrano Jirga (upper house) along with Gulbuddin Hekmatyar's former close ally, Abdul Saboor Farid. Despite these steps, however, the insurgency continued to worsen.

Key Themes

This brief overview of Afghanistan's age of insurgency highlights three factors that have contributed to the success of past insurgencies: governance challenges, external support, and variations in the quality of security forces.

Governance

Afghanistan has a long history of decentralized governance. Following the second Anglo-Afghan war in 1880, Amir Abdul Rahman Khan seized power after the departure of British troops. With British financial and military assistance, he ruthlessly attempted to defeat or manipulate tribal and ethnic groups such as the Hazaras, Aimaqs, Nuristanis, and various Pashtun tribal coalitions. However, Khan was unable to destroy tribal power and establish a strong, centrally controlled state.

Successive efforts over the next century generally failed. Afghan territory has been controlled by tribes and local strongmen, and its inhabitants have generally pledged loyalty to those with similar kinship ties and patrilineal descent rather than to a central governing authority. One consequence of this power structure is that Afghan governments have never been able to establish a monopoly on the legitimate use of force inside the country. The insurgencies that began with the 1979 Soviet invasion and continued through the Taliban conquests in the 1990s only served to increase Afghanistan's decentralized political structure. In addition, Afghan governments have never established a formal justice system. In the absence of a central government, local shuras (village councils) and tribal elders developed an informal legal system that incorporated a wide range of Islamic and customary laws.

External Support

State support and sanctuary have been critical variables in the outcome of these insurgencies. Afghan governments and opposition groups have received aid from a number of states. The Soviet Union provided a total of $1.3 billion in economic aid and $1.3 billion in military aid to the Afghan government between 1955 and 1978 and roughly $5 billion per year between 1979 and 1989.

The United States provided $533 million in economic aid to the Afghan government between 1955 and 1978, and between $4 billion and $5 billion to the mujahideen between 1980 and 1992. Both the United States and the Soviet Union suspended most aid in 1991.

The Pakistan government, especially the ISI, played a particularly active role in Afghan politics. Pakistan provided significant assistance to the mujahideen during the Soviet wars. And it provided weapons, financial aid, and other assistance such as wheat and petroleum to the Taliban and other groups from the 1990s through 2001.

Saudi Arabia gave nearly $4 billion in official aid to the mujahideen between 1980 and 1990; there was also a flow of unofficial aid from Saudi Islamic charities and foundations, the private funds of Saudi princes, and mosque collections. Saudi Arabia provided aid to the Taliban and al Qaeda in Afghanistan until 1998. Finally, Iran provided assistance to various factions, especially to Afghan commanders in the western regions of the country. Iranian military aid to the anti-Taliban alliance escalated after the fall of Kabul in 1996 and again after the fall of Mazar in 1998.

Security Forces

Afghanistan's history of weak central governments and the flow of support from external actors impacted efforts to establish strong central government forces. During the 1980s and 1990s, there was no national civilian police force in Afghanistan. Instead, local militia and tribal forces enforced the rule of law in much of the country. Among the Pashtun (who constitute a majority of Afghanistan's population), the traditional military institution has been the lashkar, or the armed tribe. Each family contributed male members and weapons to the lashkar, which was further enriched by whatever material it took in battle.

There are no precise figures for the number of militia fighters. Estimates during the 1990s ranged from about 200,000 to 600,000.20 Most were untrained, ill-equipped, illiterate, and owed their allegiance to local warlords and military commanders, not to the central government.

As a German delegation in January 2002 concluded

The police force is in a deplorable state just a few months after the dissolution of the Taliban regime. There is a total lack of equipment and supplies. No systematic training has been provided for about 20 years. At least one entire generation of trained police officers is missing. Next to constables, former Northern Alliance fighters are being put to work as police officers.

While Afghanistan has lacked a trained civilian police force, it has had secret police agencies. During the Soviet era, the Afghan government established a powerful secret police body, the State Information Services, to suppress opponents of the regime and establish order. The Taliban established the Ministry of Enforcement of Virtue and Suppression of Vice to enforce decrees regarding moral behaviour, such as those restricting women's employment, education, and dress; enforcing men's beard length and mosque attendance; and regulating the activities of the United Nations and NGOs.

The Afghan army has traditionally had little internal control over the country. During the 1980s, the Moscow-backed Democratic Republic of Afghanistan and its successor, the Republic of

Afghanistan, recruited a large number of tribal and local militias as army forces.

During the Taliban era, the army was comprised of an assortment of armed groups with varying degrees of loyalties and professional skills. There was no formal military structure. The army was not organized, armed, or commanded by the state. Mullah Mohammed Omar was commander of the armed forces and ultimately decided on military strategies, key appointments, and military budgets. A military shura sat below Omar, helping to plan strategy and implement tactical decisions. Individual Taliban commanders were responsible for recruiting men, paying them, and looking after their needs in the field. These field commanders acquired much of the money, fuel, food, transport, and weapons they needed from the military shura. The Taliban's military structure also included Pakistani officers and al Qaeda members. For example, the elite Brigade 055 consisted of Pakistani, Sudanese, and other foreign fighters.

Conclusion

Governance challenges, external support, and the capacity of indigenous security forces have been critical factors in the outcome of Afghanistan's insurgencies. Pakistan played two particularly important roles. First, the Pakistan government, especially the ISI, supported the victors of each insurgency: the mujahideen, Taliban, and U.S. forces during the initial stages of Operation Enduring Freedom. Since Afghanistan and Pakistan share a 1,160-mile border, Pakistani leaders have historically viewed the ability to influence Afghanistan as critical for strategic depth. Second, Afghan insurgent groups have repeatedly used Pakistan as a sanctuary. These findings have significant implications for understanding the Taliban's resurgence and assessing how they can be defeated.

THE INSURGENCY

The Taliban's penetration into Baghlan was facilitated by the political marginalization and persecution of local Pashtuns, who saw the insurgency as a possible source of protection and resources. Disgruntled Hizb-e-Islami followers allied with the Taliban and facilitated their penetration into key Hizb-dominated areas of

Baghlan. However, in provinces dominated by non-Pashtuns, as in Baghlan, the Taliban worked with the clergy to transcend ethnic divisions rather than solely championing the cause of disaffected Pashtuns. The rerouting of NATO supplies through northern Afghanistan after attacks on NATO convoys increased in Pakistan enhanced the strategic significance of Baghlan for both NATO and the insurgents, resulting in increased Taliban and Hizb-e-Islami military operations in Dand-e-Shahabuddin and Dand-e-Ghori areas of Puli Khumri aimed at disrupting ISAF supply lines.

Taliban penetration began in the districts of Nahrin, Khost-wa-Fering, and Andarab as early as 2008, but the first serious signs of insecurity appeared in the spring of 2009 in Puli Khumri and Baghlan-e-Jadid. In Puli Khumri, Dahan-e-Ghori, and Baghlan-e-Jadid, the Taliban relied on local Hizb-e-Islami commanders to gain a foothold. The situation deteriorated further in the lead-up to the August presidential elections. For example, in Dand-e-Ghori area of Puli Khumri, Taliban and Hizb-e-Islami fighters attacked police patrols and captured police vehicles and ammunition without much resistance. Local power brokers such as Mullah Alam believed the attacks against police convoys and capture of vehicles and weapons were orchestrated by those aligned with Atta Mohammed Noor, who wished to create insecurity so voting could not take place in Pashtun areas and thereby hurt Karzai's chances of reelection.

Security continued to deteriorate after the elections. In November 2009, the Taliban felt confident enough to try a military takeover of Baghlan-e-Jadid. Hundreds of Taliban fighters stormed the district center and the home of the district governor in a conventional-style military attack. The attack was repulsed after the district governor, Amir Gul, asked his former Hizb-e-Islami commanders for help against the Taliban. A jihadi militia of more than four hundred, many having successfully avoided the UN-supported DDR program, fought pitched battles lasting for days before the government regained control of the district. According to Abdul Rahman Rahimi—the police chief of Baghlan from April 2010 to September 2011—in the spring of 2009, the Taliban's influence had reached the center of Puli Khumri. They regularly infiltrated the city at night and launched random attacks on government posts and then withdrew without much resistance.

In 2010, newly arrived surge troops, including U.S. special operations forces, showed growing NATO concerns for the situation in the north. Although Baghlan was of strategic importance to NATO supplies, the ISAF presence in the province had been negligible until spring 2010 when a 126-man German Quick Reaction Force (QRF) was deployed. Earlier, in 2006, a small contingent of Hungarian military had taken over the PRT in Baghlan, but it lacked both the political will and the financial and military resources to aggressively police large parts of the province or take on the Taliban. Furthermore, the limited number of Afghan regular forces made it easier for the Taliban to spread its influence unchallenged. In the run-up to the August 2009 presidential elections, the provincial police, made up of a coterie of local militias belonging to Jamiat commanders Mustafa and Kabir Andarabi, were used in an attempt to stabilize the situation. But the police chief, Abdul Rahman Rahimi, described the local force as ill disciplined, poorly led, in poor fighting spirit, and under the influence of local strongmen.

The Rise of Arbaki Militias

Puli Khumri was mostly threatened from Dand-e-Ghori and Dand-e-Shahabuddin areas, located a few kilometers to the north of the provincial capital, along the Baghlan-Kunduz and Baghlan-Mazar highways. The so-called arbaki militias in Baghlan grew out of a specific security context, initially involving a small band of local fighters who adopted the Hizb-e-Islami banner to attract resources. Although they originally cooperated with the Taliban, after making unsuccessful overtures to the local administration, the Taliban, suspecting them of collaboration with the government, launched a military operation in March 2010 and defeated the Hizb-e-Islami fighters in Dand-e-Shahabuddin. Afterward, around seventy fighters surrendered to the government. They were housed in an NDS compound in Puli Khumri, and after a few months, small groups began to return to their villages. On returning to their villages, the self-styled arbaki militias, numbering around forty, lacked proper training and were ill equipped to face off against a better-armed Taliban. Only a few of them got back their arms from the NDS.

The Taliban then launched a second and much larger attack in mid-September against Sher and his band of arbaki militias. The battle of Shahabuddin lasted for three days and ended in Sher's death by an ISAF air strike, which was called in to disperse an estimated Taliban force of sixty fighters.

The battle also highlighted the overdependence of lightly armed government-backed militias on regular or special forces, be they government or ISAF, when they come under insurgent attack. After Sher's death, Nurul Haq took over as arbaki commander and established his base at Gaji, a small distance from the spot where the battle had occurred. The arbaki militias emerged around the same time as NATO supplies started coming through Baghlan and Kunduz.

These steps led to an improvement in security as a force of around seven hundred local arbaki was gradually built up and deployed by the local administration in Dand-e-Shahabuddin, Dand-e-Ghori, and Baghlan-e-Markazi. Initially, the arbaki mostly relied on whatever resources local villagers were willing to provide, but over time, they resorted to more coercive tactics to extract resources, including forced taxation of farmers. Otherwise, they lacked regular government support, which is one explanation for why such militias regularly abused the local population and committed human rights abuses. The German military knew that the arbaki forces they were working with regularly engaged in criminal activities. According to a *Spiegel* report, "None of these men are angels.

Until recently, Sher and his men used brutal methods, including the threat of slicing off ears, noses and heads, to exact protection money from their victims". They appeared to play a relatively limited role in military operations against Taliban insurgents in Puli Khumri. Most of the fighting was actually done by regular troops from the government and ISAF. The Afghan police and army and the SOFs played a far more important role in clearing central and northern Baghlan from the Taliban.

Rahimi claimed that his first act after taking over as police chief in the spring of 2010 was to increase the number of police check points in the city where the Taliban had influence and that he gradually expanded the security cordon out to Dand-e-Shahabuddin and Dand-e-Ghori. However, because of the shortage of police, especially from among the Pashtun community, and general distrust of a factionalized police force to hold territory and set up check points in Pashtun-dominated areas, the government inevitably relied on local fighters to hold key areas around Puli Khumri.

Following Sher's death, Nurul Haq emerged as a prominent arbaki commander in Puli Khumri, especially after he established links with recently arrived SOFs. Embedded SOFs built new bases and began joint operations with arbaki militias. The arbaki could now get access to regular pay and supplies and, most important, get SOFs' military backing if attacked. The relationship with SOFs made Nurul Haq a formidable figure in Baghlan politics. After the addition of the coercive power of SOFs and the spread of arbaki militia in key areas, the security situation saw gradual improvements. In 2009 and 2010, the road to Kunduz and Mazar was "impossible to travel on." However, both roads later became safe enough for travel, including at night in late 2011 and again in the spring and summer of 2012. Travel within Puli Khumri and to former insurgent strongholds in Dand-e-Shahabuddin and Dand-e-Ghori and Dahana-e-Ghori remained safe during the day. In fact, most fighting in Baghlan ended after the 2009 presidential and 2010 parliamentary elections. A similar pattern of conflict escalation seems very likely as the 2014 elections approach.

From Arbaki to aLP

Pashtuns switched to the government side when the local balance of power changed, particularly after the pressure from SOFs on insurgents increased in late 2010 and early 2011. Many joined the government's peace and reintegration program. The first group to benefit from the program was purported to be made up of Hizb-e-Islami fighters under Sher. Those arbaki fighters who survived the battle of Shahabuddin were later rebranded as ALP when the program was first established in February 2011 in Dand-e-Shahabuddin. Other insurgents joined the ALP later on. Newly hired ALP members interviewed in Puli Khumri in June 2012 admitted to being, until recently, with the Taliban. They displayed open loyalty to the Taliban when asked whether they would ever side with Americans to fight the Taliban. They dismissed suggestions about any possible role given to local shuras or the provincial council—which is dominated by Rasoul Mohsini, the powerful former Jamiat-e-Islami commander from Andarab and a strong critic of the ALP—in recruiting new ALP members in Puli Khumri. Most of them had bypassed any vetting process and directly entered the ALP along with their commanders after formally surrendering to the government, following the example of Sher's Hizb-e-Islami fighters forming an arbaki unit.

After Nurul Haq and his arbaki fighters became the first recruits to join the ALP without vetting or approval from either elders or local shuras or the provincial council, the ALP program was expanded to Dand-e-Ghori in June–July 2011 and subsequently to Baghlan-e-Jadid and Dahana-e-Ghori districts. In the official MOI structure, the ALP covers three districts in Baghlan: Puli Khumri (Dand-e-Shahabuddin and Dand-e-Ghori), Baghlan-e-Jadid, and Danhana-e-Ghori. All three districts have majority Pashtun populations. Tajik-dominated districts like Andarab and Khinjan, which largely remained free of Taliban insurgency, have not been allotted ALP units, despite the presence of many illegal armed groups and insecurity. According to SOFs, the ALP numbered 325 in Puli Khumri and 300 each in the other two districts, for a total force of 900 in Baghlan. When asked about the number of ALP in Puli Khumri and Dahan-e-Ghori, Nurul Haq reported 425 in Puli Khumri and 300 in Dahana-e-Ghori. He claimed that the 725 ALP recruits commanded by 33 commanders in both districts reported to him, though he admitted he was no longer officially an ALP commander. By this time, the ALP was part of a much larger security architecture in Baghlan that included 2,500 ANP and 1,200 ANA along with the 900 ALP.

According to the head of the ASOP shura in Baghlan, the ALP was established in Dand-e-Ghori about a year after the battle of Shahabuddin. A local shura, which was supposed to vet ALP recruits in Dand-e-Ghori, was established months later and played no meaningful role in selection. The arbaki fighters were simply given a new ALP label. Mullah Alam, a former Hizb-e-Islami commander, reportedly used his own *shura-e-sulh-wa-musharikat-e-mili,* a local development shura, to rubber-stamp decisions regarding the ALP. The recruitment and vetting papers of some recruits were signed by ASOP shura and others by a special committee in the provincial council, where Rasoul Mohsini tried to oppose the process. The ALP recruitment procedure was controversial in that provincial authorities felt that the U.S. forces took the lead in these decisions and left little room for the input of local authorities. The head of the provincial council, Rasoul Mohsini, was a strong opponent of the ALP and the role of SOFs, which according to him empowered men like Nurul Haq and undermined the authority of the provincial police, which were dominated by his Andarabi clan. The Andarabis view the ALP as a Pashtun militia and a threat to their local power base. In this province, therefore, the ALP dynamic has intensified Tajik-Pashtun power struggles.

Occasional armed rivalries between the ALP and ANP in Baghlan undermined the rationale for the program as a supplementary force to the ANSF. Although relations have improved since U.S. SOFs partly ceded control over the ALP to the provincial police chief, enabling him to subordinate the ALP to his command, rivalries between the two forces in the past have been serious. During one incident in late September 2011, an ALP unit backed by SOFs launched a full-scale attack against a QRF unit of the ANP in the center of Puli Khumri. The armed confrontation erupted after the ANP unit shot and killed an ALP member. It quickly escalated, and when U.S. forces came under fire, a NATO air strike was called against the QRF unit. The air strike was called off at the last minute following direct intervention by a top-ranking police official in the northern region. The action narrowly avoided a massacre of police at the hands of their ALP subordinates and their SOF mentors. After the incident, Nurul Haq and his ALP commanders threatened an armed attack against the Andarabis in Puli Khumri. Pashtun politicians, notably Mullah Alam and Alam Jan, called for more patience and tried to resolve the issue without resorting to force. Although the Pashtuns insisted on the arrest and prosecution of commander Ghani, the head of the QRF unit, the case was eventually settled by the decision of a jirga and an award of 3.5 million Afghanis to the family of the bereaved. Major power brokers in the north—notably General Baba Jan, the head of the ANP in the north (Pamir 303 regional command), and Governor Atta and Vice President Fahim Qasim—intervened in support of the Andarabis. The Pashtuns were told that they should not insist on Ghani's arrest and criminal prosecution and were instead advised to settle for less.

Incidents like this reflect and accentuate lines of conflict. When Nurul Haq was asked whether he would turn his weapon in and demobilize when the ALP program ended, he responded that he would do so if the elders made that decision. He added, however, that "as long as the government in Pul-i-Khumri remains the way it is now—an Andarabi organization—we are going to protect ourselves however we can". As far as Nurul Haq is concerned, the state of war between the Pashtuns and Tajiks in Baghlan is perpetual, even though not all Pashtuns see the conflict in such terms. Other Pashtun power brokers, such as Mullah Alam and Alam Jan, have resisted Nurul Haq's efforts by trying to act as brokers and mediators because they calculate that armed conflict with Andarabis would strengthen Nurul Haq and undermine their position in the local power setup. Pashtun power brokers who have benefited from the ALP, however, view it as a chance to regain power when the regular police and security sector remain in the hands of Andarabi Tajiks. The ALP has become an instrument of political aspirations for those Pashtuns, whose interests overlap with factions in the central government that wish to curtail the power of the Andarabi elite. The ostensible aim of the ALP to connect the population in insecure areas to the provincial government and enhance government legitimacy is secondary to the political game of ethnically aligned patronage politics. To some extent, all sides in this game have an interest in durable disorder. As long as the politics of difference and the notion of the hostile "other" are kept alive and struggles over power and resources continue, entrepreneurs of violence and politicians on both sides can be sure of the support of their fellow ethnics.

The U.S. SOFs shared the view of most Pashtuns that the dominance of the security sector by the Tajik-Jamiat faction was illegitimate. By siding with the Pashtuns and isolating the process from political interference by the dominant power brokers from Jamiat, the U.S. military made the ALP program in Baghlan even more controversial. One paradoxical outcome of the U.S. military's role in the formation and support to the ALP in Baghlan has been the reinforcement of two separate but interconnected governing orders, one for Tajiks and one for Pashtuns.

Once this was acknowledged, the U.S. military began working on bridging the divide between the two sets of power holders in Puli Khumri and Dand-e-Shahabuddin—the former in the control of the ANP, and the regular police and the latter controlled by ALP forces. Few Afghan politicians, however, are convinced by the SOF commander's efforts in this direction.

Alam Jan, deputy head of the provincial council, dismissed claims that the U.S. military's presence in Baghlan had resulted in progress in all three aspects of the VSO-ALP initiative—namely, security, governance, and development. He stressed that the only positive outcome of the U.S. forces' presence in Baghlan was in preventing ALP militias from turning to *chur-au-chapawul,* or open banditry, and in preventing armed hostilities from erupting between the ANP and ALP.

The Americans did so largely by wedging themselves between the two forces, which raises the question of what will happen when they are eventually withdrawn. Although in public the former governor of Baghlan, Munshi Majid, supported the ALP, in private, he had a poor view of Nurul Haq, the role of U.S. special forces, and the ALP, whose members he considered no better than criminals and murderers.

Although the ALP might have a role to play in protecting local villages against Taliban attacks or preventing abuses by Jamiat-dominated government security forces, they have also engaged in abuses against civilians, including beatings, murder, land grabbing, rape, and forced taxation. The predominantly Pashtun ALP in Baghlan, for example, has a record of harming and abusing the Pashtun communities it is purportedly protecting. According to a local elder, the ALP played a role in improving security, illustrated by the fact that he could drive to Dand-e-Ghori, Shahabuddin, and Dahana-e-Ghori areas, which were off limits before the establishment of the arbaki and ALP. But he also pointed out that the ALP was mostly made of former Hizb and Taliban fighters—only the labels had changed. This improvement in security is independent of, and even despite, the various police formations.

Many other illegal armed groups are in the province, particularly in Andarab and Nahrin districts. The ALP by comparison has less than one thousand men, a lightly armed force scattered over three districts. As a local elder lamented, although everyone complained about the ALP, no one was willing to discuss the much bigger problem of illegal armed groups in Baghlan. The biggest threat to public security and state power may be from the so-called illegal armed groups, who have had a continued presence in the local security architecture and enjoy the protection of powerful regional and Kabul-based strongmen. Intra-and intergroup struggles are likely to intensify ahead of the NATO withdrawal and upcoming elections. This conflict will also create openings for the return of the Taliban.

Kunduz

Kunduz province borders Tajikistan in the north and the provinces of Takhar in the east, Baghlan in the south, and Balkh in the west. Its ethnically mixed population, the result of successive immigration waves, is estimated to number some 820,000 people. The province is composed of seven districts. It is an economically and strategically important region. Before the war erupted in 1979, it was part of the wider region of Qataghan—presentday Takhar, Kunduz, and Baghlan provinces—and was a major agricultural and industrial zone. Kunduz city, in spite of the destruction of the war, remains a major population center and economic hub and is strategically important given its location on the northern supply route for NATO forces.

With the emergence of a new transitional authority in Kabul after 2001 was dominated by Northern Alliance figures, jihadiera commanders returned to power in Kunduz, including Mir Alam, from Jamiat. As a commander of the Northern Alliance army's 54th division, Mir Alam established himself in the provincial capital and his former stronghold of Khanabad. The political bargain struck between Jamiat and Junbish involved divvying up the rest of the province to local commanders with ostensible loyalty to one of the two parties.

Pashtuns were largely excluded from the local political settlement, and the channeling of patronage in the form of resources and government positions reflected a new power balance dominated by Jamiat commanders. Jihadi factions folded their militias into local security structures, and although UN-supported DDR programs were launched, they did not significantly alter the coercive power of local commanders like Mir Alam. For example, by the end of the decade, an estimated forty-five hundred to ten thousand militias remained throughout the province, and some three thousand to four thousand militiamen in Khanabad district alone. A German-led PRT became the center for security sector reform and reconstruction efforts, but German troops maintained a passive role, which involved working with commander power structures rather than challenging them. In spite of international efforts to build up the regular security and police forces, the ANP has maintained a total force of some seventeen hundred personnel in Kunduz.

The Insurgency

From the mid-2000s onward, the Taliban insurgency in the south intensified and over time spread beyond the Pashtun heartlands. By 2009, the Taliban presence in Kunduz had grown, partly because of the increased strategic importance of the city with the rerouting of NATO supplies through northern Afghanistan. The Taliban expanded its presence in the north by exploiting Pashtun feelings of marginalization and by manipulating local conflicts. In the spring of 2009, Kunduz experienced a wave of Taliban violence, and insurgents established a presence in Chahardara, from which they expanded military operations to Aliabad, Imam Sahib, Dasht-e-Archi, and central Kunduz, all of which have a significant Pashtun presence.

The Emergence of Arbaki Militias

By the summer of 2009, the provincial authorities had become sufficiently alarmed by the Taliban penetration to request additional police and army personnel, partly because Germanled ISAF forces were reluctant to fight the Taliban. When the central government ignored the request, the provincial governor, engineer Mohammad Omar, asked for Kunduz to be included as part of the APPF, which at the time was being piloted in Wardak province. When this request was refused, the governor began arming local jihadi commanders, many of whom had fought the Taliban in 2001, to contain the insurgency and improve security. This was a local initiative and was not pushed by the Afghan MOI or U.S. forces. In fact, Karzai and his minister of defense were opposed to the initiative, although the minister of interior at the time, Haneef Atmar, who had supported the AP3 initiative in Wardak, was more agnostic about militias and prepared to support them as long as they remained under central government control. The German military command suggested sending 2,500 additional police to Kunduz instead of arming local militias, which they thought risked undermining the formal security structures and reversing the modest progress made through the DDR and DIAG programs.

Events on the ground generated their own momentum, however. Local commanders took advantage of the fluid and insecure situation to reactivate their old networks. General Mohammad Daud, the NDS chief and brother-in-law of Mir Alam, the powerful Kunduz-based Jamiat commander, was put in charge of recruiting local commanders and their private militias. The NDS became a coordinating office for local militias, and Daud relied almost exclusively on Mir Alam to recruit local commanders loyal to himself. Government efforts to arm local commanders initially focused on Imam Sahib, Khanabad, and Qala-e-Zal districts. The Taliban stronghold of Chahardara was considered too insecure to initiate a local arbaki force. In Kunduz, the anti-Taliban militias were mainly drawn from Turkmen, Tajik, and Uzbek communities. Only a few Pashtun commanders in Khanabad, such as Mohammad Omar from Sayyaf 's Itihad faction, set up arbaki militias. In Imam

Sahib, the Uzbek Ibrahimi family, which controlled the district, played a key role in mobilizing local militias. In Qala-e-Zal, a former mujahideen commander, Nabi Gichi, was asked by the district governor to form local militias ahead of the August 2009 presidential elections.

With Mir Alam's militia of some five hundred, in addition to his local allies fighting alongside government forces, the Taliban were driven out from most parts of Kunduz. The main effort in pushing back the Taliban from Kunduz is attributed to the arbaki forces, including Mir Alam's, recruited by the then governor, Mohammad Omar. At this stage, the SOFs did not play a role because they did not arrive in Kunduz until late 2010. The local militias had a clear incentive to fight the Taliban because their power was directly threatened by the rise of the Taliban in the north. Mir Alam thus consolidated his position as the provincial strongman. The real blow to the Taliban's control came in September 2010, in the leadup to parliamentary elections, when a much larger effort was launched to clear the Taliban from Kunduz. On his arrival in September 2010, a month after Omar had been killed, Abdul Rahman Sayedkhaili, the new police chief, began to hand out cash to arbaki commanders to fight the Taliban. The interior minister, Besmillah Khan, reportedly provided $100,000 to Sayedkhaili to pay local commanders and buy off insurgents willing to switch sides. Before he launched his offensive, Sayedkhaili delivered an ultimatum to local Taliban commanders to stop fighting and switch to the government's side. Many insurgent commanders took up his offer and crossed over.

The situation was turned around less by fighting and more by bribing Taliban commanders to switch sides, which heavily depleted the ranks of the insurgency. Sayedkhaili's efforts received a further boost when the ISAF deployed U.S. SOFs to Kunduz ahead of the September 2010 parliamentary elections. The arrival of the SOFs coupled with Sayedkhaili's campaign against the Taliban dramatically reduced the power of the Taliban and dislodged them from some of the most contested areas around central Kunduz, in particular the Gore Tepa area and in Imam Sahib, Dasht-e-Archi, and Chahardara. SOFs' night raids and killcapture operations also had a major military impact. By late 2010, Taliban commanders in Kunduz were under great pressure and had to constantly change their locations to avoid being targeted by SOFs. In January 2011, Sayedkhaili declared Kunduz cleansed of Taliban. Two months later, he was killed in a suicide attack.

After Sayedkhaili's death, the funding from the MOI stopped, and Sayedkhaili's successor could not continue the payment to hundreds of arbaki militias. This unsurprisingly led to predatory behaviour from the militias. Many local militias resorted to extorting local farmers and traders and engaged in internal power struggles and turf battles. The government responded with disarmament efforts, but in 2011, only fifty-one people were disarmed. In August 2012, a second effort was made to disarm abusive commanders in Khanabad, but after a three-day operation, only twelve weapons were collected. Militia proliferation had reached such a level by April 2011 that German forces in Kunduz resorted to bringing some of them onto the ISAF's payroll, using the U.S. military's CERP funds.

The incorporation of existing militias by the ISAF happened in parallel to SOFs' efforts to establish the ALP. These militias were renamed the Critical Infrastructure Protection (CIP) Force and located mainly in Qala-e-Zal, Chahardara, and Aliabad districts. CIP was another ad hoc response to deal with problems that might have been anticipated.

The program was implemented without any clear policy direction from the ISAF. The total CIP force was slightly over 500: 225 in Qala-e-Zal, 150 in Chahardara, and 150 in Aliabad. However, the Germans' policy of bringing local militias under the U.S. military's patronage did not sit well with Karzai's objective of centralizing the means of patronage. When Karzai learned about the initiative in late December 2011, he issued a decree disbanding CIP. In June 2012, SOFs informed the German PRT in Kunduz that the U.S. military had decided to stop payments to CIP units in Kunduz. In April 2013, a member of parliament from Qala-e-Zal confirmed the cessation of U.S. military payments to CIP units in the district. No longer paid, the CIP members "had gone back to what they were doing before they became CIP. They steal, collect *ushr,* and abuse civilians. Whereas a few years ago they drove the Taliban out and brought security, these days the arbaki militias have become a source of insecurity."

Arbaki's Transition to aLP

The final incarnation of militias in Kunduz was the creation of the ALP program. Compared with other provinces, the ALP was implemented relatively late in Kunduz. The strategic rationale was to serve, alongside arbaki militias, as a holding force to maintain the gains that had been made against the Taliban insurgency. The first ALP *tashkil* (the formal staffing structure of government ministries) for central Kunduz was approved in November 2010. A month later, three more districts were added: Imam Sahib, Dasht-e-Archi, and Chahardara, each being allotted three hundred ALP. The total ALP tashkil for Kunduz in June 2012 was 1,125. Khanabad, Aliabad, and Qala-e-Zal districts were left out of the tashkil.

It appears that existing arbaki militias were promised inclusion in the ALP, which in turn prompted SOFs to delay ALP implementation. A number of consequences followed. It is possible that delays prompted police chief Sayedkhaili to mobilize local arbaki militias to retain the initiative against insurgents. The restrictions on arbaki militias probably led to the decision to establish CIP as a way of removing pressure on the ALP as well as accommodating a large number of arbaki militias, which could not be included in the ALP. On the other hand, senior provincial officials accused SOFs of violating ALP guidelines when they began implementing the ALP in central Kunduz. The deputy governor, a Jamiat loyalist, resigned from a joint commission with the U.S. forces in protest when he realized that the Americans had already recruited preselected armed groups but expected the provincial government to approve them, in clear violation of ALP procedure.

Despite these initial delays, the implementation of the ALP went ahead. By September 2011, 105 of 225 ALP recruits had been trained and deployed in central Kunduz and ALP recruitment in Imam Sahib had begun. By January 2012, the ALP in Dasht-e-

Archi district was rolled out. In June 2012, the process had moved on to Chahardara district. As of June 2012, the ALP had been completed in two of four districts: central Kunduz and Imam Sahib. The ALP focused on both Pashtun and non-Pashtun districts where the Taliban insurgency had been strongest. Because ALP forces were deployed after arbaki militias had done most of the fighting alongside SOFs, their role in direct combat was minimal, and security for the most part had improved. At this point, two very different kinds of local militia programs were going on in Kunduz: the ALP, which was officially approved by the Afghan government, and the CIP, which was run by ISAF but lacked central government sanction, even though in theory CIP units were subordinated to district police chiefs.

Arming Pashtuns through the ALP, as had happened in Baghlan province, was viewed with concern by Tajik-dominated Jamiat, who were determined to avoid such an outcome. As with the arbaki militias, the ALP in Kunduz was disproportionately captured by Tajik (mainly Jamiat) and Uzbek commanders, especially in central Kunduz, which is ethnically mixed. According to former interior minister Haneef Atmar, the ALP in Baghlan and Kunduz was hijacked by local power brokers because commanders rather than local elders and shuras became the channel for recruitment and selection of ALP members. Senior government officials, in particular Interior Minister Besmillah Khan, are believed to have used ALP resources to strengthen Jamiat's jihadi networks.

In central Kunduz, for example, where the first ALP units were established in early 2011, all the ALP commanders were former jihadi and arbaki commanders linked to Mir Alam and Mohammad Omar, a Sayyaf loyalist and Itihad commander in Khanabad. Other prominent ALP commanders include Amir Shah, Aziz, Ghulam Ali, Juma Khan, Ishaq Nizami, and Ala Nazar, all of whom had fought the Taliban in 2009 and 2010 and maintained arbaki militias.

Ala Nazar is an Uzbek jihadi commander, at one point disarmed under the DDR program. In mid-2012, he was in charge of an ALP unit of twenty-five to thirty men in Dam Shakh village in the Alchin area of central Kunduz. All of his men serving in the ALP unit are close relatives. In 2009, he was asked by the head of NDS to start a local arbaki militia to fight the Taliban. Discussions with Ala Nazar in June 2012 revealed that he was approached by SOFs in the summer of 2011 to join the ALP. He and his men were given three weeks' training and then introduced to local elders as the new ALP unit in his village.

The ALP has also absorbed former insurgents, though sometimes with ambiguous effects, as illustrated by the case of Ishaq Nizami, a former Taliban commander and Sayyaf loyalist. After reconciling with the government, Nizami joined the ALP and emerged as a commander of five ALP units in the Tobrakash area of central Kunduz. He served as deputy to commander Hafiz Cherik. His men were involved in a highly publicized case of the rape of a Kuchi (Pashtun nomad) woman named Lal Bibi. Two years earlier, Nizami had been fighting alongside the Taliban and eventually joined the government when military pressure on the Taliban increased. Like many other Taliban commanders, Nizami emerged as a progovernment arbaki commander. Eventually, he found his way into the ALP when SOFs began the program in central Kunduz in early 2011. In June 2012, he was named as a suspect in Lal Bibi's case. As ALP commander, he was invited to mediate between one of his subcommanders and the family of Lal Bibi. He ruled in favour of his deputy and arranged a forced marriage between the deputy and Lal Bibi.

Nizami's subsequent trial and conviction in November 2012 was the result of Karzai's direct intervention. Although a prominent jihadi leader and the provincial police chief, Samiullah Qatrah, tried to protect Nizami from prosecution, Karzai intervened after a public outcry and ordered Nizami's and his cohorts' arrest and disbanded the particular ALP unit in Tobrakash. The conviction of Nizami and his men for rape, rather than a settlement through *baad,* also shows that when the government had the will to act, it also had the power to bring perpetrators to account. Nizami and his four accomplices were sentenced to sixteen years in prison for the crime.

These brief accounts of the ALP units under commanders Ala Nazar and Nizami reveal the extent to which the ALP program has been manipulated to serve divergent agendas. They point to a lack of transparency in recruitment, vetting, command, and control and suggest how the power of a host of armed groups—including so-called illegal armed groups, former insurgents, and proxy forces linked to U.S. SOFs—has been reinforced by the ALP program.

Local human rights activists following the case confirmed that the vetting of ALP recruits under Nizami had been done by Kunduz police without any community engagement. This appears to be the case for most other units. The provincial peace council is only involved if Taliban insurgents are being transitioned from the insurgency into the ALP. According to a prominent member of the provincial council, despite repeated objections from the Kunduz governor, deputy governor, chief of police, and council members regarding violations of ALP procedure, the recruitment forms of ALP members in central Kunduz were brought to the council only after they had been selected, trained, and armed by SOFs, and then council members were asked to sign them.

In conclusion, in Kunduz arbaki militias and the ALP emerged out of a specific set of security conditions associated with the reemergence of the Taliban, the deployment of U.S. forces, the holding of elections, and a precarious political settlement involving local, provincial, and national players. The counterresponse to the insurgency was organized by armed groups of Northern Alliance factions, whose power was directly threatened by the reemergence of the Taliban. Militia formation therefore had little to do with protecting communities and was primarily about protecting the new power structure at the provincial level. As a result, it was initially a local initiative with little involvement from the central government or U.S. or NATO forces.

This dynamic is quite unlike that in Wardak. Once remobilized, the arbaki militias remained a prominent element of the local security environment. After temporarily pushing the Taliban back and bringing a measure of security, their abusive activities gave rise to significant law-and-order problems. The presence of so many armed groups consolidated a highly variegated and decentralized security landscape where multiple armed groups were competing for power and resources. The ALP was just a small part of this landscape. The arbaki militias of local power brokers were well placed to co-opt the ALP program when it was implemented in Kunduz in early 2011, demonstrating how the programs tended to follow existing lines of power and feed into local struggles for control of coercive resources. By the end of 2012, this power game had been won by the dominant military force, Jamiat-e-Islami and Northern Alliance factions.

The dominance of the security and administrative structures in the province by non-Pashtuns in a majority Pashtun province in the north was already a problematic issue before the Taliban reemerged in 2009. It is likely to further contribute to Pashtun feelings of marginalization and in turn may invite overtures of protection from the Taliban, in which case further clashes can be expected. When the time comes for the withdrawal of U.S. forces, the balance of power among local armed groups may change once again in favour of Taliban insurgents. For the foreseeable future, the Pashtun populations of Kunduz will remain caught between the Taliban and a hostile local power structure from which they are excluded, a dynamic that will increase their dependence on the Taliban for protection.

Findings and Analysis

A great deal of effort has been invested in assessing the impacts of various forms of intervention in Afghanistan. Defining and evaluating success or failure is not merely a technical or scientific exercise, it is also tied up with particular normative and political judgments about what is desirable. NATO troop-providing countries keen to facilitate a hasty withdrawal have a vested interest in presenting an optimistic picture. This metanarrative of success may also shape how the ALP is conceptualized and is seen to be delivering on a set of targets, which are defined differently by international and domestic actors. There are strong institutional pressures to ignore evidence that declared goals are not being met. This is particularly relevant to programs like the ALP, which, as shown, is the latest iteration in a series of experiments involving the constant recycling and reinvention of projects. The apparent failure to learn, though true across the board, may be a particularly acute problem in the military because of the rapid turnover of staff.

Lessons derived from the program will depend partly on how success is formulated and judged. The program was itself the result of a messy compromise involving different actors with competing rationales and interests. The motivations of those involved varied and included fighting the Taliban, securing the state, protecting self or community, maintaining the status quo, renegotiating power relations, extending patronage relationships, accessing external resources, and settling scores.

Even when stated goals are met, they are achieved at a severe cost—most obviously in terms of human lives but also the trade-offs and opportunity costs involved in prioritizing one goal or area of intervention over another. A trade-off may also be temporal, in the sense that success in the short term may have severe and irreversible costs in the long term.

The difficulty of making judgments is also compounded by the challenges of accessing reliable data and evidence. Independent evaluation of the ALP and other militia programs has been limited. This is partly because of the sensitivity of the topic, related to problems of access to information, and the likelihood that data will be politicized or manipulated. Those with the most critical attitude at the outset are the least able to gain access, and those with the best access are often too close to the military to provide independent and critical analysis. Moreover, the literature is full of essentialized and simplified narratives about Afghan culture and society that clouds critical analysis.

Explaining Different Outcomes

The case studies illustrate the heterogeneity and complexity of the local security architecture in Afghanistan; the same program looks very different in one context over another. How does one explain this variability over time and space? What were the key variables that shaped the dynamics and outcomes of the ALP program? We have attempted to show through the case studies how the ALP is mediated and translated through complex bargaining relationships between international actors and both national and provincial elites in the context of an intensifying insurgency. These are ineluctable political processes, shaped of course by the security environment and the economic interests of diverse actors.

In Baghlan, for example, the ALP became a vehicle for politically marginalized local Pashtuns to renegotiate the Tajik Jamiat-e-Islami dominated post-2001 order. It can be seen as an attempt by the excluded to leverage external support to increase their access to power and resources.

In Kunduz, a former Taliban stronghold in the north with a majority Pashtun population, the expansion of the Taliban insurgency threatened the power of the dominant coalition. Arbaki militias and later the ALP became the instrument to preserve the existing order against the threat of the Taliban. This brought shortterm security but further marginalized the Pashtun population and thus increased the likelihood of a violent contestation of the political settlement in the future.

In Wardak, the ALP program was an implant by foreign forces aiming to stabilize a security context that was far more complex than originally imagined. Unlike Kunduz and Baghlan, where a dominant group had emerged, the political landscape in Wardak was open, fragmented, and contested.

The fault lines in the struggle for ascendency were more complex than the Pashtun-Tajik and Pashtun-Uzbek dynamics seen in Baghlan and Kunduz. Wardak remains a hotbed of internal factional power struggles among armed groups of more or less equal strength, all belonging to the same ethnic group—although Hizb-e-Islami remains the dominant political force in many districts.

Pashtun communities are divided in support for the government and the insurgency, and close family members may stand on opposite sides. The Hazara and Tajik power brokers used access to AP3 and ALP resources to ensure the exclusion of Pashtuns from the economic resources of the Central Highland region. One might have predicted a counterresponse by the Pashtuns to rearm, but this did not occur, possibly because most Pashtuns feared Taliban reprisals if they joined government militias.

Impacts on Security

The role of the ALP needs to be kept in perspective. In terms of funding and size, the program is relatively insignificant and certainly does not compare with the militias of the Najibullah era. In addition, the difference between the ALP and the ANP should not be overstated: The distinction in Afghanistan between state and nonstate, regular and irregular, is blurred in terms of the status, behaviour, capacity, and legitimacy of the various "specialists in violence." The same actors may be constantly switching sides or even simultaneously be a member of both. The ANP is also in part composed of militias that have simply been rebranded as national police after 2001, as the Baghlan case clearly illustrates, and at times the ANP has been more abusive than the ALP toward civilians. The greatest threat to stability in Afghanistan is less the existence of a few hundred militias per district in the form of the ALP and more the danger that after 2014 an oversized and unevenly trained armed force will decompose and fragment into myriad competing militia groups, as it did after the collapse of the Najibullah regime. The ANSF in their current form are not fiscally sustainable, which raises the question of how long Western donors can continue to fund the estimated $6 billion per annum to sustain them.

When making judgments about the ALP's impacts on security, different conceptualizations of security are frequently conflated. The first is security in relation to the fight against the Taliban and whether the ALP is an effective force in gaining a tactical or strategic advantage in the war effort. Second is the security of the state and whether the ALP plays a role in strengthening the institutions and legitimacy of the state (not just the regime). Third is the security of the Afghan population and whether the ALP provides a form of protection to the rural Afghan population or acts as a magnet for insurgent attacks (as Karzai has argued).

Making judgments about the effects of the ALP on any of these three dimensions of security is extremely difficult given the problems of data, counterfactuals, attribution, and time frames. The ALP may positively affect one dimension but adversely affect another: For example, the program may be effective at countering the Taliban, but at the expense of the population's security and ultimately undermining the security of the state if it leads to the uncontrolled fragmentation of the means of violence, as the Kunduz case illustrates.

Supporters of the program point to the fact that the ALP has been disproportionately targeted by the Taliban as a metric of success. According to ISAF data, 6.2 percent of ALP members have been wounded or killed versus fewer than 3 percent of the Afghan army and police. It is no coincidence that in 2012 the death rate of foreign forces declined markedly in parallel with the significant increase in the toll on Afghan forces. The number of ANSF forces being hit by IEDs increased by 124 percent, and an average of nearly three hundred Afghan security forces were killed on a monthly basis in late 2012 and early 2013.

Although the UN Assistance Mission in Afghanistan (UNAMA) reported a 12 percent decline in civilian casualties in 2012, the Afghanistan NGO Safety Office data for the first quarter of 2013 showed a dramatic increase in violence, 47 percent more attacks by the armed opposition compared with the same period in 2012. The majority of these attacks targeted Afghan civilians and security forces. Attacks by the insurgents against international troops constituted only 4 percent of the total versus 73 percent against the Afghan security forces. In the first three months of 2013, 1,183 Afghan soldiers were killed, an increase of 40 percent versus the same period in 2012.

The ALP data can be interpreted in various ways:

- Lightly armed ALP units are located in exposed, frontline, contested areas and, as the first line of defense against better armed insurgents, are most likely to be attacked.
- The Taliban see them as challengers to their rule in the villages, more so than the regular forces—hence, for example, Taliban statements that the killing of one ALP member is worth ten U.S. soldiers.
- ALP forces are easier targets because they have less weaponry to protect themselves and nowhere to run because they live in the villages.

- The ALP units have fewer financial resources than regular forces and therefore are less able to buy off or negotiate spot bargains or conflict management pacts with the Taliban—though they do have the capacity to generate revenues through local taxation, as do the regular forces and the Taliban.

NATO's shift back toward counterterrorism rather than counterinsurgency following McChrystal's removal involved rebalancing the terms of engagement and a concomitant increased reliance on kinetic power. This shift is reflected in the upward trends in security incidents, night raids, and aerial bombardments in the three provinces studied, which, combined with buying off the loyalties of antigovernment elements, appeared to quell the insurgency.

Although the military strategy achieved some tactical successes in terms of pushing back the Taliban, the extent to which the creation of ALP units contributed to the clearing and holding of these areas is difficult to ascertain. Interviewees maintained that the ALP were more effective than regular forces in outlying areas because they knew the lay of the land and were an important source of intelligence. Some evidence, though not very systematic evidence, indicates that the ALP constituted a useful military asset that contributed at least temporarily to the Taliban's having to cede territory.

And though militias may be effective militarily and costeffective in resource use, they can be politically costly; they are supposedly formed to engage in protective violence—though in practice have often been used as a combat force—but often mete out predatory and abusive violence, as shown in other cases. In the long term, increased insecurity of communities is likely to act as a further catalyst for the insurgency. An association between the ISAF and these militia forces increases resentment toward international forces and the government. For example, ALP forces in Baghlan were perceived locally as a criminal network involved in the forced extraction of *zakat* and kidnappings. In spite of the protestations of their supporters that "the misconduct is extremely low in comparison to the numbers that are out there," community perceptions are important, and a small number of incidents can have a disproportionate impact.

The positive gains in relation to the Taliban must be balanced against other costs. Over the war years, a patronage-based political marketplace has become monetized and regionalized, and shifting alliances are shaped by contending resource flows and changing power dynamics, making it an extremely volatile system. In some places, the ALP has created a perverse incentive structure in which groups compete for resources, including from the insurgency, to strengthen their position with respect to other local power holders and groups, as in the case of Hazaras in Jalrez and Pashtuns in Puli Khumri. In this context, the program may encourage a dynamic of competitive rearmament or an armament spiral in one place, but in another content, it may provide coercive resources to weaker actors to balance the power of stronger rivals. The ability and willingness of the government to disarm militias that have gone rogue varied across the cases. Nizami in Kunduz was ultimately dealt with, for example, but other arbaki militias linked to local and national power brokers were not. Local conflicts frequently transcend the local. Smallscale conflicts usually become enmeshed in and influence wider conflicts at the provincial, interprovincial, or national levels. For example, conflicts in Baghlan were intimately connected to wider power dynamics, specifically in relation to the role of Atta Mohammad Noor, the governor of Balkh, and Pashtun power brokers around the president in Kabul.

Finally, although much of the critical writing about the ALP focuses on how it endangers rural communities, there is little acknowledgment that the program puts those who are recruited in extreme danger. It is worth remembering that many of those who join do so because they have little choice, being forced into militias as a result of coercive pressure or economic necessity. The risks for ALP members and their communities are likely to increase with the drawdown of foreign troops.

Impacts on Statebuilding and Governance

The case studies have highlighted how militias are influenced by and shape the spatial dynamics of conflict and statebuilding.

They show the need to think carefully about how the state, including foreign forces, and counterstate formations seek to territorialize power and how peripheral elites collude with or resist the projects of political elites at the center. COIN analysts frequently claim that the insurgency and counterinsurgency have led to the bifurcation of territory into state and nonstate spaces. State space, according to several interviewees, contains the major population centres, critical infrastructure, and roads that are prioritized, defended, and protected by the state. It is commonly asserted that 80 percent of the fighting occurs where only 20 percent of the population live. Conversely, 80 percent of the population are assumed to live in relatively secure areas. To some extent, this follows the historical pattern, in which state spaces have been restricted to the major population centres and the most accessible areas of the country that can be most profitably administered. Nonstate or antistate spaces have always tended to be peripheral, rural areas, where tribal structures remain strong and where administration and governance is difficult and, thus, where the state has a comparative disadvantage.

The general literature on insurgency and counterinsurgency supports a more complex picture that is also evident in the case studies. At one level, this might be conceptualized as a threeway division of territory into state, nonstate, and gray zones, reflecting the fact that political actors in irregular warfare face three distinct population sets: populations they control, populations they share, and populations belonging to rivals. They are also constantly faced with an identification problem: Who is on our side? Who can be trusted? It is in the gray zones that defection is most likely and that the highest levels of indiscriminate violence are experienced. Yet this also simplifies a more complex reality. The boundaries between state and nonstate are blurred to the extent that they become almost meaningless. Gray zones can be state spaces during the day and antistate spaces during the night, and the correlation between peripherality and antistate status is not straightforward.

The stated aim of NATO forces has been to create what they call white space in the nonstate spaces and gray zones in which to clear, hold, and build. In many places, though, holding has been difficult when allies have been predatory. Outsourcing community protection and defense to the ALP may, far from extending state power and legitimacy, have the opposite effect.

To understand this issue, we need to appreciate the ways that the ALP reflects and helps shape coreperiphery and intraperiphery bargaining relationships over access to resources and the means of coercion. State and nonstate actors compete with one another to gain access to what might be called violence rights and economic assets, and this competition in turn recalibrates coreperiphery relations. The ALP influences politics at the local level by empowering and disempowering particular groups. To a large extent, there is a disjuncture between outsiders' idealized notions of traditional shura, elder, and tribal institutions and the real power structures and actual practices of commanders who are key ALP members. Evidently, the extent to which the ALP has consolidated or undermined political order has varied from district to district and over time.

The Wardak, Baghlan, and Kunduz examples support studies showing that elections have shortened the time frames and destabilized the dynamics of elite pacts (Giustozzi and Orsini 2009). Elections have been important turning points in relation to the insurgency and local politics. The Taliban have made advances during these periods, partly because the state is even less coherent at these times, and corruption in the voting process further delegitimizes state officials in the eyes of the population. Militia formation may also be directly linked to election campaigns—the 2009 presidential election campaign, for example. Local militias also become entwined with parliamentary politics, with MPs often lobbying to have their people included within the ALP program.

The ALP may also become a vehicle for ethnic assertion as in Baghlan. In this case, Pashtuns were excluded from the state security architecture, as shown by the ANP tashkil, in which 2,400 of 2,800 are from one district, and consequently the excluded groups saw the ALP as a way to leverage power and protection. The resulting security arrangements pitted Tajiks in the regular forces against Pashtuns in the irregular forces, thus working at odds with declared statebuilding goals. Following a long-standing pattern, the weaker party (the Pashtuns) seek to leverage external support from more powerful actors, whether the Taliban or central government.

As the three case studies show, the picture is far more complex than a Taliban–anti-Taliban fault line. The micro cleavages of conflict get caught up in the meta cleavages of civil war, as Stathis Kalyvas shows in relation to the civil war in Greece (2006). Politics becomes privatized as individuals and groups seek to settle scores by drawing on wider discourses around the national conflict. Hizb-e-Islami and Taliban clashes in Wardak are one example of mobilizing the population for selfdefense, constituting a means of fermenting old factional differences. In this context, the ALP can be an instrument to settle old scores. As such, it may prolong and intensify conflict, undermine state authority, and create competing power structures difficult for the state to control. International forces are also sucked into these local power games—for example, the U.S. SOF support for ALP units in a firefight with the ANP in Baghlan. One might contrast the haphazard attempts of the SOFs to identify and arm proxies with the patient and systematic efforts of the Taliban to penetrate areas of the north (Giustozzi and Reuter 2011).

As other studies have shown, in Helmand, the ALP has become inseparable from longstanding conflicts between indigenous and settler communities. The settlers see the program as an external force that has become involved in poppy eradication to further the interests of powerful actors linked to the state. In Jalrez district in Wardak, as discussed, Hazaras and Tajiks were keen to join the ALP to keep Taliban and Pashtun nomads (often conflated) out of Hazara areas, but Pashtuns were more reticent, in fear of Taliban reprisals. Subsequently, when Pashtuns joined the ALP, recruits were dominated by one particular clan with links to a local jihadi commander, Ghulam Mohammad Hotak.

If COIN is truly a battle for justice, then the effects of the ALP are at best ambiguous or mixed. This situation is exacerbated by the absence of effective and timely state justice. Although the ALP program may be relatively cheap in resource terms, it involves significant opportunity costs. As a number of European informants argued, deploying the police as a paramilitary force leads to the neglect of what should be the primary peace mission, which involves protecting the public from serious crime.

The ALP is symptomatic of a wider deficiency of the post-2001 intervention in Afghanistan; there has been a constant search for temporary solutions that end up creating more problems, which are in turn dealt with pragmatically and superficially. The creation and then disbanding of the CIP force in Kunduz, which in some cases were simply renamed as the ALP, is a case in point. Temporary solutions nevertheless create path dependencies. The ALP will not go away, and it will leave a longterm legacy that others, above all the Afghans, will have to deal with.

Implications

This study has aimed to uncover and analyse the complex political and security dynamics surrounding the ALP program in three provinces. Rather than seek to extract generalizable policy lessons and prescriptions, the case studies aim to show the complexity and contingency of individual contexts and thus highlight the redundancy of off the-peg policy advice in Afghanistan and elsewhere. However, the findings do have relevance for debates on transition in Afghanistan and statebuilding and state consolidation more broadly.

Statebuilding has historically been a violent, largely endogenous, and unplanned process that takes a long time and follows varied and unpredictable trajectories. Research on state formation in Afghanistan and other latedeveloping countries shows that the impact of violence devolution is also varied and unpredictable. Historically, states have frequently franchised the means of violence to nonstate actors, and in the long term, this strategy may extend rather than diminish the authority of the state. Yet in other contexts, or at other times, violence devolution has contributed to processes of state collapse. A key variable is the role and capacity of the state and the extent to which it has the coercive power, resources, and legitimacy to enforce and shape political settlements and regulate the decentralized violence its agents exercise. State capacity is in turn shaped by processes occurring above and below the state—including the level and type of engagement of international and regional actors and the orientation and capacities of armed nonstate or antistate actors. It is important to appreciate the specific origins and characteristics of militias and their patrons, including their internal organization, leadership, and incentive systems, as well as the external context in which they emerged and evolved.

Analytically, it also seems to be important to distinguish between militias constituted as part of a process of endogenous statebuilding, characterized by Charles Tilly as coercion intensive statebuilding (1992), and those funded externally in the context of imperial wars or counterinsurgency operations. In some cases, imperial powers have successfully mobilized militias to prop up regimes in the context of decolonization struggles or in more recent statebuilding interventions such as Iraq. However, apart from the immediate costs in terms of human lives and rights abuses, such experiments in surrogate forces have often left baleful longterm legacies for the successor governments.

The positive albeit brutal examples of militia formation have involved states playing the preeminent role in creating, funding, and controlling their militias. This depends on a level of state leadership, coherence, and capacity based on a sufficiently inclusive political settlement, which currently does not exist in Afghanistan. The Afghan case has experienced both types of militia formation and is a powerful illustration of the deleterious effects of exogenous, militarized statebuilding, which at many different levels has undermined the statebuilding endeavor. This is reflected in the paramilitarization of the national police, the skewed distribution of aid funding, and the plethora of aid projects driven by a military rather than a development logic.

COIN experts are correct in highlighting the illiberal ways in which states have successfully dealt with internal insurgencies and consolidated their power; this more closely resembles historical experience than the liberal version of "nice statebuilding" (Mayall and de Oliviera 2011). Such reading of the evidence is highly selective, however, and these experts have rescued from the dustbin of history a set of colonial practices that, putting aside ethical concerns, have at best a mixed track record of success, particularly when applied in the contemporary context to expeditionary statebuilding. The paradox at the heart of this doctrine is that successful COIN depends on the existence of a highcapacity regime to put it into practice, but exogenous statebuilding prevents the emergence of such a regime in the first place.

The three case studies presented here suggest that U.S. special forces and other external military actors lack the capacity or legitimacy to make informed decisions about whom to support and why and, as the case of the ALP has demonstrated, that they have undermined efforts directed toward state consolidation.

This is not to reify or romanticize indigenous actors. The simple fact is that they have a different opportunity-risk calculus from external players, who need not, in the long term, live with the consequences of their decisions.

Choices have been made with little appreciation of either the longterm consequences for the state or the immediate consequences for the local populations. The primary driver has been the search for tactical advantage; the special forces have supported whomever they felt at the time was most effective in the fight against the Taliban, whether Abdul Raziq or Nurul Haq, even though they have a track record of human rights abuses and predation against the wider population.

Based on the criteria of shortterm tactical advantage, the ALP has on occasion worked as intended. Yet these positive impacts have often been short lived and often at the cost of the perceived legitimacy and capacity of the Afghan state.

A central paradox of the ALP program is that it is least likely to work in the areas where the program is believed to be most needed. In other words, when the state presence—particularly a credible ANP presence, which can back up the ALP and monitor its activities—is strong, it may play a useful auxiliary role in holding ground and preventing Taliban penetration.

However, in the outlying areas, where the state presence has always been limited and contested, the ALP is likely to live off the land and contribute to an existing lawand-order problem.

Recommendations

Clearly, the problem of militias has no straightforward solution. Militias grow like a mold in a particular security environment, and the long-term solution lies in changing that environment. To a large extent, the solutions are not military but political, ultimately depending on the forging of a more inclusive political settlement.

It is not realistic to disarm these groups, and of course the problem extends well beyond the ALP. In Afghanistan today, there exists a mass of other armed groups, all of which will remained armed, and this will continue to be the case while there is widespread insecurity, concerns about the future, and a lack of alternative forms of protection and sustenance. The longterm future of the ALP program at the time of writing remains uncertain. However, if the program continues, some practical measures can and should be pursued.

First, the program should not be expanded. President Karzai has made this clear, especially in his repeated requests to strengthen the regular forces, the ANA, and the ANP. U.S. and other foreign special forces are likely to remain engaged in Afghanistan after the transition, and it is important that they resist the temptation to form more local militias, whether within or outside the ALP program.

Second, stronger state oversight and support of the ALP program is needed. This may mean retrenching the program to areas where the ANA-ANP presence is strong, community support is substantial, and stability is sufficient to enable the ALP to hold ground. The incor-poration of the ALP into the ANSF is key to its playing a state-supporting role and preventing further fragmentation of violence and the intensification of local power struggles. Strengthening the ANSF-ALP nexus is also critical, as is avoiding placing the ALP in an isolation ward. ISAF statements regarding cutting ANSF numbers in favour of the ALP because it is cheaper would be detrimental in the long run.

Third, in the medium to long term, plans should be developed to facilitate the ALP's absorption into the ANP. International donors must be willing to pay the additional costs for this to happen. In terms of centralization versus fragmentation of violence, much is tied to dependence on resource flows. Whilst ALP forces and other militias are part of the tashkil and salaries are paid through the center, ALP arguably acts as a centripetal force. In the absence of centralized patronage, however, it can rapidly change into a centrifugal force and contribute to the unraveling of centralizing efforts. Greater clarity is needed regarding long-term funding options for the ALP, as currently they are off budget and directly paid by the U.S. military. A multidonor funding source might be necessary to facilitate ALP-ANSF integration.

In the final analysis, the ALP is a second-order question. Dealing with it depends on whether international actors are prepared to deal with the first-order questions. This essentially boils down to two interrelated issues. First, will international actors accept and support a political process that involves negotiating a new political settlement in Afghanistan? This process would necessarily involve peace talks with the Taliban and negotiation of a post-Karzai political dispensation. It will not come about as a result of democratic elections but instead would involve backroom bargains and deal making that may be unpalatable to Western actors. The result would not be a government of reformers but a coalition of power holders with unsavory pasts and powerful patrons. Second, will donors continue to provide the resources to fund such a state? A sudden reduction in funding will not only create incentives for the ALP to go rogue but also and more significantly lead to the unraveling of the regular forces.

LIMITING OUTSIDE SUPPORT FOR THE INSURGENCY

It is hard to overstate the significance of outside support for insurgencies. Military and political counterinsurgency initiatives, no matter how well formulated or executed, can have limited effect on an insurgency if it is sustained by substantial support from outside sources. Bernard Fall, Roger Trinquier and others discuss this issue in their works on counterinsurgency. Both Fall and Trinquier assert the importance of limiting outside support and the active targeting of enemy supply sources and sanctuaries with the use of guerilla tactics (even if these supply sources and sanctuaries are in other countries).

Outside support was a central issue in the Soviet Afghan experience. This is evident in a letter from Leonid Brezhnev to Fidel Castro that "On our end we are for political normalization, but genuine normalization, aimed at... the effective and guaranteed cessation of aggression an all forms of interference in the matters of Afghanistan". General Gromov writes that the question of patrolling Afghanistan's borders was the first item of discussion in the morning meetings of the 40th Army's headquarters.

Not only was outside support an incendiary geopolitical issue, it had a great effect on the mujahedeen forces. Weapons, ammunition and fighters from Iran and Pakistan were important logistical supports for the Afghan resistance. This became especially true after the Soviets commenced increased aviation strikes on mujahedeen friendly areas within Afghanistan, destroying many domestic bases of support. It is also important to note that the outside support extended to the mujahedeen was considerable – as high as hundreds of millions of dollars per year coming from the United States, China, Saudi Arabia and other wealthy nations.

Many in the United States saw the situation in Afghanistan as an opportunity to deliver a defeat to the Soviet Union. This is confirmed by Milt Bearden, a CIA officer in charge of a support program for the mujahedeen, who recounts that CIA director William Casey told him to 'go over there and win'. Afghan war veteran Major General Liakhovsky saw the outside support for the mujahedeen as a mean spirited campaign perpetrated by those with deep hatred for Russia, considering CIA director William Casey the incarnation of the devil, and noting pointedly that his efforts helped support the rise of Osama bin Laden.

Soviet leaders understood that eliminating outside support would severely weaken the mujahedeen. Bernard Fall writes, "A guerrilla force's logistical requirements may be simpler than that of a large regular force, but it has some rock bottom needs which must be filled through outside support, or it dies". Accordingly, significant time and effort was devoted to condemning outside support for the Afghan insurgency and coaxing foreign countries to end their activities. In 1980 Brezhnev authorized the withdrawal of certain units from Afghanistan with the expressed intent of using this move to win greater cooperation from Pakistan and Iran and the ceasing of their support for the mujahedeen.

This did not bring the desired results. Sealing the borders of Afghanistan by military means was an exceedingly difficult task. Roger Trinquier notes that frontier borders are a tough issue for the counterinsurgent; Afghanistan is a particularly difficult case due to difficult terrain and ethnic factors. When asked in 1979 why the border was not more closely controlled, President Taraki replied that "We are unable to do it due to the absence of the necessary means.

Besides this, closing the Afghan Pakistani borders would evoke dissatisfaction on the part of both Afghan and Pakistani Pashtuns and Baluchis, which maintain close family ties, and it would ultimately hurt the prestige of the current government in Afghanistan". These same issues continued throughout the war. Supplies and personnel entered Afghanistan through difficult mountain passes, in small caravans of pack animals, and over a long border unrecognized by tribes on either side. In a Politburo meeting in 1986, General Akhromeev noted this issue saying that "Soviet soldiers are working to seal the border [with Pakistan], but they are unable to close off all channels, through which supplies come across". This task was so difficult, and the border so porous, that it was noted in a Politburo meeting that mujahedeen controlled areas often had better supplies (which came from Pakistan) than government controlled areas that supposedly had access to the resources of the Afghan state.

Trinquier stresses the importance of working to combat outside support through closing borders to illicit traffic and attacking enemy bases in the fashion of guerilla fighters. The Soviet strategy in Afghanistan followed both these points of recommendation, indicating sound elements of strategy on the part of Soviet leaders. Soviet leaders were discussing this issue from the beginning of the occupation. In April of 1980 a report to the CPSU mentioned the need for Soviet and Afghan forces to control Afghanistan's borders to protect the country from outside threats. Vasiliy Mitrokhin notes that KGB leaders "insisted on the complete... sealing of the borders with Pakistan, Iran, China". To this end, five thousand additional forces were emplaced on patrol duty, carrying out ambushes and otherwise intercepting mujahedeen caravans. In May of 1980, additional border troops were emplaced in the key areas bordering Pakistan and China; these troops were successful in securing a four hundred kilometre stretch of the border, closing off sixteen passes and routes into Afghanistan. In 1981, Andropov authorized intensification of efforts against enemy caravans. Five additional border troop brigades were assigned as a second line of intercept against the mujahedeen in 1981 by the order of Defense Minister Ustinov. These forces, as well as KGB special units, set ambushes and mined paths used by the enemy. These measures were substantial enough to prompt Babrak Karmal to say that, "Now, that in the name of saving the Afghan revolution the Soviet Union has taken such a serious step, the fates of our nations have indeed merged together".

Efforts to close the borders of Afghanistan and limit support for the Afghan resistance continued for the duration of the conflict. Operation 'Curtain' began in 1984, and consisted of increased patrolling and ambushing of mujahedeen caravans. This effort, in revamped form, was renamed 'Barrier' in 1987. Special forces and KGB special units were increasingly used for these tasks. General Gromov notes that in 1985 two spetsnaz brigades were assigned to reinforce the effort to close off the border with Pakistan.

Teams of helicopters were also used to patrol from the air, and would land with search crews to inspect caravans. Trinquier's point that "with the methods of *modern warfare*, we must carry the war to the enemy" is echoed by Bernard Fall, who asserts that infiltrating enemy sanctuaries is necessary for undercutting an insurgency. The Soviets actively pursued this approach as well, cultivating agent networks and conducting special operations in Pakistan.

Soviet efforts to close the border and limit insurgent supply processes did bring some success. Alexander Liakhovsky notes that in many regions in 1985 the mujahedeen "were deprived of large supply bases... military supplies, provisions, [and] medical equipment". Shortages in supply were so intense at times that mujahedeen leadership organized special units specifically for maneuvering caravans past Soviet troops and into Afghanistan. Despite all the measures undertaken by the Soviets and their moments of efficacy, Afghanistan's borders were still crossed by mujahedeen reinforcements and supplies throughout the conflict. The enduring sanctuaries in Pakistan and influx of support were major reasons the mujahedeen were able to withstand the Soviet army, and persist in spite of military defeats. The Soviet strategy regarding the borders and mujahedeen caravans clearly shows, however, that substantial attempts were made to address this problem. The Soviet command simply did not have enough troops to complete the task.

Monitoring the Population

Whether one approaches counterinsurgency from the population centric or enemy centric approach, or somewhere in between, monitoring the population remains a vital element in the counterinsurgency effort. Monitoring and controlling the population helps the counterinsurgent limit contacts between the insurgent and the population. If the counterinsurgent is successful in limiting these contacts, this becomes a significant blow to the insurgent's support system. Monitoring the population is also a vital element in intelligence gathering; in the context of counterinsurgency, understanding the mood of the population is often as important as accessing more classified information about the enemy. Roger Trinquier maintains that establishing strict curfews, issuing census cards and conducting broad ranging searches and interrogations are necessary for controlling the population and isolating it from the insurgency. Soviet forces implemented all of these measures.

Afghan war veteran and historian Major General Alexander Liakhovsky notes that all males over the age of thirteen were required to register with the Soviet authorities overseeing the area; it was required to carry documentation of this registration at all times. Curfews were maintained, as well as a mandatory registration process for any visitors or supplies entering the area. General V.A. Bogdanov notes that curfews were typically set for eleven pm and that the implementation of a personal identification document was completely new for Afghanistan. It was also necessary for Afghan citizens to receive special permission to host non family members in their homes. Law enforcement and intelligence agencies played an important role in monitoring the population. KGB trained Afghan law enforcement and security agencies were built up to significant numbers. In a meeting of Soviet leaders in 1986, General Akhromeev mentioned that there were 115,000 Afghan police troops and 20,000 Khad and other agency forces.

Training local law enforcement and participating in police work is vital to the counterinsurgent, even though it is not traditionally a role played by the military. Trinquier notes that in counterinsurgency "Police action will... be actual operational warfare". Security agencies conducted extensive search and interrogation operations in areas where the Kabul government projected its influence. Vasiliy Mitrokhin notes that these agencies helped create some two hundred self defense units that acted in support of the government, providing agents and information. For example, in the first quarter of 1983 Afghan government agencies were using eight hundred agents that had infiltrated insurgent groups. Their information directed government forces in 140 air strikes and 360 local attacks. These forces also conducted many search operations to locate and destroy insurgent organizations.

While the Soviets had a sound strategy in this area in many respects, they did not project influence into enough of the country to see the benefits of these measures. Lack of troops, poor infrastructure and Afghanistan's rural society made it very difficult to sufficiently control the peaceful Afghan population and isolate them from the mujahedeen. One of the reasons that Soviets had difficulty projecting their influence throughout the country was that their forces were too few and spread too thinly. Soviet forces were often spread out in small remote outposts, having as many as 862 guarded objectives manned by some 20,200 troops. In order to address this problem, the Soviet command tried to consolidate forces and efforts in specific areas, as it was clear that relatively low troop levels precluded effective control of the entire country.

Soviet leaders started with more peaceful regions in northern Afghanistan, establishing good surveillance of the population, local self defense watch groups, and promoting economic and social initiatives. It was envisioned that sustained success in these regions would spread incrementally through the country. The attempt at consolidating aligns exactly with the recommendations of classical and modern counterinsurgency theorists. Starting efforts in the more peaceful areas follows the paradigm of the 'ink blot', a term used by Marshal Hubert Lyautey as a metaphor for the slow spread of the counterinsurgent's influence throughout a region. The Soviets' strategy in this respect also dovetails with David Kilcullen's recommendation that the counterinsurgent "start from secure areas and work slowly outwards". David Galula also promotes this method of incrementally spreading control over the country as well, noting that "Order having been re established in the area, the process may be repeated elsewhere". In modern day Afghanistan, U.S and NATO forces are encountering issues similar to those that faced the Soviets: there are not enough troops to provide adequate security over the entire country. Counterinsurgency experts are advocating consolidation of efforts in key areas in similar fashion to the Soviet strategy described above. In a report on Afghanistan from June 2009, experts recommended that the military "focus available forces where the fewest number of government and coalition troops can protect the greatest number of Afghans. This will require the coalition to depart some areas it currently occupies".

Soviet forces did adopt sound strategy aimed at controlling the population and concentrating their resources on defined areas. The Soviets, however, were unable to implement these measures effectively or broadly enough to see overall success.

Units and Training

As it became increasingly apparent that the Soviet army was ill suited to the conditions in Afghanistan, the Soviet command worked to restructure the force to be more effective. One area of adjustments involved changes to units and training. Early on in the Soviet occupation it became clear that motorized rifle units of conscript soldiers were not well suited to the tough guerilla fighting and infantry tasks necessary to engage and destroy the mujahedeen in difficult terrain. The Soviet military suffered not only from an overall lack of troops in Afghanistan, but also from a lack of *qualified* troops. Overall, it became clear that mobile, highly trained, and fit troops were needed to carry out the difficult missions required in Afghanistan. As a result, the Soviet command expanded the use of elite units, re oriented the mission and use of motorized rifle troops, and changed military training to better prepare soldiers for duty in Afghanistan. While these adjustments were well thought out, institution wide change was difficult to achieve.

The Soviet command's shift towards the use of elite units aligns with classical counterinsurgency theory. David Galula, who is often cited regarding the need to win over the support of the population, did not exclude the use of military force. He advocates the need for elite units that are "highly mobile and lightly armed". These mobile units, according to Galula, should be used to engage the enemy, while other static units should provide security for key infrastructure and population centres. Roger Trinquier promotes a similar concept of 'interval troops' and 'intervention troops', mobile units that are tasked with engaging the enemy and operating freely throughout a region; interval troops functioned in larger units and in a more defined area than the intervention troops. Soviet airborne troops were similar in concept to Trinquier's interval troops, while the Soviet special forces (spetsnaz) corresponded loosely to intervention units.

Soviet troop levels were low for the mission in Afghanistan; this was most felt when trying to hold territory already cleared in large operations. Trinquier designated this task for what he calls 'grid troops'. Soviet forces or Afghan government units were often too few to effectively maintain security after the bulk of Soviet forces left. For this reason, tactical successes were often reversed because insufficient resources were expended on securing gains. Soviet military leaders learned early in 1980 that the situation in Afghanistan would require more effort than initially anticipated. General Gromov writes that Soviet casualties in January of 1980 were a sharp reminder to the Soviet Command that it would be necessary to view the situation in Afghanistan as nothing less than a war. The types of units employed in Afghanistan were shifted accordingly. Soviet leaders quickly learned that heavy equipment and tanks were not effective against the Afghan insurgency.

The Soviet command therefore relegated many heavy armour units to static security and fire support units; lighter armoured vehicles were used to accompany and transport infantry near to their mission objectives. In 1980, many tank units were being sent back to the USSR and replaced by lighter troops, reducing their numbers by over half. For example, in July 1980, two tank regiments and an anti aircraft brigade were sent back to the USSR. The Soviet command replaced many of the reserve troops that had been mobilized for the invasion. General Gromov recounts that in 1980 many units were filled with as much as 80% reservists, which made conducting challenging combat missions very difficult. Soviet leaders quickly began to fill the ranks of the Limited Contingent with specialists and full time soldiers in an effort to position the Limited Contingent for a more substantial and active role in Afghanistan.

Despite limited resources and initial miscalculations, the Soviet Command did come to a good understanding of the units necessary for the tasks at hand in Afghanistan. The mobile units were expanded and trained for the specifics of Afghanistan's conflict. For example, Major General Luchinsky recalls that the difficult task of intercepting and ambushing mujahedeen caravans coming from Pakistan came to be conducted almost solely by spetnaz and other specialized forces. In an official letter describing the situation in Afghanistan, General Varennikov mentions the need for specialized quick reaction forces to respond to situations around the country. Such units were increasingly used for challenging missions against the mujahedeen. This shift aligned with the principles of counterinsurgency theory.

With each passing year airborne and air assault troops were increasingly used in Afghanistan. Parachute jumps were not conducted in Afghanistan's mountainous terrain, but insertion by helicopter was necessary for many of the tactics employed by the Soviets. Extreme terrain often made air landings the only way to emplace troops swiftly enough to block and intercept mujahedeen forces. Airborne troops were not the only troops that were air landed; motorized rifle troops were also used in this manner. The increased use of airborne troops had more to do with their level of training and mentality than parachuting capabilities. The Soviet army had significantly developed training and selection for airborne units since World War II, and as a result the quality of soldier was much higher in these units than in others. Soviet airborne units were akin to United States Army Ranger units in terms of training and mindset. Airborne units chose from top quality conscripts when augmenting their units. General Gromov notes that airborne troops went through specialized and very rigorous training. The contrast between airborne soldiers and those of other units was very noticeable. One Soviet conscript recounts that:

"A landing-assault brigade differs from a motorized rifle regiment in that it has more people who also have better training and more specialization. Their assignments are more serious and strict than for the regular units. Many of these fellows were good athletes and some even knew karate".

The Soviet command increasingly relied on these tougher troops to conduct combat operations in Afghanistan. Missions in Afghanistan were exceedingly difficult. Soldiers had to carry 30 40 kilograms of weight, and missions often lasted for several days. Soldiers would typically lose 7 10 kilograms of body weight after a week in the field, and after longer missions would require medical help. These conditions made it very difficult for average conscripts to remain combat effective in the field.

This shift in strategy and the contrast between the troops was evident to Afghan insurgent forces as well. A Pakistani officer, who spent time in Afghanistan with the mujahedeen notes that, "The paratroop (air assault) units fought much more aggressively.... In the months following my arrival the Soviets committed more Special Operations Forces to the conflict.... we noticed there was a high proportion of paratroops in the Soviet order of battle, indicating that these units would play a key role in offensive sweeps.... This was invariably the case".

Soviet leaders also relied heavily on spetsnaz and KGB special units for missions against the mujahedeen. These troops, even more than airborne, were trained to engage Afghan insurgents on their own terms. General Gromov writes that the officers and soldiers of these units had "fantastic military and physical training", and worked to receive good intelligence through establishing ties with the local population. KGB units, such as 'Grom' (literally trans.: 'thunder') and 'Zenit' (literally trans.: 'zenith') proved themselves during operations in Kabul at the start of the invasion in 1979. In 1980, Andropov approved the expansion of such units to one thousand people. At this time, two additional units –'Kaskad' and 'Omega' – were established. In July 1981 the Politburo approved the creation of yet another such specialized group – 'Vimpel' – to augment Soviet Special Forces. These units maintained very rigorous selection processes; Soviet Special Forces troops were not only physically and tactically superior to regular forces, but were often trained in foreign languages and cultures. The capabilities of these units are similar to those of French SAS units, which were assigned experts in Arabic language and culture, and noted as being successful in counterinsurgency in Algeria for this reason.

Soviet special units participated in many offensive and intelligence operations, even creating groups of Afghan fighters who posed as mujahedeen. Vasiliy Mitrokhin reports that there were eighty six such groups by January of 1983. Similar groups had success in other counterinsurgencies. General Crook, who fought in the American Indian wars of the 19th century, is known to have planted teams of friendly Apaches into hostile areas in order to foment confusion and conflict. The Selous Scouts of Rhodesia were another indigenous outfit used in counterinsurgency with great success: they were credited with more than two thirds of insurgent casualties within Rhodesia. Concrete information regarding particular actions of specialized Afghan units is scarce, but the concept of employing such forces is one that has historically been beneficial to the counterinsurgent. The Soviet command worked hard to improve training both for elite and for regular troops. At the time of the invasion, even spetsnaz forces had very little specialized mountain training or equipment. This was obviously a significant disadvantage for an army waging counterinsurgency in Afghanistan. General Gromov writes that the skills previously taught for mountain warfare were ineffective in Afghanistan, and clearly of use only in European areas. Directive No. D 314/3/00655 of the General Staff ordered the creation of special mountain warfare battalions. In addition, programs in mountain and convoy operations were instituted in 1980 for cadets and current motorized rifle troops.

These programs were run by trainers chosen because of their combat experience in Afghanistan. Training sites were established in Central Asian areas near Termez, Ashkabad, Almaty and Fergana, since conditions in these areas were closer to actual conditions in Afghanistan than sites deeper within Russia. In 1981, Defense Minister Ustinov formally directed Soviet troops to enhance training programs based on combat experience in Afghanistan, and top leaders were scheduled to visit Afghanistan in order to better understand the relevant conditions and issues. The Soviet military community increasingly studied tactics for irregular warfare and mountain and desert conditions. The appearance of articles on such topics in Soviet military journals reflected this shift in focus. In October of 1985 specialized officer training was implemented specifically to prepare officers for Afghanistan.

The training included classes on Afghan political and cultural aspects, mountain warfare and autonomous and independent action. Starting in 1984, basic training for recruits was substantially improved and lengthened (in 1984 it was lengthened to three months, in 1985 it was lengthened to five months). Training incorporated more and more concrete tasks necessary in Afghanistan, such as night missions and mountain actions – one source notes that 40% of training time was conducted in a mountain environment. Soldiers were trained in tactics like bounding overwatch and encircling movements. Training included challenging field exercises and special emphasis on key specialties, such as sniper skills and the use of the AGS 17 (an automatic grenade launcher). Not only did newly developed training programs stress the tactics of irregular warfare and the need for creative and independent solutions to combat challenges, they addressed the acceptance of reasonable risk. Accepting risk is a key aspect of counterinsurgency success, as willingness to accept risk often translates into greater security in the long run.

For example, Soviet motorized troops that instinctively stayed close to road bound armoured vehicles actually became more vulnerable targets. Accepting risk by relying less on large fortifications or armour units actually meant greater overall safety. Many counterinsurgency experts make this point, which is just as relevant today as it was for the Soviets. David Kilcullen summarizes the concept well in the following excerpt:

"Movement on foot, sleeping in local villages, night patrolling: all these seem more dangerous than they are. They establish links with the locals, who see you as real people... not as aliens who descend from an armoured box. Driving around in an armoured convoy and day-tripping like a tourist in hell degrades situational awareness, makes you a target and is ultimately more dangerous".

This concept is often hard to promote in large armies, however, as they tend to be more reluctant in taking risks in the context of counterinsurgency than in familiar conventional combat. The burden on the Soviet military's training system was considerable. Each year 40,000 to 50,000 soldiers had to receive basic training in order to maintain troop levels. In addition to casualties, there was significant turnover in personnel, as soldiers and NCOs had limited service requirements; after time in training, their combat tours lasted eighteen to twenty one months. Not only was this a significant strain on the Soviet training system, it meant that Soviet soldiers were consistently less experienced than their opponents, since Soviet combat veterans were routinely replaced by inexperienced recruits. Afghan resistance fighters, of course, did not rotate out and became increasingly experienced in fighting the Soviets.

In the face of these challenges, however, the Soviet command pursued very promising ideas in terms of unit organization and training. The initiatives outlined above indicate that Soviet leaders understood the kinds of units and training necessary for success in Afghanistan. Limited troops and institutional inertia, among other factors, prevented these changes from having the broad effects the Soviet command desired.

6

Counterinsurgency Theory

The dynamic nature of insurgencies and counterinsurgencies is highly complex, as every expert is quick to note. Moreover, this inherent complexity and the accelerated pace of events and modern communications make it very difficult to propose viable generalizations or establish any hard and fast rules in counterinsurgency. In the recently published US Army and Marine Counterinsurgency Field Manual, an entire section is devoted to the paradoxes of counterinsurgency, impressing the reader with the elusiveness of an effective strategy in this form of irregular warfare. Given the resurgent interest in the subject, it is important to remember that the popularity of counterinsurgency scholarship has waxed and waned as a result of many political and institutional factors. Surprisingly little was written on the topic after the 1960s; there were even movements that limited its study within the United States military. In the United States some posit that squelching the study of counterinsurgency was part of a reflexive reaction to the war in Vietnam – a way of avoiding entanglement in similar conflicts in the future.

The notion that the study of counterinsurgency begets misadventures in counterinsurgency warfare recurs in the United States and abroad, and is a subtle, though important, factor in militaries' formulation and implementation of counterinsurgency strategy both in western countries and in Russia. Independent of institutional and scholarly interest in the subject, however, governments continue to find themselves embroiled in irregular wars and in need of methods for conducting counterinsurgency warfare. In the case of the United States and the Soviet Union in Afghanistan, the need for counterinsurgency expertise was not sufficiently anticipated.

Large militaries primarily trained for conventional war are often obliged to learn (and relearn) the complex craft of counterinsurgency 'on the job'. The study of counterinsurgency has become especially relevant in the current day. Not only do the conflicts facing the United States and NATO necessitate renewed focus on the topic, but unprecedented developments in technology and dynamic changes in world ideologies change the very nature of the subject itself. As greater detail, the principles discussed by authorities such as Callwell, Lawrence, Thompson, Trinquier and Galula do not fully address the realities of today or those of tomorrow.

As is often repeated in relation to counterinsurgency, 'If it works today, it is obsolete'. The insurgency and counterinsurgency in the 1980s in Afghanistan represent an important step in this progression toward modern realities. Many phenomena that distinguish modern insurgencies from their antecedents began to reveal themselves in the mountains and deserts where the mujahedeen fought against the Soviet 40th army. The main elements of insurgency and counterinsurgency as put forth by historical authorities as well as by modern scholars and practitioners. The main debates and developments in the field. With this basic foundation it will be possible to place Soviet efforts in Afghanistan into the broader context of insurgency and counterinsurgency, allowing a clearer and more fruitful analysis of the conflict. In reading about counterinsurgency, it is interesting to note that most authors on the subject have significant personal experience in irregular warfare dealing with insurgencies and counterinsurgencies.

John Nagl writes that "The best writings on counterinsurgency share with the best sex manuals the fact that their authors generally have some personal experience of their subject matter". Divergence of opinion among authors with comparable experience in the field is a testament to the highly variable, and at times subjective, nature of conducting counterinsurgency campaigns. Two major schools of thought on counterinsurgency are: *population-centric* and *enemy-centric*. The former stipulates that winning the support of the local population must be the first priority.

Once the support of the population has been won through the provision of physical security and social and economic opportunities, the insurgent forces will cease to be relevant; at this point, one can easily eradicate whatever part of the insurgency that has not already withered away. Experts of the mid 20th century, such as David Galula and Roger Trinquier, subscribe to this approach to varying degrees. The principles of population centric strategy are currently widely accepted in the field.

Enemy centric counterinsurgency theory maintains that engaging and destroying the enemy should be the main focus of effort, and that after this has been accomplished, other needed developments will proceed naturally. This approach has its roots in imperial and colonial wars, such as those carried out by Russia, Britain and France in the 18th, 19th and early 20th centuries. The character of enemy centric counterinsurgency generally tends to be closer to that of conventional war in that it emphasizes fighting more than winning 'hearts and minds'. The principles of enemy centric counterinsurgency are far less popular today than those of population centric counterinsurgency due to their sometimes severe character, and due to powerful arguments for population centric strategies.

In the context of many new developments in technologies, ideologies and the geopolitical landscape, a new 'hybrid' approach to counterinsurgency is also emerging. This approach, discussed by experts such as David Kilcullen, requires a highly adaptive posture in counterinsurgency that employs the principles of both enemy and population centric strategies depending on the situation. This pragmatic counterinsurgency approach further emphasizes the need for military institutions to cultivate an ethos of learning and adaptability.

Enemy-Centric Counterinsurgency

Colonel C.E. Callwell's treatise, *Small Wars,* is a classic enemy centric counterinsurgency manual, and is still relevant to those with preference for this school of counterinsurgency theory. While current scholars tend not to accept Callwell's ideas wholesale, those who favour the enemy centric approach support many of the principles he sets forth. Callwell formulated his ideas in an era when large powers projected their power around the globe with a heavy hand.

Small Wars, first published in 1896, was his most famous work, and is one of the most substantial treatises that espouse an enemy centric approach to counterinsurgency. An officer in the British Army with experience combating insurgents in Afghanistan and elsewhere, Callwell does not express the sensitivity for the population so carefully detailed in other manuals for counterinsurgency. Changes in press coverage and geopolitics explain some of these differences; nevertheless, many principles that he sets forth were still supported after his death in 1928 and in the current day. Callwell phrases the essence of counterinsurgency as such: "The enemy must not only be beaten. He must be beaten thoroughly". This remains the core of the enemy centric approach to counterinsurgency. Callwell states that the small war differs from the conventional one in that "The mere expulsion of the opponent from ground where he has thought fit to accept battle is of small account; what is wanted is a big casualty list in the hostile ranks". Callwell is primarily concerned with finding ways to engage the enemy in battle and not with securing the population's compliance.

Generally, adherents to the enemy centric approach maintain that the larger power plays to its advantage by seeking out battle with the insurgent so that it can utilize its superiority in firepower, troop numbers and discipline. Callwell asserts that decisiveness and violence of action by the counterinsurgent will win the support of those who are wavering and looking to align themselves with the strongest side. Callwell details the methods of bringing the fight to the enemy, laying out a framework for dividing the territory so that a relatively autonomous, local unit is responsible for a particular geographical area. Callwell also emphasizes the idea of encircling the enemy's flank to prevent his retreat and maximize the casualties inflicted.

When the enemy refuses to fight and continues to elude capture, Callwell prescribes the destruction of villages, crops and the appropriation of livestock and other goods: "If the enemy cannot be touched [on the battlefield]... he can be touched through his pocket". These harsh measures are aimed at crushing resistance quickly and avoiding a prolonged conflict, which introduces problems for the counterinsurgent in terms of supply and care for troops in long deployment.

Callwell's approach embodies the main points of the enemy centric theory of counterinsurgency: finding, engaging and destroying the enemy. It is interesting to note that Callwell continuously includes cases from the Tsarist military's actions in Central Asia to illustrate his points. He quotes the famous general Mikhail Skobelev to articulate the necessity of quick and powerful action against the insurgent, "Do not forget that in Asia he is ... master who seizes the people pitilessly by the throat and imposes upon their imagination".

Callwell's take on counterinsurgency is the starting point for many proponents of the enemy centric school of counterinsurgency. Large powers such as Britain and Russia that waged wars in Central Asia employed many enemy centric principles.

The enemy centric approach is appealing to those of a more typically 'military' mind in the sense that it includes more kinetic action and actual fighting than the population centric school of counterinsurgency. Imperial armies did incorporate population centric principles as well.

No counterinsurgency campaign can be categorized as strictly enemy or population centric. For example, in the 18th and 19th Centuries, Tsarist forces in the Caucasus and Central Asia pursued highly kinetic and enemy centric tactics aimed at decimating resistance to their rule, but also worked to co-opt the local population, and create religious and economic structures that were acceptable to the populace and designed to preserve stability. Counterinsurgencies generally continue to incorporate varying approaches into their campaign. This can be observed both in the Soviet counterinsurgency in Afghanistan as well as in current US and NATO operations.

POPULATION-CENTRIC COUNTERINSURGENCY

The enemy centric model for counterinsurgency warfare focuses on decisive victories through the use of military power. The main thrust of the theory is to crush the insurgency as effectively as possible, usually through military means. It does not exclude the ideas of winning over the population, but the population is not the main priority. The population centric model for counterinsurgency is more announced. According to this theory, the participation and compliance of the population is the single most important element in defeating the insurgency.

The population centric approach does not exclude the use of military force against the insurgent, but firmly asserts that this is only one piece of the strategy, and, if relied upon solely, will not produce lasting results.

Population centric counterinsurgency theory was significantly developed in the French army, which acquired substantial experience with irregular warfare in French colonies in the 19th and 20th Centuries. Military officers returning from these theatres would share their experiences of foreign cultures with inquisitive ethnologists and other academics, often gaining insights from the scholars that they found useful for conducting counterinsurgency operations.

Two French officers, Marshals Hubert Lyautey and Henri Gallieni compiled principles of irregular warfare in treatises based on their experiences fighting small wars in Africa and Asia. Gallieni and Lyautey were instrumental in establishing the Ecole Militaire Spécialisée dans l'outre Mer et l'etranger in 1906, a school devoted to integrating the study of foreign cultures into training for officers deploying to theatres of irregular war. Gallieni and Lyautey were important figures in the development of population centric counterinsurgency theory in the French Army.

Both Gallieni and Lyautey maintained that excessive reliance on force could be counterproductive in counterinsurgency, as collateral damage and resulting harm to the army's public image could undercut important working relationships with the indigenous population. The population centric approach stresses the need for officers to understand the surrounding culture and complete non military tasks aimed at winning the support of the people. The British officer T.E. Lawrence also held to this attitude, emphasizing that the officer working in the context of irregular warfare must learn the culture of the area. Lawrence notes that the only way to influence the indigenous people is through "unremitting study of them". For Lawrence, as well as for others who tended towards population centric counterinsurgency, the ability to comprehend the human terrain was paramount and understood as the basis for finding ways to convince the population to withdraw support from the insurgency.

Population centric counterinsurgency orients focus away from the goal of destroying the enemy, establishing the officer's first priority as the painstaking and careful process of developing mutually beneficial relationships with the local people. Lawrence comments on this process in his notes on working with Bedouin tribesmen: "hear all that passes, search out what is going on beneath the surface, read their characters, discover their tastes and their weaknesses.... Bury yourself in Arab circles, have no interests and no ideas except the work in hand, so that... you realize your part deeply enough to avoid the little slips that would counteract the painful work of weeks. Your success will be proportioned to the amount of mental effort you devote to it".

This intellectual vector in military thinking greatly influenced two prominent French officers and scholars of the mid 20th century, Roger Trinquier and David Galula, who both completed important works on counterinsurgency based on combat experience in Indochina and Algeria in the 1940s and 1950s. Whereas the enemy centric theory seeks to capitalize on the counterinsurgent's fire superiority by finding ways to engage and destroy the insurgent, Galula and Trinquier argue that such a strategy is ineffective. They point out that the insurgent can generally choose the time and place of such an engagement, waiting for conditions that will give him the advantage. According to Galula and Trinquier, whose theories are now referred to as 'classical' counterinsurgency theory, the counterinsurgent's power should primarily be employed to protect the civilian population rather than chasing down the insurgent forces.

The shift from offensive to defensive focus, according to Galula, plays to the counterinsurgent's strengths. The counterinsurgent will likely fail in hunting down insurgent forces that are typically very mobile and familiar with the terrain. By focusing on protecting the population in a more static posture, the counterinsurgent's relative immobility is not such a disadvantage and he can rely on superior firepower to repel attacks. More importantly, the primary objective in this model is not the annihilation of insurgent forces, but the support of the population: "the *sine qua non* of victory in *modern warfare* is the unconditional support of a population". This being the stated goal, military actions are only important insofar as they help secure the support of the people.

Winning civilian support is outlined as a political endeavor that must be started by the military and then continued by civilians. This endeavor requires that the counterinsurgent convince the people that his rule is 1) legitimate and 2) that it will provide a better life than the rule of the insurgent.

The persuasion of the population requires traditional military action to provide security, but relies most on a comprehensive program of non military activities.

Such activities include publicizing the counterinsurgent message, supporting political institutions and developing economic opportunities.

As Galula famously repeated, "a revolutionary war is only 20 percent military action and 80 percent political". It is thus important that military officers function effectively in non military roles; cooperation with civilian development workers is crucial. Galula posits that a counterinsurgency is "not an addition but a multiplication of... various programs; they are all essential and if one is nil, the product will be zero".

Classical population centric theory generally prescribes that the counterinsurgent start his operations in limited areas where he can concentrate his attention and where he considers success readily attainable. Once the counterinsurgent has achieved success in these areas he expands his sphere of influence incrementally. Lyautey coined the term 'ink blot' or 'ink stain' to describe this incremental expansion of influence. Galula, Trinquier and others advocate that the counterinsurgent systematically divide territory into zones, appointing administrative teams for each zone. The division of territory implicitly suggests the decentralized nature of counterinsurgency, where more junior leaders have more control over the course of events in any given area.

The importance of the junior leader and local solutions to issues in counterinsurgency is echoed by David Kilcullen, who notes that programs should be specifically oriented to each area. Population centric counterinsurgency theory would suggest that operations in a given area proceed in the following general pattern: the counterinsurgent expels the main body of armed insurgents, establishes posts for maintaining security in the area, makes contact with and controls the population with the intent of isolating it from the insurgents, gathers intelligence from the population and uses it to target the insurgent organization, holds elections and tests new leaders, organizes local defense units, eradicates remaining insurgents with help of indigenous forces.

Theorists such as Bernard Fall, Frank Kitson and Roger Trinquier emphasize other key aspects of vital importance such as: establishing an apparatus for collecting and handling intelligence, proactively infiltrating and eliminating active sanctuaries for insurgents, disseminating information in support of the counterinsurgent's cause and promoting political and economic progress.

The population centric theory is complex and regularly requires the military to act in non military capacities.

The diversity of tasks and the necessity to cooperate with so many entities make population centric counterinsurgency hard to execute successfully. In some ways the military mentality is more comfortable with the offensive nature of the enemy centric approach.

Some of the principles of enemy centric theory, however, are too harsh to be viable for many countries in the modern context. For this reason, the principles of population centric counterinsurgency theory are most widely accepted today. Current

U.S. military counterinsurgency doctrine is largely based on the theories of Galula, though adapted somewhat for current operations. There is considerable debate about the efficacy of enemy centric counterinsurgent strategy versus that of the population centric approach, however. This is a longstanding debate that is almost inherent to discourse amongst military professionals and theorists and often rooted in deeply held beliefs about foreign policy and the role of the military.

Some military officers and theorists claim that emphasizing population centric counterinsurgency is a denial of basic truths about the nature of warfare, negatively affects the capabilities of militaries that should remain ready for conventional battle, and ultimately leads to long entanglements in conflicts that do not serve greater security needs.

Conclusions vary, ranging from support for more kinetic enemy centric counterinsurgency campaigns to avoidance of counterinsurgency altogether. In response to prevailing support for population centric counterinsurgency, some military theorists, such as Gian P. Gentile and Ralph Peters, point out that many historical cases routinely used to show the merits of population centric counterinsurgency included many enemy centric qualities.

It is also posited that successes in many cases, such as during the surge in Iraq, are not necessarily a result of protecting the population, but of other factors such as reconciliation with key tribes and successful operations against the enemy. Paul Dixon points out that the British counterinsurgency in Malaya – a case used to argue for population centric approaches included many coercive aspects.

Dixon suggests that winning over 'hearts and minds' was not the driving force behind the success in Malaya, and that coercive measures fundamentally shaped the situation. It is argued that coercive measures are extremely necessary in counterinsurgency and that softer approaches are often touted for public consumption. As insurgencies, international politics and the political goals of nations and non state actors evolve and while debates continue, some form of counterinsurgency is unavoidable, at least in the near term. It is also clear that theories based on past counterinsurgency experience are not always effective in the context of current realities. Many of the insurgencies experienced by twentieth century counterinsurgency theorists and practitioners centered on the insurgents' efforts at developing their forces sufficiently to obtain power through military action.

Some theorists who work within the framework of generational warfare, however, claim that fourth generation warfare has introduced an evolved kind of insurgency. Military action is often only one tool in the hands of insurgents for shaping the opinions of distant governments and peoples. The war of information is increasingly the determining factor in asymmetrical conflicts involving major powers. Victory for the insurgent in this situation is persuading the counterinsurgent's nation that, "their strategic goals are either unachievable or too costly for the perceived benefit".

Despite the merits or demerits of the generational war paradigm, developments in world politics and technology affect insurgencies in significant ways. General David Petraeus acknowledges such developments and their impact on insurgencies, "If you look, as we did, at what [French military officer] David Galula faced in Algeria, you find, obviously, that he and his colleagues did not have to deal with a transnational extremist network enabled by access to the Internet". Many theorists and practitioners maintain that the highly agile and technologically adept character of modern insurgencies calls for a hybrid and adaptive approach to counterinsurgency – one that is neither solely population or enemy centric. Representative of this trend toward 'whatever works' is the attitude expressed by David Kilcullen, a retired military officer closely working with the United States military on questions of counterinsurgency. He claims that "my experience has been that both [enemy centric and population centric approaches] are applicable in varying degrees in most insurgencies.... The real art is to "read the battle" and understand how it is developing, fast enough to adapt.

Neither the enemy centric nor the population centric approaches are always or universally appropriate.... the correct approach is situation dependent". While Kilcullen cannot be separated from the ongoing debate on counterinsurgency strategies, many of his views do indicate a shift in the discourse towards comprehensive solutions that involve elements from a wide range of approaches.

There are certain aspects of counterinsurgency strategy that remain important regardless of what approach is favoured. Using the many tools of the state and not only military force is crucial. Integrating political, social and economic initiatives in a coordinated effort is important for addressing the many levels upon which insurgencies challenge the counterinsurgent's power. Such aspects include: understanding the local culture and people, cultivation of networks for intelligence, control of the population, elimination of active sanctuaries, adopting local solutions through junior leaders, information campaigns to support the counterinsurgent effort, and development of governmental and economic structures.

7

Civil Military Cooperation in Post-Taliban Afghanistan

After the fall of Taliban regime, development and humanitarian assistance have been recognized as one of the essential commitments of the international community towards reconstruction and development of Afghanistan. Another aspect of this strategic commitment was launching counterinsurgency and peacekeeping operations to ensure security. Therefore, one of the initiatives of the international coalition was introducing the PRT model with the objective of providing security and facilitating humanitarian and development interventions at the provincial level. After this model was successfully implemented in Garzdiz Province in 2003, the PRTs soon expanded and started operating in 26 provinces under the command of North Atlantic Treaty Organization (NATO).

Establishment of PRTs in Afghanistan rapidly led to the massive involvement of military, through the PRTs, in delivering humanitarian and development assistance. This humanitarian nature of PRTs raised intense debates concerning Civil-Military Cooperation trend among the humanitarian actors, especially due to the fact that the military humanitarian activities has blurred the line between humanitarian and military actors in the ground and seriously affected the neutral and impartial image of NGHAs among the local Afghan communities.

It is worth to mention here that in recent years several civil-military cooperation guidelines have been developed by the UN agencies and other NGHAs to improve the trend but none of these guidelines proved to be effective in improving Civil-Military Cooperation in Post-Taliban Afghanistan.

In contrast to what Thomas G. Weis, the author of *Military-Civilian Interactions* (1999) argues that the main role of military in the humanitarian space is to provide security and logistics. In Afghanistan, the PRTs have conversely accelerated their "winning hearts and minds" operations by launching a huge number of quick-impact programmes, aiming to gain community support. These operations, however, did not adhere to the humanitarian organizations standards, as constantly claimed by NGHAs (.

Surprisingly, it is not only the NGHAs who criticise the PRTs involvement in development and humanitarian affairs, very precise criticisms were made by the Afghan president, Hamid Karzai who mentioned that:

"Afghanistan clearly explained its viewpoint on Provincial Reconstruction Teams and structures parallel to the Afghan government ... bodies which are hindering the Afghan government's development and hindering the governance of Afghanistan".

However, NGHAs are concerned and the Afghan Government is frustrated concerning the deficient civil-military cooperation in Post-Taliban Afghanistan, the United States has officially endorsed – in addition to PRT's three main areas of responsibilities: security, reconstruction and support to the central government – the principle of military engagement in humanitarian operations in certain circumstances. The issue was further publicised last year by International Security Assistance Forces (ISAF) press release emphasising that:

"ISAF is also directly involved in facilitating the development and reconstruction of Afghanistan through Provincial Reconstruction Teams throughout the country" .

THE NGHAS PERSPECTIVE ON PRTS

In order to assess the present civil-military cooperation trend in Post-Taliban Afghanistan, it is very essential to examine the perception of NGHAs on the involvement of PRTs in delivering aid. The establishment of PRTs in Afghanistan has seriously increased the discontent of the NGHAs operating in Afghanistan under the international humanitarian principles. One of the commentaries made by NGHAs and further supported by ICRC is the issue of blurring line between the responsibilities of military and NGHAs in most of the local Afghan communities. The ICRC, while criticising this trend, described the "blurring line" phenomenon as follows:

"The distinction between humanitarian, political and military action becomes blurred when armed forces are perceived as being humanitarian actors, when civilians are embedded into military structures, and when the impression is created that humanitarian organizations and their personnel are merely tools within integrated approaches to conflict management".

In another scenario, the simultaneous dropping of bombs and aid packages by the US military in 2001, which were later justified as military relief operations, is another instance showing how has the line between responsibility and identity of military and civilian humanitarian actors been blurred.

This situation manifests that the civil-military cooperation has been affected and weakened from the very beginning, after the international community and coalition forces intervened in Afghanistan.

Furthermore, the uncoordinated humanitarian interventions, launched and implemented by PRTs, have contributed in endangering the lives of NGHAs aid workers in many ways. The civilian divisions of military teams, for instance, have made it difficult to physically distinguish the military personal from the aid workers.

This ambiguity has led the insurgents to target NGHAs staff, quite frequently assuming them as military. Similarly, when the UN Under-Secretary General for Humanitarian Affairs and Emergency Relief Coordinator, John Holmes, visited Afghanistan in June 2008, he expressed:

"I agree that there has been and there is to some extent a blurring of lines between military operations and, for example, humanitarian assistance by the PRTs. I think it is very important that PRTs do not

involve themselves in humanitarian assistance unless there is absolutely no other alternative for security reasons".

However, such emphasis never proved effective for convincing PRTs to terminate their relief operations.

At this point, the essay outlines four specific areas where NGHAs have increasingly suffered from the instrumentalisation of humanitarian aid by the military, on the one hand, and the blurred line of responsibilities between civilian and military actors, on the other.

The current military approach towards the civil-military cooperation trend and the military involvement in development and humanitarian activities undermined the humanitarian principles, overlapped the implemented projects, fuelled the violence and finally reduced the space for humanitarian actors in most of the Afghan local communities to operate.

Undermining Humanitarian Principles

Humanitarian aid is based on the principles drawn in the humanitarian code of conduct in which all NGHAs are committed to act accordingly.

The essence of these principles – Humanity, Neutrality and Impartiality – is to deliver humanitarian assistance to the vulnerable and needy population regardless of race, ethnic, nationality and political background.

Since the PRTs are deployed in Afghanistan for a military and political purpose, therefore; they cannot be perceived as humanitarian actors. The humanitarian actors expressed their concerns continuously about the issue. Save the Children Fund, for instance, declared the humanitarian involvement of military as: "*inappropriate and contrary to the fundamental humanitarian principles of independence and impartiality*". Some may argue that the military occupying power has a mandate to ensure the safety and security of the civilian population or NGHAs in the unstable and unsecure environments based on International Humanitarian Law and the 4th Geneva Convention.

This never means that the occupying military power can deliver humanitarian aid directly, nor it can legally justify involvement of military in relief operations. In contrast, the present military involvement in delivering humanitarian and development assistance is in violation of international humanitarian principles.

In another instance, a press release by NATO/ISAF on December 2007, declared that: "Humanitarian assistance operations are helping both the people of Afghanistan and coalition forces to fight the global war on terror". The integration of humanitarian assistance with a political agenda of war on terror has significantly undermined the principle of neutrality of NGHAs among the local Afghan population. Moreover, according to Donini ICRC is the only international organization that is able to operate neutrally, impartially and independently on both sides of the warring parties. However, thousands of NGHAs are operating in Afghanistan after the fall of Taliban.

Overlapping Interventions

In principle, the roles and responsibilities of PRTs and NGHAs are sharply different, however; in practice these responsibilities are extremely blurred. Under this circumstance, development and humanitarian actors have expressed their concerns about the overlapping of certain implemented projects in the field.

An assessment conducted by the Asian Development Bank (ADB) on Security of ADB Projects in Afghanistan in 2007 revealed a couple of substantial PRT interventions that contradict Article 32.4 of the United Nations Guideline for Civil-Military Cooperation. Here, the paper quotes some of the ADB assessment findings:

"Some PRTs include projects linked to health care, education, water supply or waste clearance, in this, there is an overlap with NGO programmes" (Marsden & Arnold, 2007; p.30)

"There is some evidence that some PRTs have provided cash to power holders or individual villagers in an effort to win influence" (Marsden & Arnold, 2005; p.31).

"Some PRTs, including those led by Spain and Italy, use military personnel for development work" (Marsden & Arnold, 2007, p.30).

As a result of PRT's constant intrusions without respecting the enacted civil-military cooperation guidelines, the United Nations

Office for the Coordination of Humanitarian Aid (UNOCHA) described the increasing influence of military in humanitarian activities as follows:

"In NATO and elsewhere there has been an evolution of the doctrine of military–civilian operations, with an increasing tendency for military forces being used to support the delivery of humanitarian aid, and sometimes even to provide this aid directly (Barry and Jefferys,2001, p. 1).

Moreover, another critique against the PRTs involvement in the development and humanitarian sphere is their unprofessionalism.

The military actors are not well-trained to implement complex cross-cutting and mutually reinforcing projects at the community level. This awkwardness is bolded in the areas of rebuilding the political institutions and effectively engaging with civil society actors.

Fuelling Violence

Increased violence against humanitarian aid workers is another consequence of the current ineffective civil-military cooperation in Post-Taliban Afghanistan. In the list of fragile countries where the level of violence against aid workers is enormously high, Afghanistan is positioned in third place. Relief operations by PRTs notably raised acts of violence against NGHAs. In 2004, for instance, five employee of Médecins Sans Frontières (MSF) were targeted and killed by insurgent. As a result, MSF evacuated its staff and stopped operating in Afghanistan. Moreover, an assessment conducted by the German Institute for International and Security Affairs, revealed that the security environment in northern provinces of Afghanistan has deteriorated and level of violence against aid workers has increased since the deployment of the German Military. It is noteworthy that the northern provinces of Afghanistan were considered highly secured regions after the fall of Taliban regime.

Appendix one is produced by Afghanistan NGO Security Organization (ANSO) which shows a 60% increase in the abduction of aid workers over the year 2009. According to the Afghanistan

NGO Safety Office (ANSO) the increased nature of insurgents' attacks on NGHAs, are functionally linked with a misperception that NGHAs have political and military agendas.

Such views were strongly publicised by the various international high officials like Colin Powell, the former US Secretary of States, who said: "NGOs are the force multiplier". Ultimately, the consequences of such publications were the death of 1500 civilians who were targeted by different insurgency attacks in 2010. Furthermore, a report by UNAMA contrasts the level of violence in 2001 with the level of violence in 2007. According to the report, in 2001 only 3 suicide attacks were carried out in Afghanistan, while after five years of international military presence in Afghanistan, this figure increased 53 times. In other words, 160 suicide bombing attacks were conducted by insurgents in 2006.

Reducing Humanitarian Space

The increased level of violence, is a restricting factor for the presence of NGHAs in most of the local Afghan communities. Humanitarian actors need "Humanitarian Space" in the conflict affected areas to independently and impartially identify conflict victims to assist them. This humanitarian space is getting limited, especially when PRTs interfere in providing aid by wearing civilian uniforms and driving unmarked vehicles in the local communities.

This humanitarian nature of the military posed another serious threat to the security of NGHAs since there is no distinguishing indicator left between them and the PRTs. MSF, for instance, was among those NGHAs that found itself in an eroded humanitarian space.

The justification given by MSF, after evacuating its staff and stopping all its operations in Afghanistan, was increased level of violence against their employees as a consequence of military involvement in providing humanitarian aid in the ground.

In another instance, a UK quartered NGO left its projects and withdrew from Kamdesh District because a US armed team visited the community without informing the local authorities in advance and prior consultation with the NGO (Afghanistan Group, 2008, p. 22).

In appendix two, the figures shown in the circles are the total number of armed NATO forces in each province. Regions that are coloured in red means a 50% of growth in Armed Opposition Groups (AOG) attacks. It is interesting to see in Herat Province, for instance, the number of NATO forces is fewer – 6,700 forces – compared to Helmand – 31,000 forces – but still the level of violence in Helmand had a 50% growth over the year 2009. This shows that the presence of military in the local Afghan communities have contributed to the growth of violence.

To condemn the erosion of humanitarian space in Afghanistan, The Agency Coordinating Body for Afghan Relief (ACBAR) released a statement in 2007, mentioning that:

"Humanitarian actors are increasingly unable to provide adequate protection and assistance to displaced people and other populations at risk in the south and east of Afghanistan due to the significant deterioration in the security situation. Humanitarian space and humanitarian access continues to be seriously limited".

Moreover, existence of great insecurity against the NGHAs significantly decreased the possibilities of accessing the needy population in most of the Afghan communities. Studies carried out by UNHCR and ICRC demonstrates that large part of the country is inaccessible by NGHAs. UNHCR claimed that in 2008, they only had access to 55% of the country and ICRC declared that the humanitarian access situation was the worst in the last 27 years in Afghanistan in 2008.

REGIONAL STRATEGY

Any strategy for Afghanistan should be integrated into a broader approach to the Central Asia region. Afghanistan's neighbours are capable of helping or harming Afghanistan's stability and development, and, simultaneously, are themselves affected by developments in the country. International attention to Afghanistan and its neighbours should be calibrated to maintain strategic balance in the region and to minimize threats to stability and security emanating from the territory of any state. This includes serious attention to radical Islamic movements not only in Afghanistan, but also in Uzbekistan, and Pakistan. Among other things, this will require significant support for secular education systems and law enforcement. Simply pushing the problem from one country to another is not in the U.S. or international community's interests.

On the security front, the United States and its friends must support a regional strategy to address the drug trade and arms flows that have not only fuelled conflict in Afghanistan, but that have also undermined social well-being, good governance and stability in Tajikistan, Turkmenistan, Pakistan, and even Iran.

There is also an important role for regional planning and cooperation for mutually supportive development in the region. Afghanistan's economic potential depends on economic links to neighbours for everything from markets for its agricultural products, infrastructure investments, and a possible natural gas pipeline. Given high debt burdens and severe governance challenges throughout the region, addressing economic and political development in both a regional and bilateral context is imperative.

International Division of Labour

While primary responsibility for rebuilding Afghanistan rests with the people of the country, the United States and international community must avoid repeating the costly mistake of leaving Afghanistan to its fate after military victory is secured. With its weak central structures, various factions, and covetous neighbours, Afghanistan will require significant assistance from a range of countries and international institutions.

Coordination of international actors is more important in Afghanistan than in past reconstruction efforts due to Afghanistan's notable centrifugal tendencies; tendencies that will be exacerbated if not managed properly. Indeed, so great is the danger that the international community should think more in terms of a clear "division of labour" than about simple "coordination." Key tasks should be clearly delegated to various actors based on their comparative advantages, keeping competition among donors to an absolute minimum. Ongoing oversight of the various actors should be provided by a strong, central authority in the form of the Special Representative of the Secretary-General of the United Nations.

Unfortunately, the international community is not off to a good start in terms of donor coordination. Institutional rivalries have prevented setting up common, cooperative oversight structures, and an appropriate leadership role for the Special Representative of the Secretary-General has not yet been established.

If a marked improvement is not realized by the end of the donor pledging conference in January, the entire effort in Afghanistan will be significantly compromised. This is an issue worthy of considerable diplomatic U. S. engagement.

One key area that will require special donor coordination is that of conditionalities on assistance. There are four major areas in which conditionality has already been discussed: clearing financial arrears; narcotics cooperation; human rights; and participation of women. Because the incipient Afghan government is so weak and so dependent on international assistance, conditionalities must be carefully calibrated.

A key step to effective coordination will be ensuring a comprehensive, joint assessment of Afghanistan's needs, as was successfully done in Guatemala, and at least somewhat successfully in East Timor.

This process should build on the initial World Bank/UNDP/ADB assessment prepared for the January donors' conference, and should actively involve more Afghan participation, as well as that of other international actors.

This would not only help create a common understanding of the challenges ahead among donors and Afghan leaders, it would also spare a fractured, weary Afghan society from the many repetitive and competing assessments that have already begun. This joint assessment approach should be agreed upon in January. While a joint assessment would help establish a division of labour with respect to specific responsibilities, some of the general comparative advantages of the various donors are already quite evident.

The United Nations should play a leadership role in three areas in particular: managing support for the political process in Afghanistan; overseeing donor coordination efforts; and managing humanitarian assistance programs. The Special Representative of the Secretary General should take the lead in supporting the political process, and should also be provided sufficient authority and resources to oversee coordination of all outside actors operating in Afghanistan. The UN's sponsorship of the Bonn agreement demonstrates its legitimacy and authority as a neutral representative in a politically charged environment.

This impartiality will be critical in assisting and strengthening the Afghan interim authority's ability to lay the foundations for the country's future political structure.

On the humanitarian side, UN agencies such as WFP, UNHCR, and UNICEF are already administering and disbursing humanitarian aid flows to vulnerable populations. In addition, UN agencies such as UNHCR, WHO, UNDP, and IOM have comparative advantages in everything from refugee repatriation, provision of key health services, community based social and economic development, and integration of the Afghan diaspora, among other issues.

Similarly, the World Bank, UNDP, and the Asian Development Bank should provide leadership in the economic rejuvenation of Afghanistan.

They are sufficiently resourced and experienced to provide assistance in the areas of employment generation, infrastructure, and agriculture reform that will lay the foundation for trade, investment, and sustainable economic activity. The World Bank's economic recovery programs should stress good governance practices in order to ensure efficiency and effectiveness. Additionally, the World Bank, in cooperation with the UN Special Representative of the Secretary General and UNDP, should administer and coordinate reconstruction funds through the establishment of a multi-donor "trust fund."

In addition to refraining from meddling in internal Afghan affairs, regional actors should also be prepared to play a helpful and supportive role by offering diplomatic and financial assistance for Afghanistan's emerging political reorientation. On the diplomatic side, a "Friends of Afghanistan" group, consisting at a minimum of its neighbours (Pakistan, Iran, Tajikistan, Uzbekistan, Turkmenistan, and China), plus the United States, Russia, the EU and Japan, should be assembled to provide political stability in the region, guarantee the sanctity of Afghanistan's porous borders, and prevent spoilers from jeopardizing the success of Afghanistan's government.

Assistance to regional actors in dealing with their own internal development needs should be considered part of the larger vision of post-conflict reconstruction in the region.

The United States, due to its role in the military campaign and concerns about "superpower intentions" in the region, should not establish or maintain a large, high profile presence on the ground in Afghanistan. At the same time, there are a number of important actions the U.S. government can take to help Afghanistan in order to protect its own interests.

The U.S. could avoid leaving a large "footprint" by assisting significantly through financial and diplomatic means. The U.S. will be well positioned to help promote the work of other multilateral actors through its position on the boards of international lending institutions, and its general interest in supporting open societies in Central Asia. Additionally, the U.S. has strong capacity to lead an external "over the horizon" rapid reaction force in support of the UN-authorized interim security force. Furthermore, the United States could continue to play a central role in the provision of humanitarian assistance.

Other bilateral donors, mainly EU members and Japan, should emphasize different areas for assistance. The UK is leading a UN-authorized multinational security force; Germany and France have offered significant military capabilities, and all other 12 EU members have announced their interest in participating.

In addition to meeting these security requirements, EU countries should focus their assistance on financial and technical support for UN-administered humanitarian assistance programs and for long-range social and economic development. Similarly, Japan has offered limited military resources that could be used in supporting international peacekeeping initiatives.

Japan's sponsorship of the Tokyo donors' conference is another indication of its commitment to supporting post-conflict reconstruction in Afghanistan. There may also be a role for China in supporting the regional infrastructure need. Participation by China in this larger project may be an important way to bring in a major regional actor. Turkey has indicated an interest in working with the Afghan interim administration on development of an Afghan police force and national army.

8

Change in U.S. Policy Towards Afghanistan

During the Clinton administration the U.S. had no clear policy towards Afghanistan until 1998-1999 and tended to favour Pakistani policies. In 1997, U.S. State Department's Robin Raphel told anti-Taliban leader Ahmad Shah Massoud to surrender to the Taliban. Massoud answered that as long as he controlled an area the size of his hat he would continue to defend it from the Taliban. Robin Raphel eventually became a lobbyist and adviser at Cassidy & Associates.

The firm had a $1.2 million contract with the Musharraf military regime of Pakistan. At Cassidy & Associates she lobbied and advised Congress and the State Department for Pakistan on issues such as Afghan policy, Pakistan's relations with India, judicial independence and U.S. perceptions and congressional views of the Pakistan government. In late 2009 Raphel was (again) appointed to the Af-Pak region as deputy to Richard Holbrooke, the late US. Special Representative to Afghanistan and Pakistan, by the Obama administration. Raphel will be the main person overlooking the $1.5 billion U.S. aid package "for non-military purpose" to Pakistan.

At one point in the war, in 1997, the Taliban were vulnerable and the road to the capital, Kabul, was wide open. Two top foreign policy officials in the Clinton administration flew to northern Afghanistan to convince – without success – the United Front not to take advantage of an opportunity to make crucial gains against the Taliban. Before the United Front could strike, Assistant Secretary of State Rick Indefurth and American U.N. Ambassador Bill Richardson flew to northern Afghanistan and tried to convince the leadership of the United Front that this was not the time for an offensive. Instead, they insisted this was the time for a cease-fire and an arms embargo. At the same time Pakistanis began a "Berlin-like airlift to resupply and re-equip the Taliban", financed with Saudi money.

United States policy towards Afghanistan changed after the 1998 United States embassy bombings. Subsequently, Osama Bin Laden was indicted for his involvement in the embassy bombings and in 1999 both the United States and the United Nations enacted sanctions against the Taliban via United Nations Security Council Resolution 1267 which demanded the Taliban surrender Osama Bin Laden for trial in the United States and close all Al Qaeda bases in Afghanistan. In the meantime, the only collaboration between Massoud and another U.S. intelligence service, the Central Intelligence Agency (CIA), consisted of an effort to trace Osama bin Laden following the 1998 embassy bombings. The U.S. and the European Union provided no support to Massoud for the fight against the Taliban.

A change of policy regarding support to Massoud, lobbied for by CIA officers who had visited Massoud, was underway during 2001. According to Steve Coll's book *Ghost Wars* (which won the 2005 Pulitzer Prize for General Non-Fiction):

The CIA officers admired Massoud greatly. They saw him as a Che Guevara figure, a great actor on history's stage. Massoud was a poet, a military genius, a religious man, and a leader of enormous courage who defied death and accepted its inevitability, they thought.... In his house there were thousands of books: Persian poetry, histories of the Afghan war in multiple languages, biographies of other military and guerrilla leaders. In their meetings Massoud wove sophisticated, measured references to Afghan history and global politics into his arguments. He was quiet, forceful, reserved, and full of dignity, but also light in spirit. The CIA team had gone into the Panshjir as unabashed admirers of Massoud. Now their convictions deepened. —Steve Coll in *Ghost Wars, 2004*

CIA lawyers, working with officers in the Near East Division and Counter-terrorist Center, began to draft a formal, legal presidential finding for Bush's signature authorizing a new covert action program in Afghanistan, the first in a decade that sought to influence the course of the Afghan war in favour of Massoud.

Richard A. Clarke, chair of the Counter-Terrorism Security Group under the Clinton administration, and later an official in the Bush administration, allegedly presented a plan to incoming Bush administration official Condoleezza Rice in January 2001.

A change in policy was finalized in August 2001. In late August 2001, the Bush administration, to pressure the Taliban to hand over leading al-Qaeda operatives, agreed on a plan to start giving support to the anti-Taliban forces of Ahmad Shah Massoud who sought to create a democratic form of government in Afghanistan.

Massoud until then had not received any meaningful support from Western countries. In a meeting by the Bush administration's top national security officials it was agreed that the Taliban in negotiations would be presented with a final ultimatum to hand over Osama bin Laden and other leading al-Qaeda operatives.

If the Taliban refused, covert military aid would be channeled by the U.S. to anti-Taliban groups. If both those options failed, "the deputies agreed that the United States would seek to overthrow the Taliban regime through more direct action."

9 September 2001

On his visit to Europe in March 2001 Ahmad Shah Massoud had warned that his intelligence had gathered information about a large-scale attack on U.S. soil being imminent.

Massoud's intelligence staff is aware that the attack against the U.S. will be on a scale larger than the 1998 embassy bombings, which killed over two hundred people and injured thousands.

On 9 September 2001, Massoud, then aged 48, was the target of a suicide attack by two Arabs posing as journalists detonating a bomb hidden in their video camera during an interview in Khoja Bahauddin, in the Takhar Province of Afghanistan. Massoud died in a helicopter taking him to a hospital. The funeral, though in a rather rural area, was attended by hundreds of thousands of mourning Afghans.

Massoud had survived countless assassination attempts over a period of 26 years. The assassination of Massoud is considered to have a strong connection to the 11 September 2001, attacks, which killed nearly 3,000 people, and which appeared to be the terrorist attack that Massoud had warned against in his speech to the European Parliament several months earlier. International experts and members of the United Front such as Amrullah Saleh feared that without Massoud the anti-Taliban resistance would be overrun by the Taliban.

11 September 2001

On 11 September 2001, in the early morning, a series of coordinated attacks took place on United States soil. Four commercial passenger jet airliners were hijacked. The hijackers intentionally crashed two of the airliners into the Twin Towers of the World Trade Center in New York City, killing everyone on board and many others working in the buildings. Both buildings collapsed within two hours, destroying nearby buildings and damaging others. The hijackers crashed a third airliner into the Pentagon in Arlington, Virginia, just outside Washington, D.C.

The fourth plane crashed into a field near Shanksville in rural Pennsylvania after some of its passengers and flight crew attempted to retake control of the plane, which the hijackers had redirected toward Washington, D.C to target the White House, or the Capitol. There were no survivors from any of the flights.

Nearly 3,000 people and the 19 hijackers died in the attacks. According to the New York State Health Department, 836 responders, including firefighters and police personnel, have died as of June 2009.

The United States identified members of the al-Qaeda movement based in Afghanistan as the perpetrators of the attacks.

Legal basis for war

The United Nations Charter, to which all the Coalition countries are signatories, provides that all UN member states must settle their international disputes peacefully and no member nation can use military force except in self-defence. The United States Constitution states that international treaties, such as the United Nations Charter, that are ratified by the U.S. are part of the law of the land in the U.S., though subject to effective repeal by any subsequent act of Congress (i.e., the "leges posteriores priores contrarias abrogant" or "last in time" canon of statutory interpretation). The United Nations Security Council (UNSC) did not authorize the U.S.-led military campaign in Afghanistan (Operation Enduring Freedom).

Defenders of the legitimacy of the U.S.-led invasion argue that U.N. Security Council authorization was not required since the invasion was an act of collective self-defence provided for under Article 51 of the UN Charter, and therefore was not a war of aggression. Critics maintain that the bombing and invasion of Afghanistan were not legitimate self-defence under Article 51 of the UN Charter because the 9/11 attacks were not "armed attacks" by another state, but rather were perpetrated by groups of individuals or non-state actors, and that these attackers had no proven connection to Afghanistan. Further, it is their opinion that even if a state had perpetrated the 9/11 attacks, no bombing campaign would constitute self-defence; the necessity for self-defence must be "instant, overwhelming, leaving no choice of means, and no moment for deliberation."

President George W. Bush was authorized by Congress on 14 September 2001, by legislation titled Authorization for Use of Military Force Against Terrorists which was passed and signed on 18 September 2001, by both President Bush and congress. This legislation authorized the use of United States Armed Forces against those responsible for the attacks on 11 September 2001. The authorization granted the President the authority to use all "necessary and appropriate force" against those whom he determined "planned, authorized, committed or aided" the 11 September attacks, or who harbored said persons or groups.

The Bush administration, for its part, did not seek a declaration of war by the U.S. Senate, and labeled Taliban troops as supporters of terrorists rather than soldiers, denying them the protections of the Geneva Convention and due process of law. This position was successfully challenged in the U.S. Supreme Court and questioned even by military lawyers responsible for prosecuting affected prisoners. On 20 December 2001, more than two months after the U.S.-led attack began, the UNSC authorized the creation of an International Security Assistance Force (ISAF) to take all measures necessary to fulfill its mandate of assisting the Afghan Interim Authority in maintaining security. Command of the ISAF passed to NATO on 11 August 2003.

2001: Initial attack

On 20 September 2001, U.S. president George W. Bush addressed the United States Congress and demanded that the Taliban deliver Osama bin Laden and destroy bases of al Qaeda. On 5 October 2001, the Taliban offered to try Bin Laden in an Afghan court, so long as the United States provided what it called "solid evidence" of his guilt, but the U.S. would not hand over its evidence to the Taliban. So on 7 October 2001, the U.S. government launched military operations in Afghanistan. Teams from the CIA's Special Activities Division (SAD) were the first U.S. forces to enter Afghanistan and begin combat operations. They were soon joined by U.S. Army Special Forces from the 5th Special Forces Group and other units from USSOCOM. On 7 October 2001, airstrikes were reported in the capital, Kabul (where electricity supplies were severed), at the airport, at Kandahar (home of the Taliban's Supreme Leader Mullah Omar), and in the city of Jalalabad. CNN released exclusive footage of Kabul being bombed to all the American broadcasters at approximately 5:08 pm October 7, 2001.

At 17:00 UTC, President Bush confirmed the strikes on national television and Prime Minister of the United Kingdom Tony Blair also addressed the UK. Bush stated that Taliban military sites and terrorist training grounds would be targeted. In addition, food, medicine, and supplies would be dropped to "the starving and suffering men, women and children of Afghanistan". US officials rejected a new offer from the Taliban to hand over Osama bin Laden to a third country for trial if the Americans halted the bombing of Afghanistan. A prerecorded videotape of Osama bin

Laden had been released before the attacks in which he condemned any attacks against Afghanistan. Al Jazeera, theArabic satellite news channel, reported that these tapes were received shortly before the attack.

British and American special forces worked jointly to liberate Herat in November 2001. These forces worked with Afghan opposition groups on the ground, in particular the Northern Alliance. The United Kingdom, Canada and Australia also deployed forces and several other countries provided basing, access and overflight permission.

The U.S. was able to track al-Qaeda's number three at the time Mohammed Atef who was one of the most wanted, when Atef was killed, along with his guard Abu Ali al-Yafi'i and six others, in a U.S. air-strike on his home near Kabul during the U.S. invasion of Afghanistan at some time between 14–16 November 2001. This was one of America's first and largest victories during the early stages of the war.

Air Campaigns

"Having begun the war with the greatest imaginable reservoir of moral authority, the U.S. was on the verge of letting it slip away through high-level attacks using the most ghastly inventions its scientists could come up with." —Stephen Tanner, "Afghanistan: A Military History from Alexander the Great to the War against the Taliban"

Bombers operating at high altitudes well out of range of antiaircraft guns dropped bombs at Afghan training camps and Taliban air defenses. U.S. aircraft, including Apache helicopter gunships from the 101st Combat Aviation Brigade, operated with impunity throughout the campaign with no losses due to Taliban air defenses.

The strikes initially focused on the area in and around the cities of Kabul, Jalalabad, and Kandahar. Within a few days, most Taliban training sites were severely damaged and the Taliban's air defenses were destroyed. The campaign then focused on command, control, and communication targets which weakened the ability of the Taliban forces to communicate. However, the line facing the

Afghan Northern Alliance held, and no tangible battlefield successes had yet occurred on that front. Two weeks into the campaign, the Northern Alliance demanded the air campaign focus more on the front lines.

The next stage of the campaign began with carrier based F/A-18 Hornet fighter-bombers hitting Taliban vehicles in pinpoint strikes, while other U.S. planes began cluster bombing Taliban defenses. For the first time in years, Northern Alliance commanders finally began to see the substantive results that they had long hoped for on the front lines. At the beginning of November, the Taliban front lines were bombed with daisy cutter bombs, and by AC-130gunships. The Taliban fighters had no previous experience with American firepower, and often even stood on top of bare ridgelines where Special Forces could easily spot them and call in close air support. By 2 November, Taliban frontal positions were devastated, and a Northern Alliance march on Kabul seemed possible for the first time.

However, according to author Stephen Tanner, "After a month of the U.S. bombing campaign rumblings began to reach Washington from Europe, the Mideast, and Pakistan where Musharraf had requested the bombing to cease. Having begun the war with the greatest imaginable reservoir of moral authority, the U.S. was on the verge of letting it slip away through high-level attacks using the most ghastly inventions its scientists could come up with." Then US-President George W. Bush went to New York City on 10 November 2001, "where the wreckage of the World Trade Center still smoldered with underground fires", to address the United Nations and told the assembled nations that not only the United States are in danger of further attacks of the 9/11 terrorists, but also every other countries in the world. Tanner writes: "His words had impact. Most of the world renewed its support for the American effort, including commitments of material help from Germany, France, Italy, Japan and other countries."

Fighters from al-Qaeda took over security in the Afghan cities, demonstrating the instability of the Taliban regime. Meanwhile, the Northern Alliance and their Central Intelligence Agency/Special Forces advisers planned the next stage of their offensive. Northern

Alliance troops would seize Mazari Sharif, thereby cutting off Taliban supply lines and enabling the flow of equipment from the countries to the north, followed by an attack on Kabul itself.

Areas Most Targeted

During the early months of the war the U.S. military had a limited presence on the ground. The plan was that Special Forces, and intelligence officers with a military background, would serve as liaisons with Afghan militias opposed to the Taliban, would advance after the cohesiveness of the Taliban forces was disrupted by American air power.

The Tora Bora Mountains lie roughly east of Afghanistan's capital Kabul, which is itself close to the border with Pakistan. American intelligence analysts believed that the Taliban and al-Qaeda had dug in behind fortified networks of well-supplied caves and underground bunkers. The area was subjected to a heavy continuous bombardment by B-52 bombers. The U.S. forces and the Northern Alliance also began to diverge in their objectives. While the U.S. was continuing the search for Osama bin Laden, the Northern Alliance was pressuring for more support in their efforts to finish off the Taliban and control the country.

Battle of Mazar-i Sharif

The battle for Mazari Sharif was considered important, not only because it is the home of the Shrine of Hazrat Ali or "Blue Mosque", a sacred Muslim site, but also because it is the location of a significant transportation hub with two main airports and a major supply route leading into Uzbekistan. It would also enable humanitarian aid to alleviate Afghanistan's looming food crisis, which had threatened more than six million people with starvation.

Many of those in most urgent need lived in rural areas to the south and west of Mazar-i-Sharif. On 9 November 2001, Northern Alliance forces, under the command of generals Abdul Rashid Dostum and Ustad Atta Mohammed Noor, swept across the Pul-i-Imam Bukhri bridge, meeting some resistance, and seized the city's main military base and airport. U.S. Special Operations Forces (namely Special Forces Operational Detachment A-595, CIA paramilitary officers and Air Force Combat Control Teams) on horseback and using Close Air Support platforms, took part in the push into the city of Mazari Sharif in Balkh Province by the Northern Alliance. After a bloody 90-minute battle, Taliban forces, who had held the city since 1998, withdrew from the city, triggering jubilant celebrations among the townspeople whose ethnic and political affinities are with the Northern Alliance.

The Taliban had spent three years fighting the Northern Alliance for Mazar-i-Sharif, precisely because its capture would confirm them as masters of all Afghanistan. The fall of the city was a "body blow" to the Taliban and ultimately proved to be a "major shock", since the United States Central Command (CENTCOM) had originally believed that the city would remain in Taliban hands well into the following year, and any potential battle would be "a very slow advance".

Following rumours that Mullah Dadullah was headed to recapture the city with as many as 8,000 Taliban fighters, a thousand American 10th Mountain Soldiers were airlifted into the city, which provided the first solid foothold from which Kabul and Kandahar could be reached.

While prior military flights had to be launched from Uzbekistan or Aircraft carriers in the Arabian Sea, now the Americans held their own airport in the country which allowed them to fly more frequent sorties for resupply missions and humanitarian aid. These missions allowed massive shipments of humanitarian aid to be immediately shipped to hundreds of thousands of Afghans facing starvation on the northern plain.

The American-backed forces now controlling the city began immediately broadcasting from *Radio Mazar-i-Sharif,* the former Taliban *Voice of Sharia*channel on 1584 kHz, including an address from former President Burhanuddin Rabbani.

Fall of Kabul

On the night of 12 November, Taliban forces fled from the city of Kabul, leaving under the cover of darkness. By the time Northern Alliance forces arrived in the afternoon of 13 November, only bomb craters, burned foliage, and the burnt-out shells of Taliban gun emplacements and positions were there to greet them. A group of about twenty hardline fighters hiding in the city's park were the only remaining defenders. This Taliban group was killed in a 15-minute gun battle, being heavily outnumbered and having had little more than a telescope to shield them. After these forces were neutralized Kabul was in the hands of the U.S./NATO forces and the Northern Alliance.

The fall of Kabul marked the beginning of a collapse of Taliban positions across the map. Within 24 hours, all the Afghan provinces along the Iranian border, including the key city of Herat, had fallen.

Local Pashtun commanders and warlords had taken over throughout northeastern Afghanistan, including the key city of Jalalabad. Taliban holdouts in the north, mainly Pakistani volunteers, fell back to the northern city of Kunduz to make a stand. By 16 November, the Taliban's last stronghold in northern Afghanistan was besieged by the Northern Alliance. Nearly 10,000 Taliban fighters, led by foreign fighters, refused to surrender and continued to put up resistance. By then, the Taliban had been forced back to their heartland in southeastern Afghanistan around Kandahar.

By 13 November, al-Qaeda and Taliban forces, with the possible inclusion of Osama bin Laden, had regrouped and were concentrating their forces in the Tora Bora cave complex, on the Pakistan border 50 kilometers (30 mi) southwest of Jalalabad, to prepare for a stand against the Northern Alliance and U.S./NATO forces. Nearly 2,000 al-Qaeda and Taliban fighters fortified themselves in positions within bunkers and caves, and by 16 November, U.S. bombers began bombing the mountain fortress. Around the same time, CIA and Special Forces operatives were already at work in the area, enlisting and paying local warlords to join the fight and planning an attack on the Tora Bora complex.

Fall of Kunduz

Just as the bombardment at Tora Bora was stepped up, the siege of Kunduz that began on November 16 was continuing. Finally, after nine days of heavy fighting and American aerial bombardment, Taliban fighters surrendered to Northern Alliance forces on November 25 – November 26. Shortly before the surrender, Pakistani aircraft arrived to evacuate intelligence and military personnel who had been in Afghanistan to aid the Taliban's ongoing fight against the Northern Alliance. However, during this airlift, it is alleged that up to five thousand people were evacuated from the region, including Taliban and al-Qaeda troops.

Battle of Qala-i-Jangi

On 25 November, the day that Taliban fighters holding out in Kunduz surrendered and were being herded into theQala-I-Janghi fortress near Mazar-I-Sharif, a few Taliban attacked some Northern Alliance guards, taking their weapons and opening fire. This incident soon triggered a widespread revolt by 300 prisoners, who soon seized the southern half of the complex, once a medieval fortress, including an armory stocked with small arms and crew-served weapons. One American CIA paramilitary operative who had been interrogating prisoners, Johnny Micheal Spann, was killed, marking the first American combat death in the war. The revolt was finally put down after seven days of heavy fighting between an SBS unit along with some U.S. Army Special Forces and Northern Alliance, AC-130 gunships and other aircraft took part providing strafing fire on several occasions, as well as a bombing airstrikes. A total of 86 of the Taliban prisoners survived, and around 50 Northern Alliance soldiers were killed. The squashing of the revolt marked the end of the combat in northern Afghanistan, where local Northern Alliance warlords were now firmly in control.

SECURITY POLICY: TRANSITION, AND BEYOND

The Obama Administration policy goal is to prevent Afghanistan from again becoming a safe haven for terrorist organizations. The Administration has defined that goal as enabling the Afghan government and security forces to defend the country and govern effectively and transparently. Under an agreement announced after a meeting between President Obama and President Karzai in Washington, DC, on January 11, 2013, the U.S. security mission was to change from combat leadership to a "support" role by the end of June 2013. That transition was announced on June 18, 2013. Even with Afghan forces now in the lead, many of the pillars of U.S. and NATO security strategy will remain intact at least until the end of 2014 and possibly, to some extent, beyond that. The United States remains partnered with 49 other countries and the Afghan government and security forces. On February 10, 2013, Marine General Joseph Dunford succeeded Lieutenant General John Allen as top U.S. and NATO commander in Afghanistan.

Who Is "The Enemy"? Taliban, Haqqani, Al Qaeda, and Others. Security in Afghanistan is challenged by several armed groups, loosely allied with each other. There is not agreement about the relative strength of insurgents in the areas where they operate.

Groups: The Taliban/"Quetta Shura Taliban"(QST)

The core insurgent faction in Afghanistan remains the Taliban movement, much of which remains at least nominally loyal to Mullah Muhammad Umar, leader of the Taliban regime during 19962001. Although press reports say even many of his top aides do not see him regularly, he and those subordinates reportedly still operate from Pakistan, probably the city of Quetta but possibly also Karachi. This accounts for the term usually applied to Umar and his aides: "Quetta Shura Taliban" (QST). In recent years, Umar has lost some of this top aides and commanders to U.S.-led military action or Pakistan arrests, including Mullah Dadullah, Mullah Obeidullah Akhund, and Mullah Usmani.

Some of Umar's inner circle has remained intact, and the release by Pakistan of several top Taliban figures close to Umar has helped him restore the leadership circle. Mullah Abdul Ghani Bradar, was arrested by Pakistan in February 2010 for purportedly trying to engage in negotiations with the Afghan government without Pakistani concurrence; he was released to house arrest/ close surveillance in September 2013.

Other pragmatists around Umar include Akhtar Mohammad Mansoor, a logistics expert and head of the Taliban's senior *shura* council; Shahabuddin Delawar; Noorudin Turabi; and several other figures released by Pakistan since late 2012.

Umar and the pragmatists reportedly blame their past association with Al Qaeda for their loss of power. Signals of Mullah Umar's potential for compromise have been several statements, including one on the 10th anniversary of the September 11 attacks, acknowledging there have been some settlement talks; and another on October 24, 2012, that the Taliban does not seek to regain a monopoly of power.

The pragmatists are facing debate from younger and reputedly hardline, anti-compromise leaders such as Mullah Najibullah (a.k.a. Umar Khatab) and Mullah Abdul Qayyum Zakir.

Zakir, a U.S. detainee in Guantanamo Bay, Cuba until 2007, is the top military commander of the Taliban and purportedly believes outright Taliban victory is possible after 2014. The Taliban has several official spokespersons, including Qari Yusuf Ahmadi and Zabiullah Mujahid. It operates a clandestine radio station, "Voice of Shariat" and publishes videos.

Al Qaeda/Bin Laden

U.S. officials have long considered Al Qaeda to have been largely expelled from Afghanistan itself, characterizing Al Qaeda militants in Afghanistan as facilitators of militant incursions into Afghanistan rather than active fighters.

U.S. officials put the number of Al Qaeda fighters in Afghanistan at between 50-100, who operate mostly in provinces of eastern Afghanistan such as Kunar. Some of these fighters belong to Al Qaeda affiliates such as the Islamic Movement of Uzbekistan (IMU), which is active in Faryab and Konduz provinces.

Until the death of Bin Laden at the hands of a U.S. Special Operations Force raid on May 1, 2011, there had been frustration within the U.S. government with the search for Al Qaeda's top leaders.

In December 2001, in the course of the post-September 11 major combat effort, U.S. Special Operations Forces and CIA operatives reportedly narrowed Osama Bin Laden's location to the Tora Bora mountains in Nangarhar Province (30 miles west of the Khyber Pass), but Afghan militia fighters surrounding the area did not prevent his escape into Pakistan. Some U.S. officials later publicly questioned the U.S. decision to rely mainly on Afghan forces in this engagement.

U.S. efforts to find Al Qaeda leaders reportedly focus on his close ally Ayman al-Zawahiri, who is also presumed to be on the Pakistani side of the border and who was named new leader of Al Qaeda in June 2011.

CNN reported October 18, 2010, that assessments from the U.S.-led coalition said Zawahiri was likely in a settled area, and not in a remote area. A U.S. strike reportedly missed Zawahiri by a few hours in the village of Damadola, Pakistan, in January 2006.

Many observers say that Zawahiri is increasingly focused on taking political advantage of the Arab uprisings, particularly in Egypt where a Muslim Brotherhood leader, Mohammad Morsi, became president but then was ousted by the Egyptian military in July 2013. Other senior Al Qaeda leaders are said to be in Iran, including Sayf al Adl, although another figure, Sulayman Abu Ghaith, son-in-law of bin Laden, was expelled by Iran in March 2013. The United States has called on Iran to arrest and submit any Al Qaeda operatives to international authorities for trial.

U.S. efforts—primarily through armed unmanned aerial vehicles—have killed numerous other senior Al Qaeda operatives in recent years. In August 2008, an airstrike was confirmed to have killed Al Qaeda chemical weapons expert Abu Khabab al-Masri, and two senior operatives allegedly involved in the 1998 embassy bombings in Africa reportedly were killed by an unmanned aerial vehicle strike in January 2009. Following the killing of Bin Laden, three top operational leaders, Ilyas Kashmiri, Attiyah Abd al-Rahman, and Abu Yahya al-Libi were killed in Pakistan by reported U.S. drone strikes in June and August 2011 and June 2012, respectively.

Hikmatyar Faction (HIG)

Another significant insurgent leader is former *mujahedin* party leader Gulbuddin Hikmatyar, who leads Hizb-e-Islami-Gulbuddin (HIG). The faction received extensive U.S. support against the Soviet Union, but turned against its *mujahedin* colleagues after the Communist government fell in 1992. The Taliban displaced HIG as the main opposition to the 1992-1996 Rabbani government. HIG's areas of activity include Kunar, Nuristan, Kapisa, and Nangarhar provinces, north and east of Kabul, but it is not a major factor on the Afghanistan battlefield.

The group is ideologically and politically allied with Al Qaeda and Taliban insurgents, but its fighters have sometimes clash with the Taliban over control of territory. A suicide bombing on September 18, 2012, which killed 12 persons, including eight South African nationals working for a USAID-chartered air service, was allegedly carried out by a female HIG member.

HIG claimed responsibility for a suicide bombing in Kabul on May 16, 2013, that killed six Americans, including two soldiers and four Dyncorps contractors. On February 19, 2003, the U.S. government formally designated Hikmatyar as a "specially designated global terrorist," under Executive Order 13224, subjecting it to a freeze of any U.S.-based assets. The group is *not* designated as a "Foreign Terrorist Organization" (FTO).

Although it continues to conduct attacks, HIG is widely considered amenable to a reconciliation deal with Kabul. In January 2010, Hikmatyar outlined conditions for reconciliation, including elections under a neutral caretaker government following a U.S. withdrawal. On March 22, 2010, both the Afghan government and HIG representatives confirmed talks in Kabul, including meetings with Karzai, and Karzai subsequently acknowledged additional meetings with group representatives. Some close to Hikmatyar attended the consultative peace *loya jirga* on June 2-4, 2010, which discussed the reconciliation issue. HIG figures met government representatives at a June 2012 academic conference in Paris and a follow up meeting in Chantilly, France, on December 20-21, 2012.

Haqqani Faction

Another militant faction, cited by U.S. officials as perhaps the most potent threat to Afghan security, is the "Haqqani Network," founded by Jalaludin Haqqani, a *mujahedin* commander and U.S. ally during the U.S.-backed war against the Soviet Union. He subsequently joined the Taliban regime (1996-2001), serving as its Minister of Tribal Affairs.

Since 2001, the network has staunchly opposed the Karzai government, and his faction is believed closer to Al Qaeda than to the Taliban—in part because one of the elder Haqqani's wives is Arab. Over the past few years, he has delegated operation control to his sons Siraj (Sirajjudin), Badruddin, and Nasiruddin, although Badruddin was reportedly killed in a U.S. or Pakistani strike in late August 2012.

Suggesting it may sometimes act as a tool of Pakistani interests, the Haqqani network, which reputedly has 3,000 fighters and supporters, has primarily targeted Indian interests.

It claimed responsibility for two attacks on India's embassy in Kabul (July 2008 and October 2009), and is considered likely responsible for the August 4, 2013 attack on India's consulate in Jalalabad.

No Indian diplomats were injured in the Jalalabad attack, but nine Afghans were killed. U.S. officials attribute the June 28, 2011, attack on the Intercontinental Hotel in Kabul; a September 10, 2011, truck bombing in Wardak Province (which injured 77 U.S. soldiers); and attacks on the U.S. Embassy and ISAF headquarters in Kabul on September 13, 2011 to the Haqqani group as well.

That the faction is tolerated or protected in the North Waziristan area of Pakistan and also its purported ties to Pakistan's Inter-Services Intelligence Directorate (ISI) has caused U.S. criticism of Pakistan.

The ISI is believed to see the Haqqanis as a potential ally in any Afghan political structure that might be produced by a political settlement in Afghanistan. The most widely cited criticism was by then Joint Chiefs of Staff Chairman Mullen, following September 2011 attacks on U.S. Embassy Kabul, who testified (Senate Armed Services Committee) on September 22, 2011, that the Haqqani network acts "as a veritable arm" of the ISI. Other senior officials issued more announced versions of that assertion.

Many consider the faction less ideological than the Taliban—interested primarily in earning funds through licit and illicit businesses in Pakistan and the Persian Gulf and in controlling parts of Khost Province.

Such interests could make the faction amenable to a political settlement. On November 13, 2012, a top Haqqani commander said that the Haqqani Network would participate in political settlement talks with the United States if Taliban leader Mullah Umar decided to undertake such talks, and a Haqqani representative reportedly was stationed at the Taliban office in Doha, Qatar that was opened on June 18, 2013 but later closed. It has also been reported that U.S. officials met with Haqqani representatives in 2011 in UAE.

The faction's calculations might be affected by how the United States characterizes the group. In July 2010, then-top U.S. commander in Afghanistan General David Petraeus advocated that the Haqqani network be named as an FTO under the Immigration and Naturalization Act. Some in the State Department reportedly opposed an FTO designation because that could complicate efforts to conduct reconciliation talks with the faction or create pressure for Pakistan to be named a state sponsor of terrorism.

A number of Haqqani leaders had already been sanctioned as Specially Designated Global Terrorists (SDGT) under Executive Order 13224. In the 112th Congress, S. 1959 (Haqqani Network Terrorist Designation Act of 2012), enacted on August 10, 2012 (P.L. 112-168). It required, within 30 days of enactment, an Administration report on whether the group meets the criteria for FTO designation and an explanation of a negative decision. On September 9, 2012, the Administration reported to Congress that the Haqqani Network meets the criteria for FTO designation.

Pakistani Groups

A major Pakistani group, the Pakistani Taliban (Tehrik-e-Taliban Pakistan, TTP), primarily challenges the government of Pakistan, but it supports the Afghan Taliban and some of its fighters reportedly are operating from safehavens in Taliban-controlled areas on the Afghan side of the border.

Based in part on a failed bombing in New York City in May 2010 allegedly by the TTP, the State Department designated the TTP as an FTO on September 2, 2010. Its current leader, Hakimullah

Mehsud, was named as terrorism supporting entities that day. He succeeded Baitullah Mehsud, who was killed in a U.S. drone strike in August 2009. Another Pakistani group said to be increasingly active inside Afghanistan is Laskhar-e-Tayyiba (LET, or Army of the Righteous). LET is an Islamist militant group that has previously been focused on operations against Indian control of Kashmir.

Some assess the group as increasingly active in South Asia and elsewhere, and could rival Al Qaeda or Al Qaeda affiliates as potential threat to U.S. interests. Another Pakistan-based group that is said to be somewhat active in Afghanistan is Lashkar-i-Janghvi—it was accused of several attacks on Afghanistan's Hazara Shiite community during 2011-2012.

Insurgent Tactics

As far as tactics, prior to 2011, U.S. commanders worried most about insurgent use of improvised explosive devices (IEDs), including roadside bombs. In January 2010, President Karzai issued a decree banning importation of fertilizer chemicals (ammonium nitrate) commonly used for the roadside bombs, but there reportedly is informal circumvention of the ban for certain civilian uses, and the material reportedly still comes into Afghanistan from at least two major production plants in Pakistan.

U.S. commanders have said they have verified some use of surface-to-air missiles. It does not appear that sophisticated missiles were involved in the shootdown of a U.S. Chinook helicopter that killed 30 U.S. soldiers on August 6, 2011.

Some insurgents have used bombs hidden in turbans, which had, until October 2011, generally not been searched out of respect for Afghan religious traditions. Such a bomb killed former President Rabbani on September 20, 2011. A suicide bomber who wounded intelligence chief Asadullah Khalid in December 2012 might have had explosives surgically sewn into his body. A major concern, particularly during 2012, has been "insider attacks" (attacks on ISAF forces by Afghan security personnel, also known as "green on blue" attacks). These attacks, some of which apparently were carried out by Taliban infiltrators into the Afghan forces, declined by late 2012 but have continued occasionally in 2013.

9

The Incompatibility of Counterinsurgency and Nation

PEACE-BUILDING IN IRAQ AND AFGHANISTAN

In considering why great powers fail to vanquish much weaker foes in war, as has been the case in ongoing Western counter-insurgency (COIN) efforts in Afghanistan and Iraq, it is crucial to recognize several variables, notably the changes in the nature of warfare that have occurred since the late twentieth century, the contexts in which these conflicts have taken place, and recent innovations in measuring power that have manifested themselves in contemporary International Relations (IR) theory. While realist theory predicts without controversy that the most powerful state or balancing coalition will prevail in a military conflict (Waltz, 1979; Mearsheimer, 2001), recent empirical evidence from American involvement in the War on Terror, as well as past experiences, notably that of the Soviet Union in Afghanistan, belie this expectation.

With this in mind, this essay explores the question of why great powers lose wars against smaller and weaker adversaries as is currently occurring in Afghanistan, and as occurred when America was bloodied in the context of the war in Iraq. Beginning with an overview of the changing nature of warfare, specifically as it pertains to the rise of asymmetric conflict, guerilla warfare, and non-state military actors in the post-colonial period, the essay notes how the manner in which such groups are impervious to deterrence, and impossible to defeat through traditional force-on force combat, has changed the ontology of war. Concomitantly discussing context, the essay notes how the majority of recent conflicts, in which a great power has been defeated by a smaller force, have occurred in either states without stable governments, or in the throes of an overarching great power rivalry in which another powerful state has provided aid to the weaker force. On this basis, the essay thus argues that fundamental incompatibilities between the most kinetic elements of American COIN doctrine and the nation-building mission inherent to these emergent forms of conflict lies at the root of these ongoing difficulties.

On this basis, the essay shifts to empirics by first engaging in a brief overview of the Soviet experience in Afghanistan during the 1980s. While it does not directly pertain to ongoing difficulties vis-à-vis American COIN doctrine, it nevertheless represents a baseline of failure against which ongoing American involvement in Afghanistan and Iraq can be compared. Moving forward to case studies of the incompatibility of COIN and nation-building in Afghanistan and Iraq, the essay moves forward by proposing that the reasons underlying great powers' defeats in wars against weaker states are caused by a nexus made up of the increasingly asymmetric nature of warfare propelled forward by non-state actors, of the geopolitical and domestic-level contexts in which these conflicts take place, and of our discipline's antiquated and unrealistic conceptions of power.

In the specific case of NATO's current floundering in Afghanistan, the use of tactics like night raids and drone strikes, albeit successful in their kinetic intent, are portrayed as detrimental to the type of civil society reconstruction necessary to winning a war in a society as ethnically and tribally complex as Afghanistan. Similarly, the Iraqi case demonstrates an American intervention which was dichotomized into military and civil components which were not effectively coordinated in any reasonable sense of the term. Because of this both interventions suffered significantly, and brought about high body counts, because of the specific disjuncture between their kinetic COIN components and their nation-building ones. In concluding, the essay thus notes that IR must shed its traditional obsession with parsimony and mono-causal explanation, and accept that the defeat of great powers in small wars must be explained via idiographic rather than nomothetic theories. In this regard, the case study emerges as a logical vehicle for such exploration, and for more broadly understanding and refining the process by which COIN and nation-building can be brought to exist in effective congruence.

BUILDING INDIGENOUS CAPACITY

The quality and legitimacy of Afghan security forces, and argued that there were notable problems with the ANP. This section looks more specifically at the U.S. "light footprint" approach and the use of indigenous forces during operations. Metaphorically, counterinsurgency is about teaching people to fish, not about doing it for them. One of the most significant lessons from U.S. and coalition experiences in Afghanistan is the importance of advising, training, and assisting the host nation's ministries and security forces—and helping shift popular support from the insurgents to the host nation. For insurgent groups, popular support is an overriding strategic objective. As Mao Tse-tung argued, "The richest source of power to wage war lies in the masses of the people." Counterinsurgency operations must separate insurgents from their support base.

The United States adopted a two-pronged strategy for counterin-surgency operations in Afghanistan. The first part involved the establishment of an indigenous (rather than international) government. The public opinion polls conducted in 2003 and 2004 demonstrated that roughly 85 percent of Afghans interviewed had a "very favourable" or "somewhat favourable" view of Hamid Karzai, the first post-Taliban president of Afghanistan. The United States and its allies fostered the rapid creation of a national Afghan government that included representatives from major ethnic groups. This new government began to form even before major combat operations terminated. On December 5, 2001, Afghan delegates executed the Bonn Agreement, which established an interim administration under

Hamid Karzai and called for an Emergency Loya Jirga to establish a transitional authority.

Karzai became head of state in June 2002 and president in October 2004, following the country's first national election. The establishment of an interim indigenous—rather than international—government gave the population a sense of ownership. As Zalmay Khalilzad, special envoy and former U.S. ambassador to Afghanistan, argued, "The fact that the Afghans played a key role in their own liberation gave them a sense of dignity and ownership of their destiny."

The second prong of the U.S. approach involved maintaining a light military footprint in Afghanistan. The United States did not invade Afghanistan with large numbers of forces. U.S. officials adopted a light-footprint approach for several reasons: They wanted to prevent large-scale resistance similar to what the Soviet Union encountered in the 1980s; they believed that small numbers of ground troops and air-power were sufficient to establish security; and they were deeply reluctant to become involved in nation-building. Indeed, several great powers throughout history have been defeated in Afghanistan, including the forces of Alexander the Great, Great Britain, and the Soviet Union.

U.S. GEN Tommy Franks, who put together the operational concept for Afghanistan in 2001, argued that, after major combat ended, "our footprint had to be small, for both military and geopolitical reasons. We envisioned a total of about 10,000 American soldiers, airmen, special operators, and helicopter assault crews, along with robust in-country close air support."

This strategy worked well during the overthrow of the Taliban government. But it had two drawbacks for the stability operation phase, which began after the overthrow of the Taliban regime. First, there were too few U.S. and Afghan government forces to stabilize the country. Afghan militia forces had to full the security vacuum, which, in the long run, undermined the power of the central government. The per capita level of external forces in 17 stability operations since World War II. The United States had one of the lowest per capita levels in Afghanistan among all these operations, which even included a number of UN operations in

Africa and Asia. This created a challenge in targeting Taliban, Hezb-i-Islami, and al Qaeda insurgents in the early stages of the insurgency—such as 2002 and 2003—since there were virtually no trained and legitimate Afghan military and police. Nor were there sufficient forces to secure Afghanistan's borders. Insurgent forces benefited from porous borders along the Afghanistan-Pakistan frontier, as well as from assistance from sources in Pakistan and the Muslim world channeled through Pashtun tribesmen in the border region.

Second, this strategy drew the wrong lesson from the Soviet experience. The key lesson from the Soviet experience was not the number of Soviet forces deployed, but rather how they were used. The Soviets fought the wrong war; they fought a conventional war against an unconventional opponent. As one of the most comprehensive studies of Soviet combat tactics in Afghanistan concluded, "The Soviet Army that marched into Afghanistan was trained to fight within the context of a theatre war against a modern enemy who would obligingly occupy defensive positions stretching across the northern European plain." The Soviets used massed artillery, tanks, and ground forces to destroy acres of defense positions, and "Soviet tactics and equipment were designed solely to operate within the context of this massive strategic operation."

The Soviets fundamentally misunderstood the nature of counterinsurgency warfare. They terrorized the population instead of working to win the people over to the government's side. The United States, Pakistan, Saudi Arabia, and other governments exploited this resentment by providing military and financial assistance to the mujahideen. This brings up an important dilemma. A lead indigenous effort is critical over the long run for successful counterinsurgency operations. Even if tactically successful, a unilateral external operation may ultimately lead to failure by unseating the very indigenous capability that the external actor is trying to build. But what if there is no competent government force in the early stages of an insurgency? In the Afghan case, there were no Afghan army forces and no trained police. While there are no ideal options in these situations, the most effective strategy may be to (a) work with those legitimate indigenous forces (especially police) that exist; (b) effectively train and mentor them as quickly as possible; and (c) temporarily back-full indigenous security forces with sufficient numbers of U.S. and other international forces to accomplish key security tasks. These tasks include patrolling streets and villages, monitoring borders, and protecting critical infrastructure. Higher per capita levels of U.S. and coalition military and police forces might have been useful in the immediate aftermath of the Taliban's overthrow. Preparations for the war in Iraq made this increasingly difficult, because U.S. troops were needed for combat operations there.

Once counterinsurgency operations began, the United States experienced varying degrees of success in working with indigenous forces. Special forces were particularly successful at integrating ANA, ANP, and Afghan militia forces in virtually all aspects of combat and civil-military operations. Indigenous forces were involved in conducting strike operations; interdicting enemy forces along the border; participating in reconstruction efforts; and gathering intelligence.

Some conventional units were also successful in working with indigenous forces. For example, forces from the U.S. Army's 82nd Air-borne Division in the Bermel Valley involved Afghan militia forces and ANA forces in mine detection, mounted patrols, intelligence collection, vehicle checkpoints, combat operations, and search-and-seize missions. As one assessment summarized, Afghan forces "led every joint mounted patrol and most major operations," especially since they "knew the ground better and could more easily spot something that was out of place or suspicious." But others were less successful. During Operation Mountain Sweep, for example, paratroopers from the 82nd Airborne conducted operations unilaterally; their heavy-handed tactics created significant resentment among locals in Khowst Province. U.S. soldiers angered Afghan villagers on numerous occasions out of naiveté of Afghan social and cultural traditions, leading one Afghan government report to conclude,

It will be difficult for ever for the coalition forces to fully befriend the people. Instead they should try to minimize their contact with the local population and increasingly empower the Afghan forces to do the job. The more they try to be in touch with people the more they will be prone to make cultural mistakes.

DIRECT ACTION AGAINST INSURGENTS

U.S. military forces succeeded to varying degrees in four areas of combat operations: the use of a "clear, hold, and expand" approach; the use of armed reconnaissance and raiding; close air support; and command and control arrangements. Direct action was most effective when the aim was to reduce the use of force, to use force in ways considered legitimate, and to get locals to use force instead of U.S. and coalition forces.

Clear, Hold, and Expand

Counterinsurgents achieve success by destroying insurgent forces and their political organization in a given area over the long run. This involves the permanent isolation of the insurgents from the population. Ideally, this isolation is not enforced on the population but maintained by and with them.

One of the most successful approaches in Afghanistan (when it was applied) was "clear, hold, and expand." This has also been referred to as an "ink-spot" strategy, in which military forces set up secure zones and then slowly expanded them outward like ink spots on blotting paper. Forces were assigned to contested areas to regain government presence and control and then conducted military and civil-military programs to expand the control and edge out insurgents. The focus was on consolidating and holding ground that was clearly pro-Afghan and procoalition (or at least anti-Taliban); protecting the government and other key resources (such as lines of communication and major cities like Kabul); and deploying coalition counterinsurgency forces to conduct offensive operations in contested areas of Afghanistan, especially in the south and east. The deployment of forces into insurgent areas was designed to deny sanctuary, interdict the border, and expand government and coalition presence. U.S. counterinsurgency forces were kept to a bare minimum and supported with civil affairs and psychological operations personnel. A company of infantry has sometimes been provided for area patrolling and to provide security against an immediate threat to the unit. Quick reaction forces in the form of close air support assets or reinforcing units have backed up the outposts whenever insurgent forces have threatened to overrun them.

Clear, hold, and expand forces conducted operations in everincreasing zones, or ink spots, around their bases. In the first zone, forces tried to target and eliminate the insurgents living within the area. This required living among the local population for long durations to gain its trust and support and then trying to separate the locals from the insurgents. The secondary zone was the transit and support zone for the insurgents. Clear, hold, and expand forces in Afghanistan cast a wide net of operations outside their force protection zone to disrupt and interdict insurgent operations. This required patience and discreet intelligence work to ascertain the location of insurgent weapon caches, safe houses, and transit support systems. The outer zone included remote locations or areas where the population was neither friendly nor hostile to the counterinsurgency unit's efforts. Occasional operations were conducted in these areas to show the flag and to keep the population neutral to the idea of supporting the insurgents. Battalion-sized sweeps and clearing operations by conventional forces generally reaped far less than their effort because of the difficulty of finding and fixing elusive insurgents.

However, there were some challenges with clear, hold, and expand. Pakistani forces never attempted sustained clear, hold, and expand operations in the tribal areas or in Baluchistan, especially against high-and middle-level Taliban members. Even in Afghanistan, clear, hold, and expand was limited to small areas of the country, since there were too few U.S., coalition, and Afghan forces to hold and expand large areas.

Armed Reconnaissance and Raiding

An additional lesson from the Afghan counterinsurgency is the need to develop an armed reconnaissance capability and a specialized raiding force. Armed reconnaissance is the patrolling of suspected insurgent areas to glean information on their activities, initiate contact and conduct battle, or confirm that the area is clear. Armed reconnaissance in Afghanistan was accomplished with a variety of platforms and measures. These were tailored for "hunter-killer" type missions—search for, hunt down, gain contact with, and keep contact with insurgents. AC-130 gunships (operating generally at night), tactical unmanned aerial vehicles, and mounted ground reconnaissance patrols all served to accomplish this mission and keep insurgents off balance and disrupt their timing. Tactical unmanned aerial vehicles were somewhat helpful in assisting reconnaissance, force protection, viewing avenues of approach, and positive target identification.

A specialized raiding force was sometimes required to conduct time-sensitive targeting beyond the scope of conventional forces. These specialized raiding forces took various forms, including counterterrorist units, indigenous strike forces, and specially formed and trained units with personnel drawn from organic forces. In Afghanistan, raiding forces often required dedicated mobility platforms and a high level of access to intelligence assets. The sensor-to-shooter links worked best when noncontributing layers of decisionmakers were removed. The number-one role for these units was to target the insurgent's organizational structure and leadership; they also had a secondary role in the conduct of raids in sanctuaries in which political sensitivities precluded larger operations.

Close Air Support

Close air support provided a significant advantage to small groups of U.S. and Afghan forces operating against insurgents. For example, close air support was extremely effective when U.S. forces encountered unexpectedly strong resistance during Operation Anaconda in the Shah-i-Kot Valley. This lesson may not be applicable to all counter-insurgency operations, especially those conducted in urban areas. Also, in cases in which there is sufficient indigenous air capacity, the United States may choose not to provide close air support. Over the course of the Afghan counterinsurgency, a variety of aircraft provided close air support to U.S. and Afghan forces operating in the border areas. Prominent aircraft used include AH-64 attack helicopters, Spectre AC-130 gunships (which some

Afghan insurgents referred to as the "water buffalo"), A-10 and F-14 fighters, and B-52 bombers.19

Due to the effectiveness of close air support, it will be particularly useful for the United States to continue to develop technological capabilities like GPS and Special Operations Forces Laser Acquisition Markers (SOFLAMs), which proved invaluable for ground forces. For much the same reason, it will also be useful to continue to develop new and more sophisticated communication equipment, including advanced receivers and transmitters that link forces in the field to those in other areas, satellite radios carried by combat controllers to call in air strikes, and encrypted high-frequency (HF) radio. As one CIA officer involved in operations in Afghanistan remarked, "The advantage provided by SOFLAMs, smart bombs, laser-guided munitions, Spectre AC-130 gunships, Predator drones, sophisticated communications equipment, etc. tipped the balance militarily."

Command and Control

Perhaps the most significant command and control lesson that can be learned from the counterinsurgency in Afghanistan was the need to decentralize authority down to the small unit level. Command and control worked best when it was flattened out from hierarchical to more horizontal levels. The shorter sensor-to-shooter links were, the better they worked. Quicker and more responsive arrangements for command and control provided flexibility for forces on the battlefield.

This was not always well executed. In December 2001, the commander of Task Force Dagger (essentially the 5th Special Forces Group plus supporting units) was in direct contact with General Franks, the combatant commander. The subordinate elements of Task Force Dagger had the most current and accurate intelligence about the situation on the ground. But this changed when the 10th Mountain Division assumed operations in Afghanistan in March 2002 and again when 18th Airborne Corps took over control of the Afghanistan theatre of operations in June 2002. By late 2002, a special forces detachment's request to conduct an operation sometimes had to be processed through six levels of command before being approved. As one general officer put it: "Too much overhead." Tight command and control sometimes paralysed initiative. Reports from some special forces members in Afghanistan indicated that U.S. forces had to obtain approval from the Combined Joint Task Force headquarters before conducting operations six kilometers beyond their fire bases. In addition, all "named operations"—those other than routine travel—required approval from the Combined Joint Task Force headquarters, which could take as long as 48 hours. The net effect of these restrictions was to impede the flexibility and response of special forces.

The mission profiles of future counterinsurgency operations may require adapting organizational structures in several ways. One is to empower operations at the lowest level. Well-trained, small-unit manoeuvre is important to success. Afghan insurgent groups frequently dispersed their forces, making them smaller and more difficult to attack. They also used more secure communication, better camouflage, and more effective diversions. U.S. military operations most often succeeded when leaders at the smallunit level had enough leeway, specialized assets, and firepower to engage the population and develop their own intelligence. Indeed, U.S. military doctrine needs to establish far looser and more broadly distributed networks that have a high degree of individual independence and survivability. This means incorporating into counterinsurgency doctrine and training the preparation of company and battalion commanders to lead combinedarms warfare, conduct civil-military operations, and develop and exploit their own intelligence. It also means giving infantry commanders the responsibility, autonomy, and distance from higher headquarters that is now only held by special forces A-team commanders. Commanders must empower small-unit leaders to deal with the challenges encountered during counterinsurgency operations, including the authority to routinely make decisions currently made by battalion and brigade combat team commanders.

Intelligence

British Colonel C. E. Callwell, a military historian, wrote in his book *Small Wars* that "it is a very important feature in the preparation for, and the carrying out of, small wars that the regular forces are often working very much in the dark from the outset... What is known technically as 'intelligence' is defective, and unavoidably so." Intelligence is the principal source of information on insurgents, and has usually come from the population. U.S. military and intelligence forces used a variety of ways to identify insurgents: signals intelligence (SIGINT); scouts; long-range reconnaissance detachments; unmanned aerial vehicles; remote battlefield sensor systems; Q-36 Firefinder radar; Joint Land Attack Cruise Missile Defense Elevated Netted Sensor forward-looking infrared systems; and an assortment of HUMINT sources.

The U.S. military's experience in Afghanistan illustrates two key lessons: HUMINT usually provides the majority of actionable intelligence, especially at the tactical level; and civil-military operations can be a useful way to gather intelligence.

HUMINT was a critical facet of counterinsurgency operations in Afghanistan, and Afghan intelligence and security forces were vital in collecting intelligence. HUMINT provided the majority of actionable intelligence and resulted in successful bottom-up planning. Only rarely did units receive national-level intelligence leads; intelligence gathered at the tactical level was much more reliable. CIA officers, special forces, and Afghan assets armed with GPS, laser designators, and covert communication were critical in the pinpointing of targets. They helped feed intelligence to such weapons and delivery systems as joint direct-attack munitions, long-range snipers, AC-130 gunships, Afghan artillery, and thermobaric munitions.

In addition, the U.S. military's experience in Afghanistan demonstrates that civil-military operations can be an excellent way to gather intelligence. This was the case in various civil-military operations and local projects completed by members of the Coalition Joint Civil Military Task Force, other government agencies, and NGOs. A tactical commander can greatly benefit from intelligence gathered while helping civil-military soldiers accomplish their mission. Locals were often so thankful for receiving health care from U.S. military forces that they became willing to assist in the fight against insurgents. On numerous occasions, patients in health clinics and host nation personnel volunteered combat information to U.S. forces concerning IEDs and weapon caches, as well as enemy activity in the region. While intelligence gathered from locals can be useful, it should be taken with some caution. HUMINT sources may have other motives for supplying intelligence, such as tribal rivalries, and they may leak information to insurgent forces.

Information Operations

How can insurgents hope to succeed? They need to find support among the population. This support may range from active participation in the struggle to passive approval of it. The first basic need for an insurgent aiming at more than simply making trouble is an attractive cause. With a popular cause, the insurgent has a formidable, if intangible, asset that he can progressively transform into concrete strength.

Religion has been a significant part of insurgent rhetoric focused on gaining popular support. As Mullah Dadullah, a Taliban military commander killed in 2007, argued, We are not fighting here for Afghanistan, but we are fighting for all Muslims everywhere and also the Mujahideen in Iraq. The infidels attacked Muslim lands and it is a must that every Muslim should support his Muslim brothers.

This argument was echoed by other insurgents, such as former Taliban spokesman Mofti Latifollah Hakimi: "The issue of Afghanistan is connected with the ongoing war between Islam and blasphemy in the world. Mullah Mohammad is representing a huge umma [Muslim community], and a large nation is behind him." Portraying the United States and other Western countries as dedicated to the destruction of Islam was a critical part of this effort. As Mullah Dadullah argued, "God be praised, we now are aware of much of the U.S. plans. We know their target, which is within the general aim of wiping out Islam in this region." The Taliban used young Pakistan-trained mullahs to glorify their cause in mosques in the east and south.

These Taliban efforts had mixed success in Afghanistan, with more success in Pakistan. Since mosques have historically served as a tipping point for major political upheavals in Afghanistan, Afghan government officials focused on mosques. There are 107 mosques in the city of Kandahar out of which 11 are preaching anti-government themes. Our approach is to have all the pro-government mosques incorporated with the process and work on the eleven anti-government ones to change their attitude or else stop their propaganda and leave the area.

Another major factor was the public campaign by Afghan religious figures. For example, in July 2005, the Ulema Council of Afghanistan called on the Taliban to abandon violence and support the Afghan government in the name of Islam. It also called on the religious scholars of neighbouring countries—including Pakistan—to help counter the activities and ideology of the Taliban and other insurgent organizations. A number of Afghan Islamic clerics publicly supported the Afghan government and called the jihad un-Islamic. Moreover, the Ulema Council and some Afghan ulema issued fatwas, or religious decrees, that unambiguously oppose suicide bombing. They argued that suicide bombing does not lead to an eternal life in paradise, does not permit martyrs to see the face of Allah, and does not allow martyrs to have the company of 72 maidens in paradise. These efforts to counter Taliban propaganda were made easier by the populations' lingering resentment of the Taliban. Afghan support for the Taliban through 2007 was low. In one public opinion poll, for example, only 13 percent of Afghans had a favourable view of the Taliban.

Insurgent groups also failed to successfully use ethnicity—especially Pashtun nationalism—to gain support, in spite of a Taliban information campaign that included dropping leaflets, delivering night letters, and launching a radio station. This reflects successful U.S. and Afghan government efforts to balance representation in the government among the country's ethnic groups. The Taliban has long drawn its membership from the Pashtuns. In the immediate aftermath of the December 2001 Bonn Conference, the Tajiks and Uzbeks (who comprised the Northern Alliance) filled key government positions with their own personnel. They also took control of the intelligence service and ministries of defense, interior, and foreign affairs. This meant that there was a significant absence of representation from the Pashtuns, as well as the Shia Muslim Hazaras from the center. One notable exception was the decision to name Hamid Karzai, a Pashtun, as interim president. By late 2003, however, the U.S. government and President Karzai made a concerted push to redress the ethnic balance at the levels of minister and deputy minister. For example, President Karzai appointed Ali Jalali, a Pashtun, as Minister of Interior, who began to appoint ethnically diverse governors and police chiefs. In addition, the Afghanistan and Pakistan governments encouraged the organization of traditional Pashtun councils (jirgas) to solicit the aid of local tribes in fighting extremists. This included the use of tribal militias to help quell the growing power of the Taliban in Pashtun areas. The expansion of good governance and strong state institutions is probably the most effective longterm solution.

In sum, indigenous actors were most effective in conducting information operations. The U.S. and other coalition governments tried to implement information operations to degrade insurgent decisionmaking and recruitment. Key objectives were to deter, discourage, and dissuade insurgents by disrupting their unity of command while preserving Afghan and coalition command. They also involved shutting down insurgent communications and networks while protecting Afghan and coalition ones. This included employing five core capabilities: electronic warfare, psychological operations, operations security, military deception, and computer network operations. However, the most successful information operations were from indigenous actors such as religious, tribal, and political leaders—often without U.S. assistance.

Working with Coalition Partners

The U.S. experience working with coalition forces and other international actors was mixed. The counterinsurgency campaign—and security sector reform more broadly—was initially based on a "lead nation" approach. The United States was the lead donor nation for reconstructing the ANA; Germany was lead for police; the United Kingdom was lead for counternarcotics; Italy was lead for justice; and Japan (with UN assistance) was lead for the disarmament, demobilization, and reintegration of former combatants. In theory, each lead nation was supposed to contribute significant financial assistance, coordinate external assistance, and oversee reconstruction efforts in its sector. In practice, this approach did not work as well as envisioned. The United States provided the bulk of assistance in most security sectors—including counternarcotics, police, and the army. In other areas, such as the justice sector and the disarmament, demobilization, and reintegration of former combatants, there was little measurable improvement.

Counterinsurgency operations are generally complex, demanding, and expensive. Even major powers like the United States need cooperation from others, especially on such issues as basing rights, overflight rights, intelligence, combat forces, economic assistance, and political support. Bilateral donors, international organizations, development banks, and military alliances have different comparative advantages and can provide valuable resources to counterinsurgency. In the absence of broad multilateral support, counterinsurgency operations may not have sufficient military, economic, and political resources to establish security. In addition, the absence of multilateral participation may increase the likelihood that some states will undermine the operation.

NATO's forces in Afghanistan were generally competent. But the NATO experience in Afghanistan highlights several drawbacks with multilateral operations. One was the variation in political will of coalition partners. NATO's International Security Assistance Force was severely limited by the political-military rules of engagement, which constrained each of the national contingents. Some countries, such as Canada and Britain, were reliable allies who were willing to fight— and die—in Afghanistan. During Operation Medusa in 2006, for example, Canadian military forces fought a conventional battle against Taliban forces in Kandahar Province. The Taliban used crew-served weapons and rocket-propelled grenades and engaged from fixed positions. But most NATO countries, such as Germany and Norway, had national caveats that severely restricted their ability to fight. Another drawback was the variation in capabilities. Several coalition countries lacked adequate enabler forces—including attack and lift helicopters, smart munitions, intelligence, engineers, medical, logistics, and digital command and control—to fully leverage and sustain their ground combat power.

A final drawback was a lack of unity of command. In some operations, such as the one carried out in Bosnia following the signing of the 1995 Dayton Peace Accords, the international community created a "high representative" to oversee reconstruction and stabilization. This did not happen in Afghanistan on either the civilian or military side. On the civilian side, there was no unity of command among the international community or U.S. agencies. Even on the military side, there were separate U.S. and NATO chains of command—even after NATO took control over much of the counterinsurgency campaign in 2006. The result was several external forces operating in the same area with different missions and different rules of engagement.

THE CHANGING NATURE OF WAR: IMPLICATIONS FOR IR THEORY

As context for this analysis, it is crucial to note that in the twentieth century, and specifically in the post-colonial period, intrastate wars have supplanted interstate wars as the dominant form of military conflict in the international system. With this, the dominant reality of contemporary military conflict has changed from large-scale force-on-force engagements, like those associated with the wars of attrition and manoeuvre respectively embodied in WWI and WWII as well as in Korea, to wars predicated on the combating of an insurgency, defined by Fearon & Laitin as a "technology of military conflict characterized by small, lightly armed bands practicing guerilla warfare from rural base areas." Moving forward, Kaldor (2006) refers to the new types of conflict being fought by great powers as "New Wars," in which conflicts occur in areas having suffered a complete breakdown in the power of the state to maintain its sovereignty over its territory, and in which identity politics, specifically social cleavages based on identities, have emerged as the dominant causal forces underlying conflict. Thus the nature of war itself has changed and, with this, the strategies and tactics used by great powers have become inimical to success in defeating the new enemies that democracies face in places like Afghanistan.

Tangibly speaking, the changing nature of war has led to a context in which, when intervening in smaller and weaker nation states, great powers have had a historical tendency to fight traditional wars of attrition or manoeuvre, in contrast to weaker states' adoptions of strategies of "direct defense" or guerrilla warfare. In this context, the great power will emerge victorious, from a military point of view, if it adapts its military strategy to the context it is in, and fights the guerrilla force on its own terms. In contrast, if it continues to adopt the strategies and tactics associated with a war of attrition or manoeuvre, the enemy will dramatically win the conflict as, in the words of Henry Kissinger, "the guerrilla wins if he does not lose". With this, then, there is a clear indication that the strategies and tactics used by great powers in fighting conflicts against weaker entities or states are incongruent with success. Providing tangible empirical support for this assertion, Lyall & Wilson (2009)'s meta-analysis of counterinsurgencies from the nineteenth century to the current day comes to the interesting conclusion that, until WWI, the superior firepower of great powers led them to win most such wars.

In contrast, in the post-WWI period, great powers have lost most such conflicts. The authors propose that the mechanization of warfare, specifically the use of tanks and armoured personnel carriers, is responsible for this state of affairs for multiple reasons all centered on decreasing levels of contact with the population of the country in which the war is being fought. In a nutshell, because contemporary COIN infantry operations are based on either ground or airborne mechanization, infantrymen do not interact with the population, thus seeking to win proverbial hearts and minds, as frequently as they did in earlier wars. Because of this, the great power is incapable of building rapport with the locals, of gaining intelligence from them, and of using them to their advantage in defeating the opposing force.

With this, the tactics used by non-state actors in these asymmetric conflicts can often be difficult for Westerners to understand on the basis of their own traditions and cultural priors. For example, a recent high profile article by Pape (2003) makes the suggestion that suicide terrorism is not an inhumane aberration, but rather a rational response on the part of weaker parties to fighting against superior military forces, often belonging to liberal democracies that would otherwise force them to relinquish territory. With this, it is easy – within the confines of mainstream IR theory – to demonize combatants in the conflicts that great powers lose as being alien, uncivilized, and irrational entities. The fact of the matter, however, is that their rationality is simply informed by different worldviews than our own.

In sum then, the changing nature of war has led to a dramatic shift in the effectiveness of various war-fighting tactics and strategies. With this, the reasoning underlying great powers' defeats in conflicts against less powerful foes, like the one occurring in Afghanistan, is that their use of strategy and tactics has not evolved to take into consideration this changing nature of warfare and, consequently, of the enemy being fought. With this, not only do practitioners of foreign policy and war-fighters need to adjust their approaches to conflict, but theorists of IR also need to revisit their conceptions of power, as existing metrics do not provide an adequate empirical portrait of great powers' abilities to prevail in the military conflicts that they predominantly face today.

The Nature of COIN Warfare

With this changing nature of warfare in mind, COIN doctrines have emerged, in the Vietnam War period and afterward, to enhance military effectiveness in the contexts of these new conflicts. In the United States Amy's Counterinsurgency manual, written by Petraeus (2006), the emergent doctrine emphatically stresses the importance of protecting civilians from insurgents, building rapport with local leaders, and creating conditions germane to the endogenous development of responsible governance structures and civil society. Thus, according to Kaplan (2014), COIN embodied an attempt to change the American military's baseline culture, and facilitate its participation in the new bevy of operational types brought about in the wake of the Vietnam War. Given that latter's failure, as it pertained to American strategic victory, Kaplan (2014) thus argues that the development of COIN doctrine represented a longitudinal adaptation to the changes which America would face in a period of declining inter-state war.

With this, COIN is heavily focused on a population-centric approach to war which conceptualizes these types of conflicts as involving multiple stakeholders, with the target country's population representing the most important of these. Indeed, the Department of the Army's "Stability Operations" manual written by Caldwell (2008) notes that soft power must be a focus of COIN operations at both the strategic and tactical levels. With this, it is clear that an integral element of COIN warfare, in a context where such a heavy focus is placed on winning hearts and minds, also exists in terms of broadening America's military posture to include components germane to minimizing the kinetic components of its operations. Writ large, COIN doctrine as conceptualized in the contemporary American military thus represents a middle ground between civil and military operations, of which the express purpose is to use force only inasmuch as it is necessary to build a structure germane to the stabilization and potential later reconstruction of a given conflict zone (Greene-Sands & Greene-Sands, 2014).

PRELUDE: THE SOVIET INVASION OF AFGHANISTAN

Moving forward to empirics, the Soviet experience in Afghanistan is instructive in understanding the floundering which the NATO coalition is currently experiencing in Afghanistan.

While their initial conquest of Afghanistan was relatively bloodless, the Soviet force soon became bogged down in fighting an insurgency that, while initially short on military capabilities, seemed endless in terms of the number of *Mujahedeen* willing to lay their lives down to defend Afghanistan. While the Afghan resistance fighters soon began to receive relatively large covert arms shipments from the American government, as the latter turned Afghanistan into another Cold War proxy conflict, the *Mujahedeen* never gathered enough strength in military terms to allow for them to do any more than give the Soviets a proverbial black eye.

The difficulty encountered by the Soviets then, in their occupation of Afghanistan, was not related to the intensity of the conflict itself, despite the losses of armoured vehicles and helicopter gunships that they sustained subsequent to the introduction of American heavy weapons into the hands of the *Mujahedeen*. Rather, Edelstein (2008) attributes the Soviet defeat to the difficulties inherent to the occupation of any country in the modern area. Tangibly speaking, he proposes that the rise of nationalism that has occurred in the twentieth century, when combined with the fact that occupied countries like Afghanistan more often than not contain very little material wealth, leads to two consequences. In the war zone itself, resistance groups buoyed on by the ideational power of nationalism are willing to lose significant numbers of their own forces so as to preserve the existence of their nation. Simultaneously, because there is no material "treasure" to be gained from the occupation of failed states and most authoritarian regimes, the domestic population of the intervening and occupying state quickly loses patience and resolve with regards to the losses being taken by its country's forces, because of the perception that no gains are to be accrued from continued commitments to such contexts.

When these processes occur concurrently, as they did in Afghanistan, the occupying force is likely to be repelled, as the Soviets were, because of the sapping of the occupying government's resources, and of diminishing public will in the domestic sphere of the occupying country to continue fighting the conflict. Indeed, and given that the Soviets did not make use of any nation or peace-building components in the context of their invasion and occupation, their success was even further detracted from.

American Experiences in Iraq

Beginning with America's recent experience in Iraq, Kaplan (2014) notes that, after an initially smooth path to Baghdad, conducted on the basis of armour and mobile infantry operations, the insurgency which eventually took hold in the country largely took American leaders by surprise. Indeed, the increasing body count of the war, which occurred in the context of American governorship of the country, notably through the mandate afforded to Bremer in the context of the Coalitional Provisional Government, dramatically affected American support for the war at home. Evans (2011), high-ranking members of the American military were torn with regards to how to proceed in reconstructing the country. With Kaplan (2014) noting that the American Administration had uprooted and destroyed much of the Hussein-era Iraqi governmental capacity through the dismantling of its military, Iraqi civil society and government were in shambles at the war's apex. As such, America created a dualistic civic and military imperative for itself in Iraq on the basis of its actions vis-à-vis the Hussein-era Iraqi state apparatus. During this time, Kaplan (2014) notes that American forces were seeking to both reconstruct the country through nation-building efforts, and hold off an insurgency which was growing bloodier on a day-to-day basis.

With this in mind, relief for America ultimately came in the wake of the surge commanded by David Petraeus in 2007. With Kaplan (2014) noting that it simultaneously involved the deployment of additional troops to the region, alongside an increased focus on kinetic operations concomitant to a decrease in civil reconstruction ones, the core of the surge was a purely militaristic application of COIN doctrine. In this context, and where Greene-Sands & Greene-Sands (2014) note that this kinetic pace increased even further under the later command of Stanley MacChrystal, it becomes clear that America's successes, as it pertained to defeating the insurgency and stabilizing the country, occurred when it diminished the degree to which it was involved in civil reconstruction and nation-building, and instead focused on the kinetic components of population-centric COIN doctrine.

With this, Evans (2011) notes that the implementation of Petraeus' (2006) version of COIN is what ultimately stabilized Iraq in the run-up to America's withdrawal. Thus, despite the grumbling from the officer corps, which Evans (2011) notes, as it pertained to traditional war-fighters being uncomfortable with this nascent and less-militarized approach – at least in comparison to the manoeuvre warfare which was expected and trained for during the Cold War – its implementation was ultimately successful in leveraging an exit strategy for America. This said, Greene Sands

& Greene-Sands (2014) note that the surge, executed on the basis of Petraeus' version of COIN, saw a lesser degree of civil-military operations than had previously been the norm in the Iraqi theatre. Indeed, while maintaining the military aspects of COIN as it pertains to population-centric and sensitive warfare, the authors note that American military forces lessened efforts pertaining to purely civil reconstruction and nation-building.

Thus, the lessons of the Iraqi case lead to the compelling possibility that COIN can be most successful specifically when it is detached from the reconstruction-oriented peace and nation-building activities which occurred in the Bremer era. Indeed, these realities thus point to a potential case in which COIN is at its most effective when it is detached from nation-building, and wherein the latter is left in the hands of the home government of the state in which operations are occurring.

With this in mind, what becomes apparent from the Iraqi case as it pertains to the ultimate success of COIN in facilitating an American withdrawal is that the version of COIN implemented there was not a full and holistic one. Rather, in the surge and thereafter, Kaplan (2014) notes that, as the Iraqi government gained increasing powers, American forces began to engage in far more kinetic operations. From drone strikes to night raids, all conducted under the aegis of the Joint Special Operations Command, America shifted towards discrete and targeted kinetic operations oriented towards eliminating the insurgency's leadership. In so doing, it would appear that America increased the level of alienation present in some portions of the Iraqi population. At the same time, however, it also enhanced the efficiency by which it was capable of maintaining population-centric security. Thus, in reviewing America's performance in Iraq, it would very much appear that the success of its COIN operations increased as it decreased its participation in peace and nation-building activities. Ultimately, this thus provides initial support of a fundamental incompatibility between contemporary American COIN operations and the type of nation-building processes which the country has undertaken in terms of both the Afghan and Iraqi Wars which have been conducted under the broader aegis of the War on Terror.

NATO Floundering in Afghanistan

Reflecting on the theoretical discussions presented above, as well as the Iraqi case and Soviet exemplar set in its own attempt to invade and conquer Afghanistan, the contemporary NATO coalition's foibles become easier to understand. Most tangibly, America and its coalition partners are, for all intents and purposes, fighting a conflict in which they are winning every single battle, yet still losing the war. Because high-salience kinetic operations engender sentiments of discontent amongst the population, all the while killing insurgents, they represent a "no-win" approach to fighting a conflict such as the Afghan one. Thus, even in adopting a counterinsurgency-based approach to the conflict in Afghanistan, the coalition is alienating the population, and thus facing the same endgame as the Soviets in terms of the impossibility of generating a safe and peaceful civil society.

Thus, like the previous Soviet adventure in Afghanistan, the coalition's ongoing struggles all pertain to the fact that tactics and metrics for victory alike are premised on an outdated notion of war that is not congruent with the realities on the ground in Afghanistan. With this, the coalition is, despite a doctrinal change embodied by works like that of Petraeus (2006), attempting to fight a war that is premised on the notion that the Taliban and the broader insurgency can be defeated. Using traditional military tactics that end up alienating the native population, alongside night raids and drone strikes which serve to generate tremendous antipathy in the population, America and the coalition are thus fighting a conflict in a manner that will allow them to win each of its battles, but which will ultimately and inevitably lead them to lose the war in the same way that the Soviets once did.

As one tangible example of these counter-productive tactical and operational choices, drone strikes are especially problematic in attempting to win the type of asymmetric conflict being fought in Afghanistan. Beginning with an overview of the nature of drones themselves, they are unmanned aerial vehicles, UAVs, which are typically armed with air-to-surface missiles and bombs. With most of these piloted from American shores, inside the comfort of air-conditioned bases found largely in Nevada and New Mexico, these drones have fundamentally changed the nature of war, and of the killing which takes place in it. While killing an adversary used to require staring at the whites of his eyes, and seeing his blood, all that is now required is the pushing of a button thousands of miles away from the site of the battle. With this, drones have served to dehumanize war and to make the decision to kill someone a less stressful one. Thus, because using a drone for a military mission does not put a pilot at risk, and can be accomplished from half a world away, there is very little danger associated with the use of drones – at least not for the Americans who pilot them.

This said, drones have significant effects downrange, where they are used to conduct targeted extra-judicial assassinations. With this in mind, Scahill (2013) notes that drones have killed 4,700 individuals, from the Horn of Africa to Pakistan, with the greatest brunt of these casualties taking place in Afghanistan, since the beginning of the War on Terror. Out of these 4,700 casualties, a massive 1,500 of those killed have been innocent civilians, or what successive administrations have referred to as collateral damage. In this context, enormous antipathy has been generated amongst the Afghan population inasmuch as these civilian deaths have not only been seen as unnecessary, but also as having come about in a manner viewed as culturally dishonorable. Thus, while drones do not put Americans at risk, they have a very problematic tendency, even when used to hunt a true terrorist, to kill innocent Afghan civilians, and to thus alienate the population.

With this, drones have represented a problematic addition to America's national security apparatus as the country fights the war in Afghanistan. While they were originally designed for surveillance missions and were unarmed, America has rapidly used these platforms as aerial killing machines oriented towards the targeted assassination of specific individuals. On this basis, drones have thus emerged as a mainline tool of American foreign policy, and have been transformed into hunter-killer platforms in spite of their original designation as reconnaissance ones. In this role, they have killed thousands of innocents in the name of American foreign policy. In such a context, Scahill (2013) notes widespread instances where, in the wake of an American drone strike in a given Afghan village, villagers stopped cooperating with American civil and military officials and returned to the Taliban for protection. Thus, a direct causal linkage exists between these attacks and the decline of facilitating conditions germane to peace and nation-building activities.

Given that these targeted extra-judicial killings which America and NATO use in Afghanistan are very similar to political assassinations, Afghan dismay at their usage is unsurprising. They are embodied by the use of American and coalition military-or intelligence-based paramilitary forces so as to eliminate terrorist leaders via either remote drone strikes, as conducted by Predator and Reaper drones, or by special forces "wet teams" which conduct night raids on a regular basis across Afghanistan (Kessler & Werner, 290-292). These tactics, while previously used as methods of last resort against high value terrorist targets, have now become a mainstream U.S. policy in the context of the Afghan War. As such, Scahill (2013) makes the case that as America says one thing through its civil relations arm, it does another far more kinetic thing through its military apparatus. As such, the narrative ultimately experienced by the Afghan population is one of confusion and inconsistency – two factors anathema to success in counterinsurgency.

Tangibly, the purportedly rigorous process underlying this tactic requires that the President of the United States – on the basis of his advisors' guidance as well as the deliberations of a classified targeting tribunal featuring members of the Executive, Congress, and America's armed and intelligence forces – issue a "finding" indicating that the targeted individual is beyond any reasonable doubt a terrorist who has committed acts of warfare against America, and who is beyond the reach of conventional military forces. If the finding is issued, the military then attempts to eliminate the target all the while causing the least amount of civilian collateral damage that is possible, although civilian casualties are common during such operations.

Problematically, however, drone strikes and night raids are two of the most significant forces involved in the coalition's current war in Afghanistan as it pertains to the alienation of civilians. Tangibly, the struggles which the NATO coalition is currently experiencing in Afghanistan, even in places such as Kandahar, where pacification had previously been achieved by Canadian and other coalition forces, is resulting directly from the highly-kinetic policies adopted by the American military. Thus, repeating the mistakes made by the Soviets two decades ago, the NATO coalition is losing the war in Afghanistan, while winning all of its battles, because it fundamentally misunderstands the realities of winning an asymmetric conflict. Indeed, its continued attempts to engage in nation-building, all the while losing civilian trust through kinetic operations, is creating a COIN-based paradox which is ultimately inimical either to victory or achieving the conditions necessary for a safe withdrawal.

In this regard, its failure to apply COIN doctrine to the same degree of relative success which occurred in Iraq, at least as it pertained to achieving an exit strategy, can be tied to the fact that America has continued to seek to instantiate civil-military programs pertaining to nation-building, all the while engaging in these kinetic operations (Greene-Sands & Greene-Sands, 2014). Indeed, with the Iraqi case demonstrating that America's greatest successes occurred after a shift to military COIN predominance occurred, it becomes clear that America is repeating many of the Soviet Union's mistakes in its continue pursuit of the Iraq War. In a context where Scahill (2013) notes that the potential state apparatus of Afghanistan is far less than it was in Iraq, America views the reconstruction of the Afghan state as a necessity. Problematically, however, the Iraqi case made it clear that highly-kinetic operations are incompatible with nation-building. As such, America will likely have to sacrifice the type of reconstruction which it has attempted in Afghanistan if it is to succeed in the withdrawal which has been forced about by pressure from its domestic political sphere.

Conclusion

In the end, then, the theoretical examination provided above, buoyed and validated by the subsequent case studies, provides a clear indication that the defeat of great powers in conflicts against smaller states is a result of multiple independent variables acting in synergy. Beyond this, IR's failure in predicting these defeats is a result of our discipline's inability to truly understand the changing nature of military power in the international system, as determined by the changing nature of warfare itself. Merom (2003) perhaps provides the most parsimonious account of why great powers fail to win such wars in noting that success in such conflicts depends on three principle variables: the degree to which the great power's government is dependent on popular support; the level of divergence between the morality of the great power's elite and mass; and the degree to which public opinion constrains elite decision-making. The argument made here, in concluding this discussion, is that theories like Merom's are a significant element of the problem faced by our discipline.

The changing nature of war, and thus of the tactics that are effective within it, points to a need for a theorists of IR and practitioners of foreign policy to more broadly conceive of power in evaluating cases, and to focus on each great power versus weaker state conflict as a discrete empirical event, rather than as a component of a broader class. Simply put, the heterogeneity of these conflicts, manifested not only in the motivations underlying them, but also in the nature of the fighters involved in them, belies the discipline's traditional conceptions of power, which are themselves predicated on antiquated metrics. As such, there is a need to focus on the substantive and particular components of each conflict, within the overarching theoretical context of the changing nature of war, so as to properly evaluate the counter-intuitive and misleading question of why great powers lose wars against less powerful adversaries on such a regular basis.

From an empirical point of view, the disjuncture which exists within COIN operations as it pertains to the conflict imperatives associated with kinetic action and nation-building are also very salient in any such debate. COIN succeeded in Iraq when America lessened the degree to which it sought to rebuild the country, and engage in outright nation-building activities. In the Afghan case, where the country's previous status as a failed state left it bereft of governance capability, American forces have not necessarily had the luxury of adopting the more militaristic elements of COIN with such abandon. As such, the persistence of insurgent difficulties in Afghanistan can likely be attributed to America's attempts to engage in nation-building despite all the while sapping the population's trust and morale through the collateral damage of kinetic operations. Ultimately, this leaves American forces in Afghanistan between a proverbial rock and a hard place inasmuch as these two divergent components of the COIN paradigm make success in the ongoing conflict a dubious possibility.

In concluding, the theoretical discussion and empirical case studies presented above provide a compelling and multi-faceted account of the reasons underlying which big states lose ostensibly small wars. In bracketing this essay, it is crucial to note that despite the mainstream tendency to see parsimony as the dominant metric by which the value of a social scientific theory is measured, the value of this metric recedes when we consider the nature of contemporary warfare. It is clear, from both the extant literature and the forays into empirical analysis engaged in above, that mono-causal explanations of conflict are insufficient in contemporary IR, especially when we are dealing with the so-called "New Wars" that have emerged in the late 20th century. With this, then, it is imperative that the dominant analytic frame used by IR to analyse military conflict, realism, takes heed of the ideational insights provided by approaches such as constructivism, and modifies its approach so as to more fully account for the synergistic effects of ideational factors on power within warfare. In doing this, the discipline will more clearly perceive the true ontology of war in the international system, and, with this, provide more accurate accounts of these conflicts.

10

Counterinsurgency Approach for Fighting the Extensive War

The single greatest national security question currently facing the U.S. National Command Authority is choosing the best, sustainable strategy to combat al Qaeda and its affiliates. The U.S. national strategy against al Qaeda is far broader than the Department of Defense (DoD) mission. Nonetheless, DoD's contribution to the fight is substantial, both in terms of resource allocation and the net effect in reducing the al Qaeda threat.

The National Command Authority has at least four broad means of employing military resources in the overall strategy to combat al Qaeda. These choices include conducting counterinsurgency, waging counterterrorism, supporting insurgency, and strengthening antiterrorism. This Carlisle Paper focuses on counterinsurgency because that is the strategy through which the United States has expended the greatest level of military resources since September 11, 2001 (9/11). The chapter also briefly highlights the strengths and weaknesses of the other three strategies.

Counterinsurgency does not appear to be a wise, long term strategy for the United States to employ in combating al Qaeda. U.S. military resources on counterinsurgency ignores historical lessons in successfully combating terrorism and fails to utilize military resources in the most efficient, sustainable manner possible.

COUNTERTERRORISM, INSURGENCY, AND ANTITERRORISM

Counterinsurgency (COIN) is defined as "those military, paramilitary, political, economic, psychological, and civic actions taken by a government to defeat insurgency."

COIN is well known from its use during the latter stages of the second U.S. war in Iraq and from General Stanley McChrystal's 2009 recommendation as to the best means to prevail in Afghanistan. The most notable characteristics of COIN are its indirect approach to combating terrorism and its cost. COIN focuses on the local civilian population, seeking to secure the population from the enemy and to obtain popular support through effective governance, including public services, eventually defeating insurgents or making them irrelevant. Counterinsurgency's high cost begins with the large number of counterinsurgents required to provide security. Large expenditures for personnel, equipment, and materials also are required for civil works programs to support the host government. COIN conducted in a remote, rugged, insecure area, such as Afghanistan, increases costs exponentially, based on transportation and transportation security costs. Ideally, COIN should be conducted by the whole of government and nongovernmental organizations (NGOs), not merely military forces.

In practice, the DoD has conducted the vast majority of the U.S. Government's portion of the COIN efforts in Iraq and Afghanistan for a variety of reasons, including DoD resources and its ability to operate in unsecure environments. Counterterrorism is defined as "operations that include the offensive measures taken to prevent, deter, preempt, and respond to terrorism." Reported U.S. counterterrorism operations include missile strikes from unmanned aerial systems (drones), and special operations raids against high value targets, including senior leaders. Many counterterrorism successes are publically unknown because they are classified. Counterterrorism also includes nonkinetic efforts to secure weapons of mass destruction (WMD), including those held by nonallied countries, in order to deny these weapons to terrorists.

Counterterrorism is conducted by the DoD, especially the Joint Special Operations Command (JSOC) and Defense Threat

Reduction Agency, and also by the Central Intelligence Agency (CIA). Insurgency is the inverse of counterinsurgency, namely, "[t]he organized use of subversion and violence by a group or movement that seeks to overthrow or force change of a governing authority. Insurgency can also refer to the group itself." This definition includes the overthrow of legitimate and illegitimate governments. Almost immediately after 9/11, the United States openly supported an Afghan insurgency, the Northern Alliance, against the Taliban, which tolerated or supported al Qaeda. Earlier, the United States more quietly provided military aid to insurgents including the Mujahedeen who fought Soviet military forces entering Afghanistan beginning in late 1979. Since 2002, U.S. support to insurgency as a means of fighting terrorism has received little public discussion.

Antiterrorism is defined as "defensive measures used to reduce the vulnerability of individuals and property to terrorist acts, to include limited response and containment by local military and civilian forces." The Department of Homeland Security (DHS) is the primary U.S. federal antiterrorism agency. The DoD can and does support domestic antiterrorism efforts. DoD contributions to the U.S. antiterrorism efforts include providing armed National Guard Soldiers in airports shortly after the 9/11 attacks and providing support to other government agencies for high profile events, such as presidential inaugurations and Super Bowls.

COUNTERINSURGENCY AS A STRATEGY

It likely is impossible to quantify exact al Qaeda threat reduction benefits to the United States from specific COIN operations. Not knowing whether successful al Qaeda attacks in the United States would have occurred if a COIN operation had not been conducted hinders quantification. Additionally, some al Qaeda threat reduction information from COIN operations is likely classified. Consequently, this analysis evaluates the resources al Qaeda needs to successfully attack the United States and the al Qaeda resource reductions a COIN may provide through the force's presence and by solving fundamental underlying problems in an unstable society.

Reducing al Qaeda's Means to Harm the United States. COIN has immediate effects on some al Qaeda resources and also has second and third order effects. Returning to the previously discussed elements al Qaeda presumably needs to operate, it needs senior leader guidance, funding, command and control, ideology, popular support, safe havens, fighters, and weapons. How should a successful COIN affect each of these elements?

Senior Leader Guidance. Al Qaeda senior leaders do not appear to arise from the ills a COIN should fix. Osama bin Laden grew up in a wealthy family in Saudi Arabia. Ayman Al-Zawahiri was born to a prominent Egyptian family and is a doctor. Saudi Arabia and Egypt are stable states, with relatively legitimate governments, providing a middle of the world level of freedom and opportunity to their citizens. Saudi Arabia and Egypt are not Switzerland, but nor are they North Korea. Bin Laden and Zawahiri's countries of origin and economic and professional status are relatively typical for al Qaeda senior leaders.

It is possible, though by no means sure, that COIN operations might indirectly affect potential future al Qaeda senior leaders through influencing their ideology. Specifically, Western COIN operations might convince potential al Qaeda senior leaders that Western ideology, evidenced through good works in Islamic and other third world countries, is not evil. This idea is discussed in greater detail in the "Ideology" section. Information developed during COIN operations may help locate al Qaeda leaders. Counterterrorism operations have killed a substantial number of deputies and middle level leaders. Intelligence sources that led to these counterterrorism successes are classified, and there are reasons to question whether the information leading to these successes did or did not come from COIN operations in Afghanistan or Iraq. And even if COIN operations *are* the basis for intelligence successes, the intelligence would have come at very high economic, military, and political costs.

Funding. Criminal enterprises and some governments are believed to be the primary al Qaeda funding sources. Criminal enterprises tend to flourish in failed and weak states, so COIN has the potential to diminish or destroy one of the two primary funding sources for al Qaeda. Unfortunately, COIN does not appear to destroy criminal enterprises, in either the short or long term.

In the short term, COIN tends to ignore or to strengthen major existing criminal organizations, and it also spawns new criminal enterprises. The indigenous population's "hearts and minds" is the center of gravity for counterinsurgents. Because they cannot afford to alienate a large segment of the population, counterinsurgents are very hesitant to target criminal organizations that are supported by a significant segment of the indigenous society, even if the criminal enterprise causes substantial harm worldwide. For example, in Afghanistan counterinsurgents largely ignore rather than destroy poppy fields, which provide 95 percent of the world's illicit heroin and up to $400 million to the Taliban.

Warlords have long controlled critical passes and roads in Afghanistan, exacting illegal payments from merchants seeking safe passage of goods. As previously discussed, COIN requires huge amounts of resources, and in Afghanistan logistics travel is over land, via roads controlled in places by warlords and the Taliban. Illegal toll charges increase with the value of the commodities transported, and thus COIN has vastly strengthened the existing warlord and Taliban criminal enterprises. Transportation contractors for the DoD in Afghanistan received $2.2 billion from the United States during 2008-09 and are generally understood to pay some percentage of the logistics contract funds to insurgents. If 10 percent of the contracts were spent on "security" payments to insurgents to avoid attacks, this would be $220 million for 2008-09 alone.

The civil works aspect of COIN spawns new criminal enterprises. For example, development projects in Afghanistan before 2002 were so insignificant that they did not merit exploitation by significant criminal enterprise. As development in Afghanistan grew following the overthrow of the Taliban, a new criminal enterprise grew to take advantage of it. Some fraction of the billions of dollars spent in Afghanistan for development is diverted to corruption, much of it eventually flowing to warlords and the Taliban. Some estimates are that 10 to 15 percent of development funds end up with the Taliban. Similarly, in Iraq, billions of dollars in reconstruction funding could not be accounted for, and it is probable that a substantial fraction of the missing funds was lost to corruption.

It is doubtful that COIN reduces funding for criminal enterprises, and by extension to al Qaeda, in the long term. A successful COIN transforms a failed or failing state into a weak state emerging from conflict. A weak state emerging from conflict lacks the resources or the motivation to fight entrenched, well-funded criminal enterprises when there are many other more obvious, urgent priorities affecting the people. Moreover, strong links and even co-dependence between criminal enterprises and state governments may ensure that as long as the new government is in power, criminal enterprises that developed or expanded during the war will continue to flourish during peace. The narcotics and human trafficking enterprises in Albania and beyond during and after the Bosnia-Herzegovina War provide a stark example of this phenomenon. Many similar examples exist in Africa, including in the Democratic Republic of Congo. Anticorruption measures in a post conflict society often lead to instability and renewed fighting which makes anticorruption actions against powerful criminal enterprises all the more unpalatable, both within the nation itself and internationally.

Thus, even if a counterinsurgency is successful, it is unlikely to extinguish entrenched, highly profitable criminal enterprises. The vast funding COIN operations provide to criminal enterprises, insurgents, and al Qaeda is particularly troubling, given the small amount of money necessary to finance serious terrorist plots.

Command and Control. Other than al Qaeda cells whose purpose is to attack counterinsurgents, it is unlikely that COIN operations will significantly disrupt al Qaeda command and control. Al Qaeda operatives appear to be organized into discrete cells, and command and control structures from the senior leaders to the cells may be indirect, infrequent, or electronic. Al Qaeda leaders appear to relocate when COIN operations begin in their locales, as evidenced by al Qaeda leaders moving from Afghanistan to Pakistan as the insurgency in Afghanistan began in late 2001 and thereafter when the counterinsurgency commenced in earnest. Similarly, al Qaeda in Iraq leaders moved from Iraq after the "awakening." Moreover, there is no command and control between al Qaeda leaders and an increasing number of self-selected, self-radicalized, self-directed individual terrorists and terrorist cells. To the extent al Qaeda senior leadership has influence over many of these "fellow travelers," the influence is indirect and electronic, such as through terrorist websites or media broadcasts of video or audio tapes prepared by senior leadership. Some self-selected terrorists might work part way up the al Qaeda chain of command to request and obtain a specific mission or to obtain training or direction in a self-selected mission. An al Qaeda leader located in an area where COIN is being conducted who attempts to provide training to a self starter might have his efforts disrupted by counter-insurgents, but the most significant leaders will likely relocate.

Ideology. Well-executed, well-perceived COIN strikes at the heart of al Qaeda's ideology. It is far easier for al Qaeda to portray Westerners and Western ideology as evil to populations who are unfamiliar with the many positive aspects of Western people and practices. COIN provides personal contact between indigenous people, whom al Qaeda seeks to influence, and counterinsurgents whose ideology is said to be evil, but who are engaged in good works on behalf of the local people. Reporting, in the broadest sense of the word, extends the ideological effect of a COIN fought in a Muslim country to Muslims throughout the world.

At the international level both within and beyond the Muslim world, COIN has the potential to increase or decrease U.S. "soft power," which Joseph Nye defines as "the ability to get what you want through attraction rather than coercion or payments." Soft power is created through the attraction other governments or citizens may have to a country's culture, political ideals, and legitimate policies. A COIN providing good works, for sincere purposes, during a just war, particularly through international organizations or in conjunction with other nations, may increase U.S. soft power. Objectively, poor performance, not meeting expectations (reasonable or not), or international belief that an operation is unjust for any reason may diminish U.S. soft power rather than enhancing it. Increasing U.S. soft power is important because it increases the U.S. ability to obtain other nations' assistance in fighting al Qaeda.

For several reasons, it is no easy task to perform COIN well under the best of circumstances, even without interference from insurgents. General McChrystal's description of the immense complexity involved in building one well, in a single village in Afghanistan, suggests that the overall task of conducting COIN in countries with radically different cultures from the West is nearly insurmountable, even in the abstract.

A second, equally important, challenge is to convince an indigenous population that the purpose of COIN is altruistic, not imperialistic or crusading. A third, great problem is finding capable, indigenous leaders who are focused on advancing the national interest rather than enriching and empowering themselves and a small inner circle.

Austere conditions because of nonexistent or destroyed infrastructure and unrealistic expectations from the indigenous population round out the primary difficulties before considering the insurgents' "vote." Of course, al Qaeda and other insurgents do not sit idly by while Western counterin-surgents do good works for the local populace and publicize COIN successes. Al Qaeda and other insurgents conduct operations against the counterinsurgents and those who support or are allied with the counterinsurgents. This causes at least three problems for COIN in the ideological realm, some of which may have strategic effects throughout the world, and all of which, if the COIN operation is defeated, have a profoundly negative strategic effect.

First, fighting between counterinsurgents and insurgents and al Qaeda is among the people. killing local civilians and destroying their property. The number of local civilians who die during fighting between counterinsurgents and insurgents or al Qaeda can be reduced by counterinsurgent combat strategies, but it cannot be eliminated. Each civilian death related to Western forces' operations may turn the family and friends of the victim, as well as the broader populace, toward the ideology the terrorists espouse. Al Qaeda propagandists work to publicize deaths, blaming counterinsurgents alone for them, and work to discredit the overall effort, ascribing improper motives, such as a Christian conquest of the Muslim world.

Second, insurgents and al Qaeda target those who align with or support counter-insurgents. This causes direct harm to those who are targeted and their families. The people also are indirectly, but tangibly, harmed when their local leaders are killed for aligning with counterinsurgents. Additional indirect harm flows from insurgents targeting NGOs which have provided long-term local aid. As expressed in a Taliban "night letter," written to a mid level aid agency supervisor: "You are an American slave. You take money from Americans and work in a malicious campaign against Muslims, so we are warning you.... People who work with and are slaves of Americans are worth killing. You are all worth killing." Negative repercussions within the international aid community and beyond from insurgents targeting aid agencies in response to COIN may delegitimize COIN ideologically.

Third, within the local and regional communities, counterinsurgent forces may be blamed for casualties caused solely and directly by insurgents or al Qaeda. For example, General McChrystal described how the death of 30 Afghan civilians whose bus struck an insurgent placed improvised explosive device (IED) may be blamed on counterin-surgents: But for the presence of the counterinsurgents, the insurgents would not have planted the IED, and the counterinsurgents did not prevent the IED detonation. Therefore, the counterinsurgents were to blame for the 30 civilian casualties. This sentiment, correct or not, may carry weight within the broader ideological debate.

The end result in a COIN may shape the ideology of fence sitters, both individuals and nations who might directly or indirectly support al Qaeda, remain neutral, or support the United States. Because of its resource intensity, COIN is inherently perceived as a major commitment and test of the will and competence of a nation that wages it. If Osama bin Laden is correct that "people... will like the strong horse," the side that is perceived as having won a COIN stands to gain in its ideological followership and soft power. Thus, a nation or coalition that wages a counterinsurgency as part of a larger overall campaign stands to gain or lose in the overall campaign if it is perceived to have won or lost a specific COIN fight.

The Mujahedeen versus Soviet Union campaign illustrates the importance of perception in winning an insurgency-counterinsurgency. The Mujahedeen were perceived to have defeated the Soviet Union in Afghanistan in the 1980s. The fact that the Soviet Army was defeated by a coalition that included critical covert U.S. assistance, especially Stinger anti-aircraft missiles, did not become part of the common perception within the Muslim world. Consequently, as the ideology behind the Mujahedeen movement gained followership, the perception of bin Laden's link to the success against the Soviets appears to have assisted him in extending al Qaeda beyond that of an organization geared to fight the Soviets in Afghanistan.

Popular Support. Popular support is necessary for more far reaching al Qaeda ends such as establishing a radical international Islamic Caliphate or smaller versions of it. Consequently, as previously discussed regarding ideology, well-conducted COIN operations that generate positive perceptions could effectively combat such far reaching terrorist ends. However, the probability of al Qaeda establishing a radical international Islamic Caliphate appears remote, irrespective of any COIN operations.

Future national and subnational radical Islamic governments, such as the pre-9/11 Taliban in Afghanistan, remain possible. Counterinsurgency might prevent such governments, but at considerable cost and strategic risk. Enthusiasm for radical Islam often declines rapidly among host populations, as evidenced in both pre-9/11 Afghanistan and the Anbar area of post-Saddam Hussein Iraq. As next discussed, support to an insurgency in such a nation or subnation may be a less costly, less risky, but equally or more effective means of displacing a radical Islamic government that supports al Qaeda.

Very small quantities of physical and human resources are required to conduct terrorist attacks with strategic effects within the United States. Thus, popular support is not a prerequisite for al Qaeda attacks that could cause great physical or psychological harm to the United States or potentially lead it into additional overseas military operations. Consequently, COIN cannot realistically prevent al Qaeda attacks within our nation.

Safe Havens. COIN is regarded as greatly diminishing an area's ability to serve as a safe haven for al Qaeda. Large-scale al Qaeda training camps likely are impractical in areas where a COIN campaign is underway. Even more modest al Qaeda undertakings potentially could become known to the local civilian populous and be reported to COIN forces, or discovered independently by counterinsurgent forces.

However, the significance of safe havens in enabling al Qaeda operations is questionable. The strategic plan for the 9/11 attacks likely could have been formulated in a variety of locations other than Afghanistan. After all, the tactical and operational planning for the 9/11 attacks was undertaken in U.S. flight schools and in the first class sections of domestic commercial aircraft, as well as at a variety of other locations in the United States and Germany. Similarly, it appears that much, if not all, of the Madrid and London mass transit bombings were planned in Spain and England, respectively.

Moreover, al Qaeda has used the Internet as a virtual sanctuary from which to carry out activities that were formerly carried out from Afghanistan before 2002.78 A friendly third world government, failed state, ungoverned area, or under-governed area is not a prerequisite for terrorist strategic, operational, or tactical planning. To the extent ungoverned or under-governed territory enables al Qaeda, it is a mistake to believe the United States or a coalition of nations can eliminate all such areas of the world. The 2009 Failed State Index lists 60 states as critical or in danger of failing.

Moreover, many nations regarded as generally sound contain ungoverned regions. For example, Mexico, which is neither critical nor in danger according to the 2009 Failed State Index, contains significant regions over which the national and state governments lack control. Moreover, transforming a failed or failing state into a weak state does not destroy al Qaeda elements within the state. Instead, there is reason to believe that weak states are significantly more conducive for al Qaeda than are failed states.

Al Qaeda members may move from areas in which counterinsurgencies are being waged to areas in close proximity, such as moving from Afghanistan to western Pakistan. Proximity, presumably, is beneficial for al Qaeda leadership associated with opposing a COIN, particularly in an area with limited means for electronic communication, such as Afghanistan. In such cases, the area in which the COIN is being waged (Afghanistan) may serve as a base for operations against al Qaeda in the adjoining area (western Pakistan). Similarly, intelligence developed in the area where the COIN is being waged may help in identifying and locating targets in the adjoining area. Nonetheless, even for al Qaeda members who move from areas in which COIN campaigns are underway to unrelated regions (from Afghanistan to Yemen, for example) the COIN likely has only temporarily disrupted the al Qaeda member's work.

Because of its high cost and large intrusive footprint on the countries in which it is practiced, COIN is not suitable as an overall strategy to disrupt al Qaeda by keeping its members perpetually on the move. Al Qaeda already has cells in an estimated 60 countries, and the United States and its allies could never conduct COIN operations in the vast majority of these countries.

Fighters. "Fighters" for al Qaeda encompass people with a wide variety of skills, just as soldiers include people whose primary mission is combat, combat support, or combat service support, with a wide variety of specific duties within each category. Al Qaeda operatives align approximately with combat soldiers. Combat al Qaeda operatives include spies, kidnappers, gunmen, suicide bombers of various types, bomb placers, remote bomb detonators, and body guards. Al Qaeda also employs combat support members such as planners, trainers, and bomb makers, as well as combat service support members such as recruiters, propagandists, and electronic information technologists.

Some al Qaeda fighters and potential recruits live in areas where counterinsurgencies are being waged or might be waged. On balance, a well-executed COIN would be expected to kill more al Qaeda members and dissuade more potential members than it inadvertently recruits for al Qaeda through collateral casualties and serving as a basis for al Qaeda propaganda. Of course the reverse likely is true for a poorly executed COIN. Assuming counterinsurgencies are well executed, it is still unclear how significant they are in reducing important fighters for al Qaeda. Areas in which counterinsurgencies are waged presumably have significant numbers of certain types of combat and combat support personnel, as well as a few specific types of combat service support personnel.

For example, Afghanistan is a superb location for al Qaeda to obtain gunmen who are well trained for infantry operations in Afghanistan. Similarly, men with rudimentary bomb making skills may be available there. However, Afghanistan likely is not a good area for al Qaeda to obtain sophisticated propagandists, skilled cyber hackers, accomplished information technologists, or those whose skills would be useful in producing any variety of a WMD or transporting it into the United States. Moreover, operatives who are highly skilled in infantry operations in Afghanistan do not necessarily have skills that would translate even to a Mumbai-style attack in the United States. Such operatives would first have to make their way into the United States and then obtain the necessary weapons and other equipment, not an easy task for a person who only speaks Pashtu or Dari and who can neither read nor write any language. Thus, while places in which counterinsurgencies are waged are excellent locations for al Qaeda to obtain fighters who are skilled in combating local counterinsurgents, these fighters' skills likely do not translate to different missions or similar missions in significantly different environments. Once the counterinsurgents have departed the area, al Qaeda likely will have limited use for large numbers of narrowly skilled, indigenous fighters.

Weapons. Biological, nuclear, and chemical WMD pose the greatest destructive capability against the United States. A sophisticated cyber attack on key U.S. infrastructure, particularly if timed to have maximum effect, also could cause great damage to the United States. Do successful counterinsurgencies prevent al Qaeda from obtaining or developing WMD or cyber warfare capabilities? The answer depends on where and when a COIN is fought. The COIN fought in Iraq appears to have had no effect in reducing al Qaeda's access to WMD or cyber-attack capability. When the United States invaded Iraq, Iraq had neither WMD nor WMD capability. Presumably, Iraq also lacked meaningful cyber-attack capability. Thus, because there was no WMD and no WMD or cyber capability at risk in Iraq, there was nothing to secure.

As was the case in Iraq, the COIN in Afghanistan is having no direct effect in reducing al Qaeda's access to WMD or cyber-attack capability. Afghanistan has never possessed either WMD or capabilities for WMD. Afghanistan's neighbor, Pakistan has a significant nuclear arsenal and mid range ballistic missiles. Advocates of a 21st century "domino theory" argue that if the Afghanistan COIN fails, instability and al Qaeda's return to robust operations in Afghanistan will destabilize Pakistan and place Pakistan's nuclear arsenal at risk. The current Afghanistan domino theory appears as flawed as the 20th century communist version. First, there is insufficient evidence that the Afghanistani insurgents will attempt to overthrow the Pakistani government. During the years it was in power, the Taliban made no attempt to overthrow the Pakistani government. Al Qaeda's announced strategy requires defeating the United States before attempting to overthrow secular Middle Eastern governments, and al Qaeda made no attempt before or concurrent with the 9/11 attacks to attack the Pakistan government.

Second, counterinsurgent activities in Afghanistan and supporting Pakistani actions appear to have been the catalyst for terrorist attacks in Pakistan. Thus, the COIN in Afghanistan appears to be a destabilizing rather than a stabilizing force in Pakistan.

Third, regardless of the Afghanistan COIN outcome, it is highly improbable that the Taliban and al Qaeda can overthrow the Pakistani government, if they seek to do so. The Pakistani military and intelligence service are both highly capable, and believe, as evidenced by their actions in Afghanistan and western Pakistan, that India threatens Pakistan far more than the Taliban and al Qaeda. It is unlikely that Pakistan will control the Federally Administered Tribal Area of western Pakistan, but Pakistan has never controlled this area, and the area has not been an existential threat to the Pakistani government and is unlikely to be so in the future. Unless the Pakistani military is defeated, Pakistan's nuclear weapons are safe from terrorist organizations.

In short, it is possible that COIN might reduce al Qaeda's access to the weapons that could most harm the United States, but that has not been the case so far. COIN is most useful in unstable second or third world countries, countries that are not apt to possess WMD, WMD production infrastructure, and accompanying delivery systems necessary to strike the United States. Personnel with the skills to build and use WMD within the United States or to launch cyber attacks against the United States are also rare in the areas counterinsurgencies are fought. Thus, as a general proposition, COIN is unlikely to deny al Qaeda the weapons that would most harm the United States.

Costs to the United States in Employing Counterinsurgency to Combat al Qaeda. Conducting COIN operations has an effect on the United States that is equally as important as the effect COIN operations have on al Qaeda. The Long War likely will be a decades-long endeavor, and the keys to prevailing are conducting the war in an efficient, sustainable manner and avoiding defeat more than achieving victory, by avoiding overreaction, incompetence, or the *perception* that the United States is either overreacting or incompetent in prosecuting the war.

It is highly unlikely that the United States can continue to conduct the Long War at its present pace for decades to come. To be sustainable, the war must be sustainable economically, politically, and militarily. At the present time, it is questionable whether the present pace for conducting the Long War is sustainable in *any* of these three aspects, much less sustainable in all three aspects.

Moreover, even if the Long War were sustainable in its current mode, the continued use of COIN still would not be the best U.S. strategy. Waging COIN entails twin risks. First, waging repeated counterinsurgencies is likely to make the United States appear to be overreacting to the damage al Qaeda has done and the threat it poses. Second, waging COIN runs a great risk of failure, making the United States appear to be incompetent. Regarding overreaction, the presence of a small to moderate U.S. force in Saudi Arabia allegedly first prompted bin Laden to target the United States. The continued presence of large numbers of U.S. and allied forces in a series of Muslim countries, operating under the express purpose of transforming the hearts and minds of the indigenous populations, could easily be seen as an imperialist overreaction or a modern day crusade against the Muslim world.

Regarding incompetence, waging COIN is a very high risk strategy because it does not employ U.S. strengths, and ultimate success is far from U.S. control. From an economic perspective, it places an enormous burden on the nation, not only in physical resources, but also in lives lost, physical and mental damage to many returning service members, and the lost productivity of mobilized Reserve and National Guard service members. Federal government spending may also distort markets.

From a domestic political perspective, the American people are notoriously hostile toward long wars involving large numbers of troops, large expenditures, no significant battle victories, and unclear or vacillating objectives. Regardless of whether U.S. operations in Afghanistan are or are not similar to the Vietnam War, the fact that such comparisons have been seriously considered by many Americans, including at the highest levels of the U.S. Government, highlights the difficulty of sustaining domestic political support for COIN. Coalition COIN partners share similar domestic political problems.

From a military perspective, COIN does not allow the United States to employ its overwhelming technological superiority. Massing fires and maneuvering large elements is nearly irrelevant in a COIN. Instead, very large numbers of culturally and linguistically capable troops are the key elements of military power. Moreover, conventional military power is only one element in a COIN campaign, and it is not the critical element. The key, creating a viable government accepted by the indigenous people, is primarily a Department of State (DoS) mission, requiring DoD support. Unfortunately, the U.S. inter-agency process is far from seamless, or even efficient. Even if the DoS and DoD each perform well, and perform well together, creating a successful indigenous government is beyond their control. In the typical military campaign, the complication is the enemy's "vote." In COIN, the enemy has a vote, the indigenous government has a vote, and the people have a vote. Winning all three elements to prevail in the COIN presents a high risk of failure, with failure carrying grave consequences.

SUBSTITUTE TO COUNTERINSURGENCY FOR WAGE THE EXTENSIVE WAR

The military resources may be used in three other broad categories in addition to COIN: counterterrorism, support to insurgency, and antiterrorism. A discussion of each of these three strategies as they might affect the eight categories of resources al Qaeda needs to attack the United States exceeds the scope of this chapter. The shorter framework offered above: Specifically, the strategic utility of counterterrorism, support to insurgency, and antiterrorism in conducting the Long War in a way that avoids losing by being sustainable, avoiding overreaction, avoiding incompetence, and not creating the perception of either overreaction or incompetence.

Counterterrorism as a Strategy

Counterterrorism operations fit within what Michael Howard describes as "[t]he qualities needed in a serious campaign against terrorists—secrecy, intelligence, political sagacity, quiet ruthlessness, covert actions that remain covert, above all infinite patience.

..."95 Moreover, counterterrorism can be conducted in conjunction with COIN or support to an insurgency, as well as concurrently with antiterrorism. Counterterrorism can be conducted by both the DoD and the CIA.

Counterterrorism can be conducted where the United States has a substantial, formal military presence, such as Afghanistan, and where the United States lacks a military presence, such as Pakistan. Counterterrorism can be conducted remotely via unmanned aerial systems (drones) and directly by U.S. personnel, from the air, ground, or sea. These characteristics make counterterrorism a versatile, flexible strategy that may be useful for a variety of missions in a variety of areas.

Benefits of Counterterrorism. Compared to COIN, offensive counterterrorism uses minimal total resources and is extremely sustainable. Drones, a large and rapidly increasing component of the U.S. counterterrorism strategy, 96 are inexpensive to build, operate, and maintain compared to conventional aircraft. Joint Special Operations Command (JSOC) forces are a precious, limited resource, but unlike COIN, which is a relatively "all or nothing" proposition and needs to be an "all" effort to succeed, counterterrorism operations may be modulated depending on available resources. For missions that cannot be achieved via drones, conventional aircraft, or offshore missiles, if the supply of JSOC forces is too small, then these forces can be reserved for the highest value targets only, passing up lower value targets. Defensive counterterrorism, such as the work conducted by the Defense Threat Reduction Agency, is similarly easily modulated, depending on the perceived threat and available funding. The United States should be able to sustain counterterrorism operations for generations.

Offensive counterterrorism is a very precise, limited strategy compared to COIN and, thus, has a much smaller chance of constituting an overreaction. Where counterinsurgency entails tens if not hundreds of thousands of troops stationed in a foreign nation, the total counterterrorism force is exponentially smaller and not stationed prominently or hostilely. Both COIN and counterterrorism on occasion mistakenly target innocent civilians or kill innocent civilians in the process of targeting insurgents or terrorists. It is unclear whether COIN or counterterrorism operations kill more innocent civilians, but the numbers may be comparable. Defensive counterterrorism, because it is preventative and nonviolent is very unlikely to be over reactive.

Counterterrorism should pose a vastly lower risk of acting in an incompetent manner compared to COIN. Both offensive and defensive counterterrorism decisions are made at a very high level, and the total number of decisions to be made is small. On the other hand, the total number of decisions that must be made daily during a COIN is orders of magnitude greater than for counterterrorism, and the average decisionmakers in COIN, including "strategic corporals," are vastly junior to counterterrorism decisionmakers. Not surprisingly, inane actions with strategically negative consequences such as the torture at Abu Ghraib and the use of a Quran for target practice occurred during COIN operations, not counterterrorism operations.

In terms of international or domestic perceptions of overreaction or incompetence, an overarching consideration for both offensive and defensive counterterrorism operations is the publically quiet manner in which they are conducted. Many offensive counterterrorism operations are publically unknown because they are conducted with great stealth and are highly classified. The overall outline of many defensive counterterrorism operations is available, but these activities do not generate headlines because of their bureaucratic nature or classified status.

Costs of Counterterrorism. The most significant costs for counterterrorism appear to be intangible, potential costs, rather than quantifiable costs that are evident today. Offensive counterterrorism operates in a legally murky realm, and often is referred to as "extra judicial killing," "unlawful killing," "assassination," or "murder." Through its counterterrorism operations, the United States may be moving toward forging new customary international law regarding how a nation may pursue members of a terrorist organization that does not follow the law of war and whose members reside in an area that lacks a functioning government, or where the government is incapable or unwilling to take action against the terrorist organization or its members.

The process of making new customary international law is slow and uncertain. If the international community concludes that counterterrorism operations as currently practiced by the United States are illegal, counterterrorism operations may be unsustainable based on a perception that they are inherently an overreaction because they are illegal. If a consensus emerged that U.S. counterterrorism operations were illegal and the United States ignored international law and continued its counterterrorism operations, the United States would risk the loss of allies and soft power and create a strategic communications bonanza for terrorist organizations. Similarly, counterterrorism or specific counterterrorism measures might be seen as inherently so odious that they might serve as a basis to recruit terrorists who are willing and able to harm the United States. There is some evidence that predator drone strikes might have served as a catalyst for the attempted May 1, 2010, Times Square car bombing.

Covert action, even if legal, also carries significant potential strategic risks for a democratic nation. George Kennan asserted that clandestine operations are out of character for the United States because they "conflict with our own traditional standards and compromise our diplomacy in other areas." Kennan did not rule out ever conducting clandestine operations, but believed regular, routine covert operations were fundamentally corrosive to what the United States stands for as a nation. U.S military operations long have been shaped to a greater or lesser degree by public opinion, subject to the press' access to information and its opinion of the justness of a given war. A virtual absence of public information to enable public debate on a counterterrorism war waged covertly could lead decisionmakers to routinely authorize or direct military action that would be unacceptable to an informed public.

Counterterrorism in governed areas without at least the tacit permission of the foreign sovereign may be unsustainable based on such actions being perceived as an overreaction. For example, Israeli Mossad agents killed a "senior field operative for Hamas" in Dubai, apparently without either the express or tacit permission of the Dubai government. Negative international reaction appears to have been enhanced because the Mossad agents used forged British and German passports in conducting the counterterrorism operation, but the incident highlights the risks and potentially unsustainable use of counterterrorism when it is perceived as an overreaction.

The use of counterterrorism in foreign nations with only tacit, conditional permission from the foreign sovereign also may be problematic. Unclassified sources postulate that U.S. drone attacks in Pakistan have the Pakistani government's tacit approval and support, with the proviso that the Pakistani government will never publicly acknowledge that it has authorized U.S. drone attacks in western Pakistan, and the Pakistani government reserves the right to condemn any particular U.S. drone attack that creates excessive collateral damage. Whether an arrangement such as this is sustainable in the long term remains an open question.

Sustaining Insurgency as a Approach

In late 2001 and early 2002, U.S. support to an insurgency, namely the Northern Alliance in Afghanistan, almost immediately succeeded in overthrowing the Taliban government, which had supported or tolerated al Qaeda and refused to surrender its members to the U.S. after the 9/11 attacks. The success of the U.S. support to the Northern Alliance in displacing the Taliban government suggests that support to insurgency is worthy of consideration as a means to employ military power in fighting the Long War.

Benefits of Supporting Insurgency. Low economic and military costs, in dollars spent, U.S. service members' lives lost or harmed, and equipment destroyed or degraded are the primary benefits of supporting an insurgency against a hostile government, compared to invading, occupying, and waging COIN. The process of routing the Taliban militarily in late 2001 and driving it from power was achieved with minimal U.S. casualties, using air power and a relatively small number of special forces ground troops. Al Qaeda's assassination of Ahmed Shah Masoud, the Northern Alliance commander, on September 9, 2001, suggests al Qaeda may have feared the U.S. might provide support to the Northern Alliance after the 9/11 attacks as a means of attacking al Qaeda. Covert, rather than open, military assistance to the Mujahedeen drove the Soviet Union from Afghanistan in the 1980s. Based on the experience in Afghanistan, there is also a basis to believe that open, direct U.S. support to an insurgency might result in rapid results.

The potential for the United States to displace a hostile government through support to an insurgency at a minimal economic cost and with relatively few U.S. casualties, carries with it a number of potential benefits in fighting the Long War. First, it should deter foreign governments from supporting al Qaeda or tolerating al Qaeda and its affiliates openly operating in their countries, and it may make foreign governments more apt to surrender terrorists who have attacked the United States. Nations typically harbor or sponsor terrorist organizations based on pragmatic rather than altruistic reasons, and likely are focused upon the stability of their regimes. A viable, low cost, low casualty strategy available to the United States to displace a regime significantly alters the calculation of whether it benefits a foreign government to harbor or sponsor al Qaeda.

Second, support to insurgencies meets the criteria of fighting in a manner that avoids losing. From an economic and military perspective, support to an insurgency is sustainable for a very long time. From a perception point of view, supporting an existing insurgency against a regime is less likely to be perceived as overreacting than is invading a nation, occupying it, and attempting to refashion the nation to U.S. liking. The danger of appearing incompetent in supporting an insurgency that fails is substantially smaller than the danger of appearing incompetent in invading, occupying, and waging a COIN. Insurgencies are apt to fail, and investing in one is a vastly smaller undertaking than the major U.S. combat operations in Iraq or our COIN operations in Iraq and Afghanistan.

Costs of Supporting Insurgency. "Sleep with Dogs, Awake with Fleas." Support to an insurgency does entail political risk. First, there is risk in supporting an insurgency that may be perceived as being no more legitimate than the government it displaces, for example, the Northern Alliance displacing the Taliban. In such a case, if international and domestic audiences perceive the United States as being sufficiently aggrieved, as was the case in late 2001 and 2002, support to an illegitimate insurgency fighting an illegitimate government likely will be seen as acceptable. On the other hand, if the United States is not perceived as being sufficiently aggrieved, the perception of support to an illegitimate insurgency may be hostile.

If an insurgency the United States openly supports fails, there is some element of incompetence that will adhere to the United States. Covert support, in theory, might reduce the stigma of incompetence, but in practice, it likely is difficult to keep significant covert assistance to an insurgency secret.

Support to an insurgency is also risky in that the leadership characteristics that make for successful insurgent leaders likely do not translate well to a government of which the United States or the international community will be proud. Thus, when the United States supports an insurgency, it usually is best to immediately dissociate from the insurgency once it has seized power, limiting the problem of guilt by association. To the extent the United States seeks to influence a successful insurgency it has supported toward making democratic choices, this is best done via inducements from afar, treating the new government as an independent sovereign.

Likely the worst approach is to assist an illegitimate insurgency, continue to station forces in the nation, and be seen as propping up an illegitimate government or dictating its illegitimate actions. It is better to allow a new government to fail, even if this means a potential return of a government that previously harbored al Qaeda or its affiliates. In such a case, support to a new insurgency or counterterrorism measures in the country remain possible courses of action if al Qaeda is allowed to return and operate openly.

Antiterrorism as a Strategy

It is difficult to imagine a rational U.S. strategy against al Qaeda that does not include antiterrorism. The four primary antiterrorism issues are determining how much to spend, determining priorities, ensuring a rational and coherent federal, state, and local interaction, and determining how much and in what ways to employ military resources. Answers to these four complicated issues will not be addressed here, instead overarching benefits and costs of antiterrorism as a strategy, and specific benefits and costs of employing military resources for antiterrorism will be considered.

Benefits of Antiterrorism. Antiterrorism is an economically sustainable strategy. The resource commitment to antiterrorism can be modulated relatively easily. If resources or the perceived threat diminish, annual expenditures can be reduced by diminishing funding to the lowest priority antiterrorism measures, making pro rata cuts to all programs, or some combination of lowest priority and pro rata expenditure reductions.

The cost for individual active duty or mobilized service members stationed in the United States who are performing antiterrorism duties is far less than the cost of service members stationed in remote areas overseas who are performing COIN, counterterrorism, or support to insurgency missions, primarily because of the difference in logistical support costs. Further, the costs for Reserve and National Guard service members who work at civilian jobs in local communities but are available for antiterrorism duties on an as needed basis are a fraction of the costs for an active duty service member.

Antiterrorism is a politically sustainable strategy. Because antiterrorism measures are within the United States, they are subject to great scrutiny and great debate by the U.S. electorate and its elected officials. The U.S. democratic process minimizes the possibility of overreaction through antiterrorism actions. The modulation of antiterrorism based on the public's tolerance for inconvenience and civil liberties infringements, versus safety, ensures overall perceptions of overreaction are remedied promptly. Antiterrorism also is unlikely to be perceived as an overreaction by foreign audiences, who experience the antiterrorism measures only if they travel, or attempt to travel, to the United States. This greatly diminishes the foreign audience which may perceive U.S. antiterrorism measures as an overreaction. Additionally, it is universally accepted that nations may much more freely engage in actions within their borders than would be acceptable elsewhere.

Displays of governmental incompetence certainly are possible with antiterrorism measures, but unlike some other strategies, greater antiterrorism efforts should reduce the number of failures. Moreover, unsuccessful efforts to prevent terrorist attacks on U.S. soil and to minimize the consequences of completed attacks evidence a lower level of potential error than failure to foresee threats at all or to undertake any measures to forestall or mitigate them. The potential for the perception of governmental incompetence both within the United States and abroad exists if there is a successful terrorist attack by al Qaeda, particularly if the attack is serious. However, there appears to be a growing understanding both domestically and internationally that complete safety from all terrorist attacks is impossible.

From a military perspective, antiterrorism includes at least four key specific benefits. First, antiterrorism is potentially effective against an organization and individuals who cannot be deterred. Second, antiterrorism constitutes the final layer in the overall means of preventing al Qaeda from inflicting harm on the United States and its citizens. Third, antiterrorism serves as a means to limit the effects of any successful attack within the United States. Fourth, some antiterrorism measures intended to prevent a successful al Qaeda attack in the United States, or to minimize the consequences of a successful attack, serve beneficial purposes in preventing or responding to other threats and events.

The effective Cold War strategy of mutual assured destruction succeeded because both the U.S. and Soviet governments placed a high value on the continued existence of their nations. It is unclear, however, whether al Qaeda might not willingly end its existence in exchange for destroying the United States. Members of al Qaeda who successfully conduct suicide bombings are clearly willing to end their existence in the present world to achieve their missions. Antiterrorism measures that prevent al Qaeda operatives from trading their existence for the existence of the United States or its citizens thus are an essential part of the U.S. war against al Qaeda.

Antiterrorism also is essential as the last line of defense against al Qaeda operatives who have not been dissuaded by counterinsurgency, destroyed by counterterrorism, or destroyed or controlled through support to an insurgency. If a terrorist bomb is analogized to an exploding soccer ball, antiterrorism is the goalie who prevents the proximate bomb from entering the United States, or who covers the ball that has entered the United States before it explodes.

If or when a terrorist event occurs in the United States, antiterrorism is the mechanism for managing and mitigating the event's consequences, preventing a bad event from becoming far worse. In some ways the consequence management aspect of antiterrorism is a quasi second chance opportunity. After not preventing an al Qaeda attack, federal, state, and local governments have an opportunity to respond promptly, competently, and courageously to help survivors, avoid additional casualties, clean up the wreckage, and return an affected area to normal or as near normal as is possible.

Many antiterrorism measures that might prevent or mitigate the consequences of a completed al Qaeda attack also are beneficial for preventing or minimizing the consequences of other potential or actual disasters, both manmade and naturally occurring. Terrorists who are not affiliated with al Qaeda may be thwarted by antiterrorism measures, and for any attacks they complete, the quasi second chance consequence management principles apply. Many natural disasters and some human caused accidents cannot be prevented. The same consequence management systems that are beneficial for mitigating the effects of a completed terrorist attack are equally beneficial for mitigating disaster effects.

Military resources have the potential to be beneficially employed in both the preventive and consequence management aspects of antiterrorism. Forces with specialized training and equipment may be able to perform missions that civilian forces either cannot perform or that would require expending inordinate amounts of resources to obtain specialized equipment and training that rarely would be used. Military forces with specialized training and equipment may be beneficial for both preventing domestic al Qaeda attacks and also responding to completed attacks. Military forces may also provide much larger numbers of personnel and larger quantities of logistical support more rapidly than nonmilitary forces. Rapidly available, large numbers of forces, with substantial logistical support capability are particularly beneficial for the consequence management aspect of antiterrorism.

Costs of Antiterrorism. The greatest cost of antiterrorism is political. Domestic antiterrorism actions meant to prevent al Qaeda attacks would be fundamentally incompatible with U.S. values that cherish individual liberties if these actions transform the

United States from a free, open society into a police state. Civil liberties activists see even changes such as the Patriot Act as a victory for al Qaeda against the American way of life. Many antiterrorism actions designed to reduce domestic vulnerability to al Qaeda attacks may be seen by many Americans as too costly to civil liberties, absent more severe attacks.

If transforming the United States into a police state is unacceptable to the American people, transforming it into a military state is at least doubly unacceptable. Consequently, the domestic use of military resources within U.S. antiterrorism measures is significantly constrained. The Posse Comitatus Act places legal limits on the use of federal forces for police purposes, but political constraints based on the ideological underpinnings of the Act also impose constraints. A majority of the U.S. public was relatively comfortable with the presence of National Guard soldiers armed with M-16s in airports in the immediate aftermath of the 9/11 attacks. Similarly, the use of National Guard and Army Reserve units during the post Hurricane Katrina response also was acceptable to the American people. Nonetheless, it is essential to never employ military resources in domestic antiterrorism efforts beyond what the American people consider to be acceptable.

Domestic antiterrorism measures may be substantially cheaper on a per service member basis than overseas deployments, but antiterrorism measures nonetheless carry a substantial economic cost. Additionally, the efficiency of domestic antiterrorism expenditures arguably is reduced by political considerations which may dictate the division of federal expenditures based on electoral considerations and political seniority and power, rather than based solely on an impartial weighting of vulnerability, probability of attack, and magnitude of harm from a completed attack. Additionally, for each dollar expended, the bureaucracy necessary to implement and monitor expenditures in a federal, state, and local system may exceed the bureaucracy necessary to implement and monitor military expenditures for counterinsurgency, counterterrorism, and support to insurgency.

11

Rethinking Conquest in Counterinsurgency

As a general rule, Americans are averse to war and are easily frustrated with wars of limited objectives. As such, Americans have a cultural aversion to counterinsurgency (COIN) – which is ironic given our success using asymmetric tactics against the British in the Revolutionary War. Moreover, Americans have grown to expect total victory in the form of unconditional surrender as the termination of any conflict. We consider anything less as a loss or stalemate.

The nature of COIN is inherently political – David Galula posits that COIN is eighty percent political and twenty percent military. General Sir Frank Kitson posits that "there can be no such thing as a purely military solution because insurgency is not a primarily military activity." As such, the use of the term "victory" as a description of the termination of conflict when the U.S. involves itself in COIN is problematic.

The political nature of COIN and the American way of viewing war and termination of conflict require that we adopt a new definition of "victory" in a COIN operation. The term "victory," as the term is classically defined and as viewed by Americans, does not fit in COIN planning or execution owing to the nature of the objective in a COIN operation. In any conflict, the definition of what constitutes "victory" and who defines "victory" can remain fluid and this is especially true in COIN. A comparison of the British experience in Northern Ireland, which many consider victory, to the U.S. experience in Iraq, which many consider a loss, demonstrates the need for a better definition for the termination of a COIN operation.

Based on analysis of the outcomes of historical case studies of COIN operations and what portends to be the future of warfare, this chapter argues that we create a definition of "success" for the termination of a COIN operation and replace the term "victory" in COIN in the military's vocabulary.

CLASSICAL AND MODERN DEFINITIONS OF VICTORY

Carl von Clausewitz describes his concept of victory as "the enemy's greater loss of material strength, his loss of morale, and his open admission of the above by giving up his intentions." Emile Simpson's book, War from the Ground Up provides a superb analysis and application of Clausewitz view of war to war in the 21st Century. He concludes that the nature of war and the world has changed. Accordingly, Clausewitz' views and analysis of war should change to fit the new way of war. His analysis provides a starting point for the definition of success in COIN.

The major shortfalls with Clausewitz' language and definition of victory as it relates to COIN are the implication that war is a conflict between the wills of two nationstates, the limitation of polarization to twosides, and the absence of the perception of the strategic audience. Clausewitz' use of two men wrestling as an example of war as an act of force to compel the enemy to do our will evidences his reliance on the twoparty conflict model. All of the remaining analysis and discussion of war derives from this twoparty system, absolute or limited, offensive and defensive battle.

Even his incorporation of the political domain remains limited to two opposing parties or nationstates. As a result, Clausewitz treats the outcome of any war, victory or defeat and absolute or limited, as defined against the other party. Moreover, the outcome is always a military outcome, albeit connected to the achievement of some political policy. To achieve the policy, to impose one's will on the other, requires that one must break the will of the other.

Is breaking the will of an insurgency possible in the 21st Century? Can one break the will of an ideology?

Clausewitz' use of polarization in describing conflict is similarly limited to two sides, including his discussion of multiparty conflict. In polarization, again, there is a military outcome and that outcome is mutually exclusive, victory or defeat. The enemy is traditionally what a military outcome is measured against. Moreover, victory on one side necessarily excludes victory on the other. Outside of complete destruction of the other, is victory on one side to the exclusion of the other side achievable? If this result requires the complete destruction of the other, is this achievable or even desirable in the 21st Century? Is this result achievable in COIN? We think the answer to these questions is no because the end state in COIN, currently described as victory to one side and defeat to the other, is a perception, and a perception dependent on multiple views.

Clausewitz' analysis and discussion also fails to address the importance of the strategic audience. Clausewitz' interpreters of the conflict, or the perceiving parties in the conflict, are the two sides, our side and their side, and within each side, the army, people and the government. This is not the case in COIN. There are generally multiple parties in the conflict, and within those parties, there are multiple viewpoints. Polarity as described by Clausewitz is relative when dealing with multiple parties in COIN and the multiple viewpoints within each "side" in COIN. By way of example, the U.S. political leadership's view of Operation Iraqi Freedom and Operation Enduring Freedom seemed to change depending on the administration in power and party affiliation, and the views seemed to have little relation to actual success in those operations.

Clausewitz connects the desired military outcome, in terms of victory or defeat, to a political outcome. This is backwards in COIN. The military end state should not change to fit the definition of political success. Moreover, in COIN, the end state requires sustainability which in turn requires an enduring perception by the strategic audience. If victory and defeat are perceptions, then neither term is enduring. Accordingly, those terms should not be used in planning for and executing a COIN operation. B.H. Liddell Hart defines victory as "the state of peace of one's own people is better after the war than before...." "Victory is only possible if a quick result can be gained or if a long effort can be economically proportioned to the national resources the end must be adjusted to the means." This utilitarian view of employing military forces is unsustainable and is susceptible to a default position of never engaging in any war. My father, a retired Marine, told me prior to my first deployment to Iraq that he thought the life of one U.S. Marine was more valuable than any of the millions in the region. Moreover, the "peace" of a family who lost a son, daughter, mother or father, will likely always be better before the war than after. A "better peace" is simply a too stringent measure because inaction in the near term will always be the more costeffective solution in light of uncertain military outcomes.

Modern Definitions of Victory

In Winning Counterinsurgency War: The Israeli Experience, MAJGEN Yaakov Amidror provides three potential definitions of victory in COIN based on his experience in fighting Palestinian terror organizations. The first, "Total Victory," is the complete elimination of the terrorist organizations and guerrilla groups. He uses the example of the defeat of Communist guerrillas in Greece after the Second World War where the Greek army with British support completely destroyed the terror movement.

The second, "Temporary Victory," is represented by the IDF victory over Palestinian terror organizations in Gaza in the early 1970s. The IDF reduced the terrorist organizations in Gaza, and then reduced the size of the IDF in Gaza so that the IDF units could move freely. The terrorist threat resurfaced approximately fifteen years later, but with a new and different form. The third, "Sufficient Victory," achieves what he labels as a "repressed quiet," requiring the continuous effort to preserve the peace. He uses the example of the British in Northern Ireland.

Amidror acknowledges that most significant problem in defining victory is that a military victory is classically measured by the number of casualties inflicted on the enemy in manpower and equipment. He also acknowledges that in COIN, achievement of success is measured by criteria that are not clearly military, the degree of security, and indices of economic growth. Similarly, Moshe Yaalon notes that as chief of staff for the Israeli Defense Forces, he spoke of "the decisive victory." He defined decisive victory as that point when the terrorists, supporters, and political leadership come to the realization that terrorism's costs outweigh the benefits. His "decisive victory" is gained by winning tactical engagements, reducing the terrorist threat, and by strengthening society's resilience in the face of terrorism. These are not exclusively military actions.

A Theory Of Victory

Professor Bartholomees essay "Theory of Victory" does not provide a definition of victory, but provides a description of the conditions of what can be considered victory and how victory is perceived. He argues that victory in war is an assessment, not a fact or condition. In other words, victory is someone's opinion or a collection of opinions regarding the outcome. What matters is the perception of the outcome, not the facts of the outcome. In defining the conditions for victory, Professor Bartholomees posits that achieving a preferred outcome is the most basic element of conflict termination.

However, he argues that achievement of a favourable outcome, preferable to accepting alternatives or continuing the war, "does not equate to victory." He also notes that in certain circumstances a tie or stalemate may be based on conditions better than losing but something less than victory.

Finally, he notes that achievement of a desired outcome may constitute the condition for conflict termination, but the end of fighting does not necessarily signify victory. In fact, sometimes it is desirable to terminate conflicts without allowing the conflict to produce a winner. At the strategic level, Bartholomees notes that public opinion decides who wins and loses, and to what extent, based on an assessment of the postwar political conditions. The military situation plays a role, but the most important criterion is political.

He also argues that to be effective, the victory needs to be recognized and accepted by the opponent, and sustainable. He concludes that strategic victory is "a positive assessment of the postwar political situation in terms of achievement and decisiveness that is acknowledged, sustainable, and resolves underlying political issues." Professor Bartholomees also identifies the "assessors" of victory in the United States. He argues that the important opinions are "(1) the American people; (2) American political and military elites; (3) the opinion of friends and allies; and (4) world opinion." Emile Simpson would describe this collective group as the strategic audience. The affect of the strategic audience on perceived victory cannot be understated.

Emile Simpson's description of the Malayan Emergency, which according to conventional wisdom holds the blueprint for victory in COIN, demonstrates the importance of strategic audience and perception. The British viewed Malaya as a victory in 1960. However, the Communist Party in Malaya did not surrender until 1989, evidence that its will was not broken until close to 30-years following the cessation of armed conflict. However, it seems that the strategic audience was apathetic after 1960. Malaya and communism were no longer relevant to British policy.

The American Definition of Victory

It is important to note that FM 3-24 does not identify or provide a definition of "victory." This is likely owing to the fact that the classic definitions of victory fail to apply in COIN. It is also owing to another issue unrelated to the nature of COIN which should be considered in the use of language, the American view of war. Using Russell Weigley's *The American Way of War: A History of United States Military Strategy and Policy*, Colin Gray argues that the American public, strategic, and military culture does not meld with the requirements of counterinsurgency and counterterrorism. If so, the "culture" needs to be adapted and it should begin with language.

Gray addresses close to a dozen issues, but several directly relate to the notion of victory in COIN. First, he notes that there exists a cultural and skill bias contrast between the U.S. soldier and the civilian politician. In COIN, the policy and military means must work in tandem, with policy taking the lead. Moreover, the policy should be chosen and be revised in light of military probabilities. In the U.S., the professional soldier and professional politician "inhabit quite distinctive subcultural universes that have different rules and are marked by distinctive skill biases," which create problems with communication, i.e., bad news during an election cycle. A case in point is Gen. James L. Jones', the then National Security Advisor to President Obama, admonition regarding the potential request for additional forces prior to the Afghanistan "surge," or then Senator Hillary Clinton's treatment of GEN Petraeus prior to the implementation of the Iraqi surge.

Gray also highlights two issues related to how Americans treat war and peace. In the U.S., we tend to separate war and peace as two distinct conditions, i.e., we are either at war or at peace. Gray notes that this can become a lethal weakness when conducting COIN owing to the need for military action to set the conditions for a political solution. The flip side to this coin is what Gray calls America's "problem-solving faith" and optimism. COIN is based on political, religious, or ideological grievances, leading to armed struggle. These conditions are endured, maybe mitigated, but generally tolerated. A problem set can be solved. The American problem-solving spirit and optimism creates problems in COIN because terrorist-insurgents are not problems to be solved, but a condition to be addressed by direct political action and indirect military action, e.g., by providing security to the people as a means of gaining their trust. American optimism often creates situations where our military is asked and expected to achieve the impossible, do it quickly, and decisively.

Finally, the American way of war is aggressive and works best in the offensive, which are required where decisive victory is the goal, e.g., to remove enemy forces from "illgotten gains, or otherwise taught the error of their ways." Another reason is that the domestic political environment requires American participation to be completed as rapidly as possible in order to return to peace and "normalcy." America historically enters wars to stop evil regimes or evil actions, e.g. Hitler and Fascism. In COIN, the insurgent is the secondary objective and overly aggressive military action can be counterproductive.

In an interview of COL Gian Gentile regarding his book, COL Gentile encapsulates the "American Way of War" and its potential negative effect on COIN operations. COL Gentile quotes Liddell Hart's definition of the object of war is to produce a "better state of peace" at a reasonable cost in blood and treasure. He then notes that the U.S. experience in Afghanistan is a failure as against Liddell Hart's metric as too expensive in terms of lives lost and dollars spent for what is at best a corrupt and failing state. He advocates the use of military force when American vital interests in the world are threatened and the application of military force is deemed appropriate.36 If these conditions are present, the U.S. should go in quickly with decisive military force, accomplish important objectives, and then leave.

In past conflicts, U.S. adversaries accepted our view of total victory. In COIN, several different parties constitute the strategic audience and they must be convinced of success. In other words, several different actors must accept and buy into our proposed definition. Our goal should be to influence our strategic audience, either in protecting our internal strategic audience, the American people or allies, or influencing the external audience, the host nation and adversary, to accept our view of success or end state. These multiple actors will likely possess a different view of success from the U.S.'s "total military victory," and some will reject the U.S. notion of victory. Accordingly, if we are to engage in COIN, we should change our definition and terms. LtCol Daniel Lasica argues one step further in a monograph advocating a theory of victory for hybrid warfare, namely, that senior decision makers must understand the enemy's theory of victory and incorporate this understanding into their own theory of victory.

The U.S. view of war and victory must be taken into account in assessing victory in COIN and in preparing a definition of success in COIN. Historically, the U.S. views any theory of victory short of total defeat and unconditional surrender as a failure. The American way of war arguably seeks to destroy the enemy's military rather than serving as an extension of policy. It tends to ignore, or pay short shrift to the process of turning military victory into strategic gains. The idea of complete military victory is achievable in conventional threats, but is not achievable in COIN. If total military victory is a prerequisite to political outcome, there is a gap between ways, means and ends when the U.S. engages in COIN.

Assuming a Political Solution, Who defines victory in COIN?

The answer to this question demonstrates the problem with the term "victory." In the British experience in Northern Ireland, victory depends on where one sits. Both Sinn Fein and the Nationalist Party claim victory. The paramilitary organizations claim that the conflict is not over. One wonders whether the British military views the Good Friday Agreement as a victory.

During the Malayan emergency Oliver Lyttleton said "you cannot win the war without the help of the population, and you cannot get the support of the population without at least beginning the win the war." Perception and the strategic audience are two key pieces to the COIN puzzle. The population must adopt the perception that the government offers a better deal than the insurgents. Perception is vital and in the 21st Century, perception shaped by media is reality. Taking the best course of action is not always important, the perception of taking the best course of action is important.

Success in COIN cannot be Military Victory but political resolution.

Amidror's temporary victory and sufficient victory fail to provide a sustainable resolution, in large part because the means they fail to address root causes of the conflict.

He notes that so long as political, national, ethnic, economic, religious, ideological grievances exist, insurgent groups will use the grievance to recruit members. Additionally, so long as the active hard-core membership exists, the conflict will continue. A military effort cannot be expected to solve a political, national, ethnic, economic, religious, ideological grievance. As a result, short of complete destruction of the insurgent organization, resolution must be based in a political approach. Such an approach, in the American way of warfare, does not come from the military, but from politicians.

History also supports seeking a negotiated result to COIN. Sir Robert Thompson's five principles of COIN from the Malaya Emergency are (1) the government must have a clear political aim: to establish and maintain a free, independent and united country which is politically and economically stable and viable; (2) the government must function in accordance with law; (3) the government must have an overall plan; (4) the government must give priority to defeating the political subversion, not the guerillas; (5) in the guerilla phase of an emergency, a government must secure its base areas first. S.N. Bjelojac in 1966 noted that the outcome of an insurgency is not decided by decisive battles and does not end with an identifiable victory or defeat characterized by the capitulation of the enemy and surrender of its forces.

If COIN is 80% political, the end state is necessarily political. The primary instrument of power cannot be military. Therefore, victory in COIN cannot be defined by Clausewitz or Liddell Hart. Sir Robert's five principles reinforce this position with its emphasis on government action and in the political and legal realms.

The Existing Definitions are Insufficient

The Clausewitz and Liddell Hart definitions fail to address a multiparty view of "victory."

Professor Bartholomees correctly identifies the problem of perception, but admittedly does not define "victory," and does not address victory in COIN. Amidror's temporary victory and sufficient victory note that the resolution cannot be a military solution but political compromise. The American way of war and its unique view of "victory," however, require that we jettison the term "victory" from our COIN language. The more applicable term, "success," is a combination of Liddell Hart's considerations of a "better peace," the end state of Yaalon's decisive victory, and the means used to attain Amidror's "sufficient victory." This definition of success must then be accepted by Professor Bartholomees' strategic audience.

What does success in COIN look like?

Is it the elimination of the insurgent group? Or is it the perceived legitimacy of the host nation government? The basis of an insurgency is usually a complex set of problems and issues which likely cannot be solved, at least not by the U.S. These are problems which must be mitigated, "resolving a complex problem to an acceptable level." Although this sounds remarkably similar to reaching an "acceptable level of violence," one must be careful to avoid a result that is "good enough for government work."

A recent RAND analysis of historic COIN actions in modern history provides indicators of success in COIN. The study uses several factors in labeling a particular case study as government win or mixed result, government win. The deciding factors as to whether a case study was a "win," were whether the government stayed in power through the end of the conflict and whether it retained sovereignty over the region of conflict. If the government remained in power and the country remained intact, the authors then considered whether the government made concessions to the insurgents or yielded to insurgent demands. In those case studies where the government stayed in power, the country remained intact, and no major concessions were granted to the insurgents, the authors concluded that the COIN force unambiguously won. If, however, major concessions were made, then the outcome was labelled as mixed.

A second RAND study analyzed the end of eightynine separate counterinsurgencies. The authors defined "insurgent win" in those cases where the insurgent group succeeded in an overthrow of the government, successful annexation of independent territory, a marked recognition of minority rights or property rights, or, dramatic political success. This study separated outright government win from a mixed outcomes by identifying only those insurgencies that effected a political upheaval through an existing process. If the government survived but made some concessions to insurgents, it was labelled "mixed outcome."

The authors characterized a government win where the COIN force destroyed the insurgent cadre, the insurgent political structure, or both. The authors noted that in certain cases, governments crushed insurgent forces or movements only to see them reappear years or decades later. They concluded that this is "typically the case when the government fails to address the root causes of the insurgency." The authors also noted that government can achieve victory through legitimate political channels, but this usually required some accommodation to insurgent demands.

The study highlights a few interesting outcomes which support the proposed definition of success in COIN. One, of seventy three insurgencies studied, more than half were settled through negotiations. Including other means of government recognition, by ceasefires, or amnesty offers, all but 12 were settled.

Additionally, in several of the cases, "defeated" insurgencies splintered into smaller, moreviolent terrorist organizations, or went underground in order to reinitiate conflict when conditions improved. The authors referred to these people as "irredeemable," who if absorbed and protected by the local population and are able to demonstrate continuing grassroots support, continue the insurgency. However, when the government addressed the root causes of the grievance and reincorporated the insurgents into society, the insurgency ended. The authors conclude that creating a sustainable end to insurgency requires social, economic, and political change, and not solely military action. By eliminating the source of grievance, the government eliminates the grassroots support necessary to feed an insurgency, regardless of whether the insurgent cadre is wholly destroyed.

Is the British experience in N. Ireland a modern example of success in COIN?

This is not meant to be an exposition on the British experience in Northern Ireland, but a summary of the modern conflict for the purposes of analyzing the termination of the conflict, to highlight certain courses of action taken during the conflict, and to question whether the end result constitutes success.

Owing to an outgrowth of violence in response to the civil rights movement in Northern Ireland, the British government deployed the British armed forces to Northern Ireland in 1969. The view at the time was that the Royal Ulster Constabulary was unable to handle the escalating violence coupled with the perception that the Ulster Special Constabulary, known as the 'B Specials' were nothing more than a protestant army. Initially, the British troops were welcomed by Catholics. This view soon changed and the British forces became targets of violence and the source of grievance. The governments of Britain and Northern Ireland and British forces soon made several serious COIN missteps which would haunt their experience throughout the conflict.

In 1971, the British military was accused of shooting unarmed protestors in Derry. There were several allegations over the next two years of British troops killing unarmed civilians, including the infamous "Bloody Sunday" incident where the British Army is accused of killing thirteen unarmed civilians participating in a civil rights march in Derry. From the UK Doctrinal Publication 3-40 on Stabilisation Operations:

Members of the Parachute Regiment appeared to have run amok, live on TV, and the pictures of a Catholic priest running, half-crouched, through the Bogside waving a white handkerchief to try and help a fatally wounded victim will haunt the British establishment forever. Its effect was devastating. Gerry Adams later commented that on the back of Bloody Sunday 'money, guns and recruits flooded into the IRA'.

Eventually, the government in Westminster asserted control over security forces, which may have been a mixed bag given British Home Secretary Reginald Maudling's declaration that the situation in Northern Ireland amounted to "an acceptable level of violence." In 1971, the government in Northern Ireland reenacted the internment law, allowing authorities the power to indefinitely detain suspected terrorists without trial. The reintroduction of the internment power led to increased violence. Eventually, the parliament in Stormont was suspended despite an attempted power-sharing agreement in 1974 between Catholic and Protestant leaders. Unionists rejected the agreement and initiated a labour strike causing the newly formed government to resign. Westminster conducted direct rule for several years.

In the opinion of a U.S. Joint Special Operations Unit study, the major contributor in eventual pacification was Britain's nonmilitary response to the paramilitary violence coupled with a reduction in British forces. For example, public spending drastically increased with social security outlays increased by 102 percent to cope with the rise in unemployment and underdevelopment. The government in London directed money to three major areas jobs, housing, and education. London also increased expenditures on housing creating Northern Ireland Housing Executive. Britain created the Industrial Development Board to alleviate unemployment and created the Fair Employment Agency to eliminate discrimination in private hiring. London transferred control of public works from local authority to new executive boards.

They also expanded education opportunities in university and vocational schools. In local elections, they scrapped sectarian gerrymandering and established new boundaries, voting systems, and enfranchisement resulting in increased Catholic representation on District Councils. This renewed feeling of political empowerment, and the election of Bobby Sands to Westminster, led IRA leader Gerry Adams to look toward political settlement.

Britain also sought to engage the strategic audience. Its leaders dealt with people with blood on their hands. This occurred despite Prime Minister Thatcher's declaration that the British Government does not negotiate with terrorists. In 1972, Secretary of State for Northern Ireland William Whitelaw engaged in secret talks with the provisional IRA. Prime Minister Thatcher also negotiated indirectly with the IRA during the 1981 hunger strikes. Britain engaged the Republic of Ireland creating the Joint Law Enforcement Commission and discussed the extradition of terrorist suspects and other domestic legal issues, including consultative rights over British policy in Northern Ireland.

The Good Friday Agreement eventually signed in 1998 called for a transfer of power from London to Belfast, the removal of British military, a decommissioning of the paramilitary organizations and the creation of a power sharing arrangement between Unionist and Republican in the government. Over time, control of the police and justice functions would transfer from London to Belfast. After several starts and stops of governmentrule from Belfast, in 2007, Rev. Ian Paisley Sr. and Martin McGuiness were sworn in First Prime Minister and First Deputy Prime Minister. The Unionist view at the time was that the agreement was a victory because it contained an explicit acknowledgement that Northern Ireland would remain a part of the United Kingdom and because Unionists would effectively control the new Northern Ireland Assembly. David Trimble stated that "the struggle that has lasted 12 years for justice and equality for Unionists has succeeded." Ian Paisley, Jr. of the UDP takes the position that the Republicans lost and the Unionists won. He notes that the Republicans pledged their loyalty to Crown forces and to enforce Crown laws.

The Republican view is that they entered negotiation knowing that a united Ireland was not an option, but that the new Assembly would give Catholics a greater voice in Northern Ireland that at any other time in its history. The release of Catholic paramilitary prisoners and the departure of the British Army was a victory. Jennifer McCann, MP for Sinn Fein, maintains that the Republicans were not defeated, Republicans don't feel defeated, and Sinn Fein has not given up its goal of a Socialist united Ireland.

However, the rank and file on both sides feel as if their politicians let them down. The sight of Martin McGuiness shaking hands with Queen Elizabeth and the Union Jack flying in front of the Stormont government are noted as evidence of betrayal. There has been no real reconciliation between Catholics and Protestants in the province as noted by the "peace walls" which are now twice as high and long as they were when the Good Friday agreement was signed in 1998. Additionally, many Provisional IRA and UDF members fell back on criminal enterprises instead of being reintroduced into civil society. 2013 was one of the worst years of rioting in Northern Ireland for a decade and some of the highest levels of street violence and attacks by militant groups since a peace and power-sharing deal in 1998. Derry-based Republican Action Against Drugs (RAAD) enforce vigilante justice against local drug dealers but also target the Police Service of Northern Ireland (PSNI) as Crown forces.

Moreover, groups such as 32 County Sovereignty Movement make similar public statements regarding a socialist united Ireland.

Is the success sustainable? Fifteen years following the agreement, the answer is not settled. However, the result is considered success in COIN. British civic action programs, political reform and diplomatic efforts with the Republic of Ireland and the United States, brought about the cessation of armed conflict. Addressing the roots of discontent and discrimination raised in the Civil Rights movement served to create the perception that the government in Northern Ireland was offering a better deal and that it's better to participate in the new government in Northern Ireland than to destroy it. These actions "siphoned off enough anger, enticed enough collaborators, and neutralized enough opposition that it undermined much of the minority's support for IRA violence and led to a peaceful political resolution."

A LOCALIZED INSURGENCY

Afghanistan's politics and economy are extremely localized. Every area is like a separate country. It is not uncommon for major developments in one area to have little or no effect on places just miles away, or for tactics that worked in one place to fail miserably in villages nearby. Marines and Soldiers operating in Afghanistan need to understand their local environment on its own terms and tailor their operations accordingly—with the understanding that conditions vary widely from place to place.

Units required considerable autonomy, flexibility, and creativity, in order to adapt to the unique conditions in their areas of operations. It was extremely difficult for higher headquarters to develop a full picture of the conditions in remote districts. One had to be there for an extended period to develop even a basic understanding of the environment. In many cases, platoons and companies operated in places so isolated that conditions were radically different and almost entirely disconnected from the rest of the battalion's area of operations.

These differences explain a lot about why successes could apparently be achieved in some places but not others. For example, Canadian forces in Dand district south of Kandahar City made considerable progress employing sound counterinsurgency techniques. Yet Dand was also a relatively peaceful area dominated by tribes inclined to support the government. In Panjwayi to the west, the Canadians faced considerable difficulty and lost many Soldiers—in part because they employed a more heavyhanded approach, but also because the tribes of the Panjwayi had strong connections to the Taliban and a long history of armed resistance.

Sangin district in northern Helmand province was one of the most dangerous parts of Afghanistan, in part because of early operations by the British. But much of the problem was the town's unique tribal makeup and the fact that it was a major center for the drug trade. Techniques employed with some success in other parts of Helmand had little effect in Sangin.

In Nawa district in central Helmand, the US Marines met with quick success, but efforts in Marjah just a short distance away ran into serious trouble—not because of different tactics, but because Marjah was a different sort of place. In the east as well, there were places such as the Korangal Valley in Kunar province where US operations led to violent and intractable situations in some valleys but not others.

In some places, there was an identifiable leadership to work with, in others there appeared to be no one in charge. For example, in Chora district in Uruzgan province, Dutch forces were able to build relationships with some key tribal leaders, which helped stabilize the area. The Dutch then expanded into the nearby Baluchi Valley only to find that there was no discernible tribal leadership. The area was a hornet's nest of competing Ghilzai clans heavily infiltrated by the Taliban.

The area's only prominent leader had been killed in a US raid the year before. In some places, the fighting had almost nothing to do with the Taliban or other groups based in Pakistan. In some valleys in the northeast, the insurgency was about resistance to outside influence and little else. This was the case, for example, in the Korangal Valley in Kunar province, one of the most dangerous places for US forces. Similar motivations drove much of the fighting farther north in Nuristan. Pashtun tribes across the south and east have a long and proud history of taking up arms against outsiders of every stripe.

A common thread throughout all the vignettes in this book is the importance of involving the local population, communities, leaders, and existing social political and economic structures in what the unit commanders were trying to accomplish. Those units that understood the local situation and involved the local population to greater degrees were often able to reach their objectives with less conflict and fewer casualties. Local approaches worked best.

Navigating the political terrain

Insurgency is inherently political. It is about employing organized violence to achieve political objectives. The insurgents in Afghanistan are cunning political operatives. To be effective, small units needed to have an intimate knowledge of the political terrain and the ability to navigate it shrewdly. The more successful units immersed themselves in the complex politics in their areas of operation. They gathered information on tribal and ethnic groups—their viewpoints, interests, disputes, and histories of conflict.

Every district and valley of Afghanistan is an intricate web of locally-based tribal and clan rivalries, disputes over land and other resources, and feuds that go back generations. In talking to coalition forces, village leaders often spoke ill of elders in nearby hamlets. The Taliban took advantage of divisions between clans and powerbrokers, forming alliances with those who harbored grievances against the government or the coalition, or whose interests were threatened by the US presence.

Ongoing feuds between clans and tribes mirrored the fighting between insurgents and coalition troops. It was common to see one clan or tribe ally with the government and US forces, and its rival with the Taliban or other Pakistan-based insurgent groups—much like regional powers during the Cold War who joined the United States or the Soviet Union in order to gain lever-age against their neighbours. It was not possible to separate these local-level political dynamics from the insurgency writ large; they were inextricably linked. One of the unintended consequences of forming deep alliances with local tribal groups or powerbrokers was that it created suspicion and resentment among other groups who then joined the Taliban to balance the power of their rivals. By taking sides and allying with certain powerbrokers, the United States alienated others—creating opportunities that the Taliban exploited masterfully.

For example, in the Deh Rashaan Valley in Uruzgan, US and Dutch forces worked closely with Barakzai and Popalzai tribesmen and carried out raids against rival Ghilzai tribes to the north. The Ghilzais in turn allied with the Taliban. In Gulistan in southwest Afghanistan there were two rival Noorzai Pashtun clans. When the Marines arrived in the spring of 2008, the militarily weaker but better educated clan latched onto the Marines; the other kept its ties to the Taliban. In Deh Rawood district in Uruzgan province, rival factions tried constantly to use their access to coalition troops as leverage against their local enemies. US forces had allied with local strongmen, prompting others to ally with the Taliban and fire on US troops. The Dutch faced fewer attacks in part because they made neutrality a core objective.

Through these experiences, units learned that it was essential to remain neutral in local conflicts, and to be seen as an honest broker and a fair provider of public goods, such as security and infrastructure. Doing so required not taking sides, getting involved in feuds between tribes and clans, and not forming alliances of any sort. Military officers had to understand politics and be involved in it to some extent but to remain above the fray and unassociated with any particular faction—a very difficult thing to do.

Searching for political solutions

The most successful operations were those where a unit identified the political problems driving the insurgency in its area and came up with viable solutions. In these cases, further counterinsurgency operations were sometimes unnecessary. Dialogue and negotiation also reduced the amount of fighting necessary during clearhold-build operations and helped protect vulnerable forces in isolated areas.

For example, in the Mirabad Valley in Uruzgan province, a place notorious for improvised explosive devices (IEDs) detonated against Dutch forces, a mobile battlegroup of British Marines pushed in, met with the valley's elders, and determined that the people of the Mirabad had allied with the Taliban as a result of repeated abuses by the district police chief and the men under his command. The valley's leaders also felt they had been shut out of power at the provincial level, and that rival tribes were using their control over the government to exploit the people of the Mirabad.

The British Marines persuaded the Dutch to reach out to the valley's leaders, bring them into the political process in the provincial capital, fire the police chief, and rein in the local police. Soon thereafter, the IEDs in the Mirabad disappeared, and the Dutch were able to move through the valley unmolested thereafter. The valley was stabilized without any permanent deployment of forces and without firing a shot. Once the various parties had reached a political solution, further action, including clearhold-build operations, was no longer required.

Reaching out to marginalized groups proved effective elsewhere as well. For example, US Soldiers in the northeast made a point of engaging with Nuristani clans left out of power at the district and provincial levels. Evidently, earlier units deployed to this region had not dealt with these clans, many of which were responsible for attacks on US forces. Attacks on convoys in the region dropped significantly once US forces engaged with these marginalized tribes.

Political engagement lent legitimacy to combat operations, and allowed units to achieve military objectives with less fighting and loss of life. For example, as the British prepared to retake the town of Musa Qala in northern Helmand in 2007, they established contact with a prominent tribal leader whose fighters made up the bulk of the Taliban force in Musa Qala. The British persuaded the leader to defect in exchange for political power once the British took over. As the UK-led Task Force moved on the town, the leader ordered his fellow tribesmen to stand down. The remaining insurgents melted away with little fighting as the coalition swept into the town.

In Nuristan, a battalion of US Soldiers was able to project power into some of the most dangerous and hostile terrain in all of Afghanistan by negotiating with village leaders ahead of military operations. Unlike earlier units deployed to Nuristan, the battalion faced relatively little resistance as it pushed into isolated mountain valleys that had a long history of armed resistance against outsiders— valleys where there had been numerous attacks on US forces in the past. After months of painstaking talks with the elders of eastern Nuristan, the battalion was able to negotiate a peace between US forces, village leaders, and the insurgents. These negotiations allowed the battalion to push into the area without a shot being fired. These negotiations required substantial knowledge about the political terrain and considerable diplomatic skills.

ENGAGING THE POPULATION AND BUILDING POPULAR SUPPORT

Soldiers and Marines who used a population-centered approach tended to make more progress with less violence than those who focused on the enemy or the terrain. Doing so required dispersing into small outposts in or near populated areas, getting out constantly on foot, engaging and collaborating with local leaders, and implementing development projects that benefitted communities and built popular support. Units that followed this approach took on greater risk in the short term, but usually ended up safer in the long run.

The more successful units focused almost entirely on the population. Many did not bother to chase down insurgents. When the Marines cleared through Nawa in 2009, they focused on setting up outposts and beginning reconstruction. They allowed many fighters to escape, and even offered amnesty to those who agreed to lay down their arms.

On the few occasions that Afghan National Army (ANA) units led clearhold-build operations, they too focused on the population and did not give chase to fleeing insurgents. For example, in the Tagab Valley east of Kabul, Afghan Soldiers did not even shoot back when fired upon. Instead, they moved slowly up the valley, holding shuras (meetings of local leaders) in villages, setting up bases, and starting reconstruction projects. The Afghan Army managed to stabilize the valley with little fighting. Using Afghan forces to engage the population helped build relationships. Military operations that included local security forces were more effective than those that involved only coalition troops. Even more so, when US advisors were embedded with the Afghan Army—not just occasionally conducting operations with them—the effects were more positive. In many places, the local population was more willing to accept the presence of Afghan Soldiers, and they attracted fewer attacks.

Successful counterinsurgency operations involved constant interaction with local people, countless cups of tea, and sociable conversation. Relationship-building proved essential. Afghanistan, like most undeveloped rural nations, is a relationship-based society. In such places, it is necessary to build trust, which takes time, commitment, and work. It was not enough to institutionalize interactions between commanding officers and government officials. Personal rapport was essential.

Conducting foot patrols from small outposts in populated areas also proved essential. On foot, Soldiers and Marines were able to interact with people constantly—to gather useful information and understanding, and to form relationships. Small units that spread out into small outposts and patrolled every day on foot were more effective than large units that were consolidated on large bases disconnected from the local population.

Armoured vehicles and large, heavily fortified bases put barriers between local people and coalition troops. The same was true of wearing body armour and carrying weapons—especially pointing guns at civilians. In 2003, when permissive security conditions in Kandahar City allowed US troops to drive in unarmored vehicles and walk around without guns or body armour, it was much easier to engage with the people. As violence grew in later years and the coalition shifted to battle mode, coalition troops became increasingly cut off from the city's population.

Units that projected a heavier, more imposing and invasive presence often attracted more attacks. The more successful Special Forces teams operating in remote areas learned that it was important to maintain a light footprint in order to gain access to the population—otherwise, a team's actions could threaten local powerbrokers and heavily armed clans that had a penchant for taking up arms against outsiders. Providing a nonintrusive benefit won local support and therefore local protection. Leveraging Afghan leaders to mobilize the population often proved to be the best way to defeat the insurgency. The worst possible outcome for coalition troops in Afghanistan was to be seen as an army of occupation.

Foot patrols and engagement with the population also saved lives. In Kandahar province, for example, Canadian Soldiers in such districts as Zharey and Panjwayi operated out of large, heavily fortified bases and moved around in armoured vehicles. These units met with intense fighting and took many casualties. In areas where the Canadians dispersed into small bases and patrolled on foot, there were fewer attacks.

The same was true for the US Marines in Nawa in 2009. They spread out into 26 small outposts, and conducted constant foot patrols out of these bases. They were out so often that the locals wondered whether the Marines ever slept. They also held shuras nearly every day near their outposts. By doing so, the Marines in Nawa were able to dominate the areas around their positions and build support among the nearby population.

In Helmand and parts of Kandahar, the insurgents used IEDs to prevent coalition troops from interacting with the people. The aim of the IEDs was to make movement so dangerous that Soldiers and Marines would no longer patrol far from their bases—ceding control over the population to the Taliban. In most cases, the best counter to the IED threat was regular foot patrols and engagement with the population. Soldiers and Marines who were able to build support among the population found that the IED threat diminished considerably over time. On the other hand, the more troops stayed in their bases and allowed their movements to be restricted, the more intense the IED threat became. This was the case in many places, including Sangin, the notorious town in northern Helmand where thousands of IEDs stood between British forces and the population. In many remote areas, it was the population that protected US and NATO forces—not the other way around, as is suggested by the counterinsurgency manual. For many of the 12man Special Forces teams operating out of isolated firebases, building a base of support among the local population was essential for survival. Popular support, gained through sound counterinsurgency techniques, proved to be the best form of force protection. In some places, Special Forces teams moved safely in areas with substantial Taliban presence, because the local population supported the team's presence and pledged to protect it from attack.

The same was often true of general purpose forces stationed in remote and dangerous areas. For example, Soldiers in northern Kunar and eastern Nuristan managed to befriend village leaders who offered sanctuary to US forces passing through. These leaders also promised protection to US troops when inside the confines of their villages. Local elders sometimes accompanied US Army patrols outside their villages in order to deter attacks by local militants. These patrols were rarely, if ever, fired upon. However, not far away in the Korangal Valley, where the population was hostile and village leaders refused sanctuary to US forces, Soldiers were under constant fire everywhere and took many casualties. Where coalition troops had popular support, they faced little danger. Where they were looked upon as an occupying force, they were never secure, even in the apparently safe confines of their bases.

Using reconstruction funds

Many units learned to target their use of reconstruction funds toward specific objectives, rather than simply fund projects for their own sake. This meant using funds to gain and maintain support in key areas, draw fightingage males away from the insurgency, bring quarrelling factions to the negotiating table, and punish recalcitrant tribes and clans. It was not enough to simply execute a large number of reconstruction projects—to give people wells, roads, and other amenities in the hope of winning hearts and minds. Throwing money at problems rarely worked. Successful units used reconstruction funds to build relationships, in pursuit of clear political objectives. These relationships were often more important than the projects themselves.

Used unwisely, reconstruction funds frequently did more harm than good. For example, it was not uncommon for resentful tribes who did not receive funds to sabotage projects and attack US troops. Contractors who became wealthy and powerful as a result of their special relationship with US forces threatened local powerbrokers, leading to violence that was often mistaken for insurgent activity. The same was true of projects that employed outside labour.

Those units that were able to tie the local economy into the continued presence of coalition forces were particularly successful. They did this mainly by creating jobs and targeting certain leaders or segments of the population. The trick was to bring money into the community without upsetting the political and social balance of the locality. This worked even where the population was inclined to support the insurgency.

Reconstruction projects aimed at largescale job creation tended to be effective, especially where there were large numbers of landless laborers. For example, Canadian engineers in Dand district south of Kandahar City recognized early on that a few wealthy men owned all the land. Nearly all the people living in the district were sharecroppers and laborers who stood to gain little from roads, irrigation canals, wells, and other projects that promised to improve the productivity of the land. Such projects would merely enrich a few large landowners. The Canadians instead focused on low-tech, labour-intensive projects aimed at providing jobs to young men of fighting age. After six months, the Taliban was no longer able to recruit fighters in Dand district.

When it came to getting results from job creation programs, much depended on local conditions. For example, like the Canadians in Kandahar, US Soldiers in northeast Afghanistan focused on low-tech projects aimed at providing employment. Yet, insurgent facilitators based in Pakistan offered generous salaries to wouldbe recruits—far more than the US military could provide with its limited amount of funds. Reconstruction projects in the northeast did not yield the clearcut results that Canadian Soldiers saw south of Kandahar City. In Sangin in northern Helmand, a major center for the poppy trade, well-heeled drug traffickers allied with the Taliban paid handsomely for attacks on British forces. The funds available to the drug traffickers dwarfed those available to British forces.

Successful units recognized that money is power. US Soldiers in Zabul's Shinkay Valley dispensed funds as patronage—much like a patronage-based political machine. They used their money to create a network of supporters around their firebase and in villages farther beyond. Successful units gave money directly to laborers, rather than go through local contractors or powerbrokers—unless their intention was to empower these individuals. They also spread their funds around in order to avoid the appearance of favoritism that might breed resentment. In Dand district, the Canadians hired one fightingage male from every extended family. Their intention was to spread their funds out as evenly as possible, and to tie every family in the district into the reconstruction effort.

In northeast Afghanistan, US Soldiers gave funds directly to village leaders in exchange for specific concessions—such as support for upcoming operations, actionable intelligence, or reduced attacks on convoys. In this case, the battalion's objective was to empower cooperative local leaders by giving them control over reconstruction funds, and to give the battalion leverage over these leaders. The Soldiers also pushed money into outlying areas ahead of major operations in order to buy support and soften resistance. The approach worked well and saved many lives.

In Nangarhar province in the east, US forces supported a governor who paid tribal leaders to stop growing poppy. The governor combined these incentives with threats against those who refused to comply. In just one year, Nangarhar went from being one of Afghanistan's main opium cultivators to one that was declared "poppy free."

Protecting the population

Preventing the insurgents from intimidating the population was essential to building popular support and making reconstruction work. Afghans were rarely willing to cooperate with coalition troops if they (or their families) believed they might face retaliation. Where insurgents could target individuals working with the coalition, the presence of coalition troops did more harm than good. In contested areas, where coalition forces and insurgents fought for control over the same population, the plight of civilians was the worst.

Where the insurgents managed to infiltrate back into cleared areas and operate underground, reconstruction efforts faltered or failed altogether. For example, in such places as Nawa and Musa Qala in Helmand, US and British forces managed to push the insurgents out and keep them from returning. In these places, the population cooperated with the coalition, and reconstruction efforts proved relatively successful. In other areas of Helmand, such as Marjah and Sangin, where the insurgents infiltrated back in to intimidate the population and lay IEDs and ambushes, US and British forces faced considerable difficulties at rebuilding the government and getting projects underway. In such places, the population was often less secure and less wellgoverned than under the Taliban. People played both sides in order to survive.

In many places where insurgent influence remained strong, Soldiers and Marines could not trust local government officials, especially the police. For example, in Gulistan in early 2008, a US Marine platoon was forced to work with a district governor and police chief who were actively collaborating with the Taliban. The government officials tried to lure the Marines into prelaid ambushes and reportedly engineered the killing of local police who cooperated with the platoon. Only when the Marines succeeded in pushing the Taliban out of most parts of the valley—thereby ending its campaign of intimidation—did district officials start cooperating with the Marines.

Many Afghans were skeptical about the staying power of US and NATO units. Local people had to consider their lives and those of their families five or more years down the road when the Taliban might very well return to power and retaliate against those who had collaborated with the coalition.

In some areas, it was apparent that the population did not want the protection of coalition troops or Afghan Soldiers. Permanent garrisons and checkpoints attracted insurgent attacks and led to fighting that caused harm to civilian life and property. In some of the more remote areas, Taliban influence was relatively benign; violent struggles for control between insurgents and coalition troops posed a greater threat.

Employing restraint in the use of force

Restraint on the use of force was essential to every operation detailed in this book. Killing the wrong people had farreaching consequences. In many places, illin-formed or poorly conceived combat operations reversed months—and in some cases years—worth of patient effort overnight. In other places, targeting operations had second-order effects that were not apparent until months or years later. Powerbrokers close to the US often used their special relationships with coalition forces to eliminate their enemies—by passing false information naming their rivals as Taliban. Officers repeatedly fell for these tricks, carrying out raids against individuals based on information from local interlocutors whose motives were questionable. These operations—in which US and NATO units were manipulated into killing prominent local leaders whose commitment to the insurgency was uncertain—created powerful enemies, and probably caused more harm than doing nothing at all.

For example, in the Deh Rashaan Valley north of Tarin Kowt, the Ghilzai clans in the northern part of the valley allied with the Taliban after a series of airstrikes by US and Australian forces that killed several prominent tribal leaders. Their rivals among the Popalzai and Barakzai to the south—who controlled the provincial government and had regular access to coalition forces—may have fingered certain Ghilzai leaders as Taliban, when in fact their connections to the movement were tenuous and uncertain. Rather than reach out to the Ghilzai clans and try to bring them into the government, coalition troops targeted their leaders for assassination, alienating them and pushing them into alliances with the Taliban, which deepened the divide further and led to more violence.

Killing people, even insurgents, often did more harm than good. Many insurgents were related to local people, including with the government and US forces. elled demands for vengeance, even if young men were involved in the le resented the killing of their loved ctivities might have been. In many nor to avenge their deaths. It was clans targeted in earlier raids to attack US and NATO forces of their own accord without establishing any connections to the insurgency.

Military units that were successful at stabilizing an area and building popular support almost never carried out raids in populated areas they sought to influence. For example, Dutch Soldiers in Uruzgan did not conduct raids in or near the areas where they intended to build popular support. The same was true of some Special Forces teams.

Raids against enemy fighters tended to yield mixed results. In many cases, they proved counterproductive—especially in remote, mountainous areas where there were few coalition forces and little accurate and uptodate information. In the mountains, the terrain was so difficult, the road infrastructure so limited, and the distances so long that insurgent leaders often had plenty of time to flee, leaving innocent people to suffer the consequences of coalition attacks. It was nearly impossible for outside forces to move through the mountains undetected. Air assault raids in particular were a problem because most of the forces carrying out these operations were based far from their targets and knew little about the areas in which they operated.

It was not uncommon for villagers to take up arms against outsiders—any outsiders, whether rival clans or US forces—who entered the confines of their villages uninvited, especially at night. In such circumstances, it was not easy for coalition troops to distinguish between insurgents trying to protect themselves and local men seeking to defend their village. Many units just assumed that anyone firing at them was an enemy fighter. Raids in which innocent people were harmed or their honor violated created enduring enmity in many areas of the country. As a result, entire families, clans, or even tribes took up arms against the coalition and allied with the Taliban. In several cases covered in killcapture missions and other enemycentric combat op caused violence to escalate significantly. For example, se conditions in Kandahar City in 2003 were so permissive coalition troops walked around without body armour. Later uni focused on raids and measured their progress by the numbers of enemy fighters killed. Kandahar City became increasingly violent and unstable, and relations between US forces and the population grew strained.

These vicious cycles strengthened the insurgency and created problems that became increasingly difficult to solve. Misplaced combat operations caused entire clans or tribes to declare war on coalition forces, prompting the shedding of more blood and demands for more vengeance. Killing more people often made the problem worse and gave strength to the insurgency.

Large-scale sweep operations in particular were ineffective and counterproductive. These operations, which involved a battalion or more of US forces pushing into a large area from different directions in order to kill or capture a substantial number of insurgents, caused significant damage to civilian life and property yet netted few enemy fighters. Most of these sweeps were slow, clumsy, and ill-in-formed. Insurgents easily escaped through porous cordons or hid their weapons and pretended to be civilians. Since holding forces were rarely left behind, the insurgents returned to business as usual when the operations were over. Afghan militia forces involved in these operations were often accused of widespread looting. These operations alienated entire valleys, causing untold damage to the over-all US effort.

Despite these pitfalls, the discriminate use of force was often an integral part of counterinsurgency in Afghanistan. The trick was to demonstrate superior strength and will—to the insurgents and the population—while doing no harm to civilian life or property. After decades of civil war in which villages have seen one armed faction after another take power, many Afghans have learned to support whichever side happens to be the strongest. For example, when the US Marines arrived in Gulistan in southwest Afghanistan in the spring of 2008, they encountered a population that was almost entirely controlled by the Taliban. Most villages initially expressed indifference or outright hostility toward the Marines. After a number of high-profile engagements where the Marines prevailed without hurting civilians or their property, entire villages began working with the Marines. In Nawa in central Helmand, the Marines defeated the Taliban in a matter of days. Once it was clear that the insurgents stood no chance—and that the Marines were there to stay—the population turned around almost immediately.

Restraint was usually the better part of valor. Diplomacy was more important than force. The insurgents exploited local grievances to build popular support and recruit fighters. Killing insurgents often aggravated these grievances, made political solutions more difficult, and expanded the pool of enemy fighters. In the words of one battalion commander in northeast Afghanistan: " We can't fight our way out of this insurgency. The supply of fighters here is inexhaustible." Some of the vignettes in this book suggest that it may never be too late to turn the tide. It was often possible for officers to reach out to leaders whose communities had been the victims of heavy-handed operations—to offer compensation and promise that past mistakes would not be repeated. In Kunar, a US Army battalion made peace with an openly hostile village that had been the site of several botched raids during earlier years of the war. The village had since become the site of numerous attacks on US forces. Through public apologies, sustained engagement, reconstruction projects, and assurances that all future raids would cease the battalion was able to turn the village around. Attacks stopped, and insurgents were no longer able to operate there.

FINDING THE RIGHT BALANCE BETWEEN CONCENTRATION AND DISPERSION

It took time and a lot of trial and error for units to figure out how much territory and how much of the population they could reasonably control with the capabilities they had. Finding the right balance between concentration and dispersion—in order to adequately protect the population and limit insurgent safe areas, without spreading one's forces too thin—was particularly hard in

Afghanistan, with its vast expanses of rural hinterland, unforgiving terrain, and spreadout population.

Where a large number of forces were deployed in a relatively small area— such as the US Marines in Helmand after 2008—the dilemma was less acute. But in places where small units were responsible for massive areas, there were no good solutions. There were always areas of Afghanistan's vast rural hinterland where the Taliban could operate safely. That created pressure for US and NATO forces to constantly clear new areas. Once there, they could not withdraw. Otherwise, the Taliban would return and the gains made would quickly disappear.

Some battalions were spread out across an entire province, or even multiple provinces. For example, 2nd Battalion, 7th Marines (2/7) Marines, the first US Marine unit to establish a permanent presence in southern Afghanistan, was spread across eight districts in Helmand and Farah provinces. Many of the routes between bases passed through Taliban-controlled territory. The 2/7 was ordered to train the police in each of these eight districts, forcing the battalion to disperse its forces across a massive area mostly controlled by the Taliban.

In eastern Afghanistan in 2007 and 2008, a US Army battalion was responsible for all of northern Kunar and eastern Nuristan. The battalion operated across multiple mountain ranges, its forces dispersed into combat outposts that could only be reached by air. Before 2007, a single 12-man US Special Forces team was responsible for this entire region. SF teams elsewhere in Afghanistan were responsible for similarly large areas. Some coalition troops were able to follow a gradualist, oilspot strategy that involved focusing on small areas where they knew they could make a difference—rather than rapidly expand into new areas. These units met with greater success, at least in the areas where they focused their energies. The oil spot approach, which involved protecting and consolidating a base of support and then slowly expanding this base, seemed to work better than rapid expansion through largescale clearing operations.

For example, in Dand district south of Kandahar City, a reinforced company of Canadian Soldiers and engineers focused on only one village at first. Once this village and its immediate surroundings were stable, the Soldiers slowly expanded into nearby villages. The Dutch followed a similar approach in Uruzgan province. In areas where the Dutch focused their energies, they met with considerable success. The downside of the oil spot approach was that it left many areas under de facto Taliban rule. For example, the Dutch followed an oil spot strategy that involved focusing on small areas where they knew they could make a difference, recognizing that the Taliban would continue to operate further afield. Though Dutch influence in Uruzgan remained strong in certain areas, the Taliban operated freely in much of the province.

The initial British plan in 2006 was to oil spot out from Helmand's provincial capital, Lashkar Gah, but when the Taliban attacked all of the towns in northern Helmand simultaneously, the British were forced to fan out across the province in order to keep the majority of Helmand's population from falling under Taliban control. The British soon found themselves spread thin, under siege, and unable to conduct patrols and engage effectively with the population. Because British forces were so spread out, the insurgents were able to infiltrate back into many cleared areas. This was true for many US units as well.

Many units learned the hard way the perils of expanding too far too soon. In many cases, they did not know what they were getting into. The strength of the insurgents only became apparent once new areas had been cleared, new bases were set up, and new commitments had been made. Returning to a more consolidated force posture required shutting down bases under duress, which looked a lot like defeat.

Units that went too far afield or spread out too much across too large an area found their lines of communication frequently cut, their smaller bases and outposts under threat, and their influence attenuated. This was a serious problem for the British in southern Afghanistan in 2006 and 2007. It was also a problem for the US in eastern Afghanistan with its high mountains and long distances. In the northeast, insurgents actually overran two remote bases—Combat Outposts Wanat and Keating—in 2008 and 2009.

Bibliography

Abdul Qadir : *Criminal Law of Islam,* Kitab Bhavan, New Delhi, 1999.

Basrur, Rajesh M., and Hasan-Askari Rizvi, *Nuclear Terrorism and South Asia and Afghanistan,* Albuquerque, NM: Sandia National Laboratories, February 2003.

Debray, Regis. *Revolution in the Revolution.* New York: Grove Press, Inc., 1993.

Evelyn Goh, *Meeting the Afghanistan Challenge: The U.S. in Southeast Asian Regional Security Strategies,* DC: East-West Center, 2005.

Giustozzi, Antonio: *Koran, Kalashnikov, and Laptop: The Neo-Taliban Insurgency in Afghanistan,* New York: Columbia University Press, 2008.

Hoffman, Bruce, *Inside Terrorism in Afghanistan,* New York: Columbia University Press, 1998.

Ikram, S.M. : *Muslim Civilization in India,* Oxford, New York, 1981.

Keane J.: *Democracy and Civil Liberty in Afghanistan,* London, Verso, 1988.

Kilcullen, David: *Counterinsurgency,* Oxford University Press, 2010.

Krepinevich, Andrew Jr.: *The Army and Vietnam,* Johns Hopkins University Press, 1988.

Mohiuddin, Ahmad : *Saiyid Ahmad Shahid,* Modern Pub., Lucknow, 1975.

Nagl, John A.: *Learning to Eat Soup with a Knife: Counterinsurgency Lessons from Malaya to Vietnam,* University of Chicago Press, 2005.

Paget, J.: *Counter-insurgency Campaigning,* London: Faber & Faber, 1967.

Rosen, P.: *Societies and Military Power: India and its Armies,* Ithaca, Cornell University Press, 1996.

Saxena, V. K. : *Muslims and the Indian National Congress,* Discovery Publishing House, New Delhi, 1985.

Smith, W. C. : *Modern Islam in India : a Social Analysis,* Manohar Publishers, New Delhi, 1985.

Index

❑❑❑